# Awakening
## A Patriot's Diary of American Deception

**Sidney Pines**

## Table of Contents

# Copyright

# Dedication

This is for everyone who felt they didn't have a voice. You felt something deeper was occurring in our world and you followed your heart and your gut. Whether it be seeking out the truth, yearning for answers, passion for your country, or out of just sheer curiosity, you knew everything was not as it appeared. You weren't sure what was transpiring but it prompted you to research from either public announcements, highly conservative websites and even possible psyops on both sides. The result was you discovered many hard truths. Whatever intrepid routes you took to find accuracy, you were never understood. You couldn't figure out why others could not see what you have discovered- no matter how clearly you explained it. You were silenced, ousted, ridiculed, made fun of and many were even disowned from family and friends. This is for you. This is our voice, unapologetic and uninterrupted.

To my dear friend, Ella. Thank you for inspiring me to document this untraditional journal. I will always treasure our friendship and our support to each other during this momentous time in our country and in all other aspects of our lives. Thank you for just being- you.

To my family, thank you for always throwing humor in the equation and making everything in life tolerable. Your love and support are something I will value eternally.

Lastly, to the democrats and liberals. Please see us, please hear us. Listen to us from our point of view and not the stigma that was so unjustly placed upon us. We are good people; we are not domestic terrorists; we are not filled with racism and hatred. In fact, quite the opposite. In the end, everyone will realize that we all have the same characteristic. We have all been pawns in a dangerous game of chess. Hopefully, that realization will be what brings us together as a nation.

# Awakening: A Patriot's Diary of American Deception

To our adult children– Jack, Adam, Mac and Willow. The following notes and the description of what transpired in this country were all documented for you.

The reason is because there will come a day when our grandkids, and all future generations, will be studying this in school. Much like past generations have learned about the Holocaust, this travesty will also be in our history books. I have no idea how this will end. I do, however, know with certainty that we want everything that transpired in our daily lives documented. By doing so, you will have firsthand knowledge of what happened, and how we handled it.

Luckily, when I started to see certain common denominators that didn't make sense to me, I had the support of our good friend and neighbor, Ella, who felt the same way. Thankfully, our husbands, Andy and Sammy, were also on the same page. While the husbands shared the same annoyance about what was occurring in our country, I must admit that they were not as obsessed with finding out what caused this turmoil like Ella, and I were. Their lack of obsession does not diminish their sense of patriotism, by any means.

We are everyday middle-class families. We cook, we clean, we do yard work, and we pay our bills. On the weekends we enjoy going out to dinner and often have barbecues with an occasional game of bean bags and there is always enough laughter going around from all involved. The four of us love hanging out with our adult children and treasure every memory we make. We are not Harvard graduates by any means– just average citizens that love our country.

Little did we know when we started this journey, what we would unveil. Nothing could have prepared us for what we were about to discover. What I thought was just trying to get to the bottom of the corruption and a stolen election escalated quickly into an evil, dark and satanic whirlwind.

One day, Ella and I were talking about everything that we had already discovered, when she suggested I start documenting everything. So, there you have it– the birth of these notes that I hope someday our ancestors will appreciate.

At first, I thought that maybe I started them too late, but no, it is still very fresh in my head. First, allow me to fill you in and catch you up. I need to go back a few years for you to fully understand the severity of everything.

The story starts here:

When you're young, you are carefree, as it should be. In your twenties, as long as you have clean clothes for work, your hair turns out okay and you can solidify your plans for the weekend, life is good. In your thirties, you concentrate on your kids and making sure they are fed and bathed. You attend their activities, and just do your best to make sure your kids grow up to be good human beings. Like many others, politics was the last thing on my mind. That is, until my 40's. Obama won the presidential election. That's when my eyes opened and I realized I needed to do more research and be an actual adult when it came to elections. Gas prices shot up, people lost jobs, banks went under, insurance went up, the housing industry crashed, new construction came to a halt– and that is just to name a few things. A lot of people thought the economy took a dive solely because of the crooked banks, but I always felt Obama was behind it (remember that for later).

Andy was one of many that lost his job and by the grace of God, we survived it. The situation wasn't easy, but what doesn't kill you makes you stronger– isn't that what they say?

I heard that Donald Trump was going to run against Hillary Clinton. Finally, a man that did not have a mile long history of politics and more importantly, he had balls! He would put the country back on the right track, there would be fewer terrorist attacks, and he promised to bring the economy back. If he doesn't do well, it can't be worse than Obama, right?

2016–Trump wins!

New construction homes that previously had come to a halt were now being finished after eight years of standing dormant. Gas prices plummeted, thousands of jobs were created, home values went back up, there were no terrorist attacks, record for low unemployment the list goes on and on. Life was good and everyone you met, just seemed happy.

During Trump's presidency, I noticed a lot of unexplainable happenings on the news. For instance, I would see articles and videos how Ivanka Trump would visit Third World countries and help. You know, much like Princess Diana did, and it would be all over the news. They never aired Trump or his family's doings. It appeared that any good deed that anyone in the Trump family performed never received any recognition, which always seemed very odd to me. One night, on the news they showed how ex- first Lady, Michelle Obama, was spotted at a Starbucks and autographed a coffee cup for someone. During that same segment, they spoke for many minutes criticizing Trump for not holding Melania's hand while exiting Air Force one. Again, it seemed odd. Must just be me.

It was being reported on the internet about all the accomplishments that Trump had already made while in office for such a short time, and it would only get better.

Amazing. He saved the world from the implosion of Obama! That would surely make the News tonight, right? Nope.

Now, does any of that really matter? I guess not, the country was in great shape. However, it raised a red flag. Why? Why weren't the good deeds of our Commander in Chief never aired? The political world hated him, but the news–they are not supposed to biased, right? Wasn't it their job to report the truth?

The celebrities– I heard Joy Behar talking horribly about Trump, I believe even joking around about murdering him, on national television. Whoopi– the things she has said. I thought to myself, well, their career is done. They are still on. Robert DeNiro said "fuck Trump" on the Golden Globes– still working. In fact, he got an award recently.

Sure, even back in the day Johnny Carson made jokes, and many others have as well. But *EVERYONE* crossed the line with Trump. They took it too far with no repercussions. Something didn't feel right.

For years the First Lady has adorned many magazine covers. How many has Melania been on? Go ahead and look it up. I'll wait. None. Not one. The only first Lady to *not* be on a magazine cover. The Trumps were even excluded from having the White House Christmas specials like the previous presidents have always done for years.

Now you might be asking yourself, why is any of this important? And to be honest, it isn't. Who cares if someone didn't get a Christmas special? However, it does most certainly raise questions. The point is President Trump, and his family were excluded and treated poorly from day one. Never has that happened to a President of the United States. It alerted me and made my ears perk up, so to speak. Why would the news outlets dismiss and humiliate him, and *only* him? I could not think of the word for it. It appeared to be something, but I could not put my finger on it. Picking on him? Ignoring him? Nah–those terms seem too petty. It was something else.

Over the next couple of years, it got so much worse on the News. No mention that he does not take salary from the United States payroll, no mention on how he donates his own money to Veterans Homes, or the fund raisers or humanitarian projects to which his family volunteers their time. There was, however, plenty of mentions and humiliating comments about Melania's clothes, Trump's hair, false collusions, false rape allegations, and false statements.

Now I know when you're in the public eye it is impossible to have everyone "like" you. But this– no, this, this was different. Mine, and so many others, internal senses were flagged. Could not put our finger on it.

At this point I decided to get my news on non-biased stations, Newsmax & Fox. One day I saw a Trump speech, and I must admit, I do not remember verbatim what was said, but it was something along the lines of being grateful for the farmers and the military. Nice, right?

Well, that evening on the regular news or mainstream media, they replayed that speech. Yep, replayed it– they did not show it live. They played a 30 second clip of his 45-minute speech. And it was altered. Here is what it said:

"For obvious reasons, I have always thought the Military are pigs."

Since I saw the "real" speech, I was flabbergasted. My mom, who lives with us, was blown away, but not for the same reason I was. She believed he said that.

I explained to her how I saw the original speech and of course, she did not believe me. After all, she is from a generation that trusts the news.

That was the nail in the coffin for me regarding the mainstream media–true verification that I needed to avoid listening to it at all costs.

It was later proven that a tech savvy journalist reconfigured the recorded speech. He cut out words and spliced the footage to his advantage. The journalist was caught and charged with tampering with a presidential speech, violation and defamation of character. It went to court and Trump won. The only punishment that Trump instilled upon him was to never be able to work again. The journalist lost his license and is blacklisted in the journalistic world. Also, as part of his punishment he had to make a public apology explaining what he did. The journalist did that.

Did they show that on the news? Nope, they never did. His apology was useless. But it's out there. You can find it online. You can dig. You can find *EVERYTHING*.

My mom got fooled. I asked her, "Mom, even if Trump really did feel that way about the military, do you think he would be stupid enough to announce that on National TV?"

Her answer was a simple "Yes."

Ok, that's her. Again, from a different generation. But surely people in my age group or younger will have enough common sense to know that it was fudged. There is no way anyone would believe that anyone would be naive enough to call our military pigs–on the air waves. Well, people did.

Watched another Trump speech. He made a statement that since the day he started campaigning and then ran, then won, the media and Democrats have been on a "witch hunt" for him.

That's it! That's the term I had been looking for! I knew something was up, but I couldn't put my finger on it or didn't know what to call it. "Witch hunt"– perfect wording. He was right.

I will admit, sometimes hearing him speak, he is full of himself and brags, and I can see how it would bother some people. However, does he have a choice? No one has ever addressed what he has done for this country. They only report his "bad stuff"– and guess what? There was no bad; it was all falsified. He was backed into a wall, leaving him no other choice but to announce what he had done. If it sounds like he is full of himself, or bragging, so be it. It's the only way people can hear about it.

On our border, hundreds– if not thousands– of drug traffickers, criminals, human traffickers, terrorists and pedophilia ring leaders have crossed into our country for years. It was documented that 78% of illegals entering and drug trafficking had subsided when Trump was in office. Americans should be happy over that, right? Nope, they claimed he was racist.

He does not want any foreigners, that is, according to the news. Key word, people- *ILLEGALLY* coming over. If you go through the proper channels and gain residency legally, then welcome to America!

He is all for residents of other countries to come here, if it is done legally. I don't think that is too much to ask for. They would zoom in on the children's faces at the border, the camera would be right in these kids' faces and then show these minors on the news. They would criticize Trump for separating them from their parents. My first reaction was confusion as to why in the hell they were blaming Trump when it's clearly the parents' fault for putting their children in harm's way. Unfortunately, a lot of people did not feel like me. They jumped on the mainstream media band wagon and everyday people were accusing Trump of being cruel to foreign children.

But that's politics. The 2020 campaign trail was coming up and every politician tried to make the other one look bad.

As time passed, I noticed the frequency and consistency of the mainstream media utterly bashing Trump. From the tone of their voice to the reporters rolling their eyes when they mentioned his name and the constant flow of negative reports on a sitting President, it all felt staged to me. If not staged, it felt like they were purposely trying to silence him or make us despise him. What didn't they want us to know?

I thought everyone would see how ignorant the media was by being obviously one-sided, but sadly, that wasn't the case. In fact, quite the opposite. All of this led to a division between the American people, one you cannot begin to fathom.

The mainstream media was starting to speak of a virus that was starting to spread rapidly. They reported this in such a histrionic way, that it prompted Ella and I to do research on this. We started digging and discovered multiple websites offering the truth. In February of 2020, Ella and I made the gruesome discovery that there was a lab in Wuhan China.

Wuhan China was where the virus originated. The lab was partially owned by Bill Gates and Obama. Like everything else, the proof was out there. Not too many people investigated it because, well, they believe the news is a trusted source of information.

Listening to the news one night at dinner– now mind you, I had no choice– my mother is captivated with mainstream media. They started the broadcast out with how this "new Corona virus" is getting worse. Immediately, I blurted out that I did not believe it.

They said on the wonderful news to wear gloves and a mask. You were still able to go out to any store that was essentially necessary. Small businesses and restaurants had to close. Talk about schools closing.

I never understood why big box stores were able to stay open. Their items were essential, but a small hardware store or family-owned deli carried the same items as some of the megastores, but the small mom and pop stores had to close? I would have thought that would have been a wakeup call for everyone.

I also wondered what good was wearing gloves? You were touching the gloves to put them on, then touching your wallet, then touching the products in the store, then the cart, all with the same contaminated, gloved hand. Oh wait, they just said on the news that you didn't have to wear gloves anymore, statistics have shown that gloves do not help. Oh, ok, thanks for clarifying.

Then schools closed. Kids had to perform remote learning from home.

Now, whoever ends up reading this, please if after I am done with this, if you know of someone who had a bad case of Corona virus – or maybe even died of it– please do not think I am saying that Covid doesn't exist. I do believe Covid is real. I am not saying it's not.

There was Ebola, H1N1 (Swine Flu), Bird Flu, Mad Cow Disease, and a Salmonella outbreak. Those are all viruses that have emerged in the public eye within the last 15 years. Nothing shut down. No one had to stay home. No masks. No quarantine. School and school events still went on. And– are you ready for this? They were worse viruses than Covid. The survival rate was lower. We still went about our daily lives. We just sprayed our houses more with Lysol and washed our hands more and just used, well, common sense.

It was now kind of amusing to watch the news. Whatever Trump said, the Governors and Mayors would say and do the opposite. Trump said to shut down to try to stop the spread. Governors went on TV saying, "President Trump wants to shut down businesses to stop the spread. We are NOT going to do that. Our Citizens need their paycheck."

One week later, Trump said to let people go about their normal life, it will help build their immunity. Governors went on TV again saying, "President Trump does not want people to stay home, that is absurd! We are going to shut everything down to help stop the spread. Our wonderful President does not care if people get sick, but I do." This back and forth went on for weeks.

Kids need that social interaction at school. The gossiping, the talking, the laughing, the sitting with their friends at lunch, and yes, even the drama. Now that it was summer, school was out but nothing was open. Surely, they could have gone outside and made their own fun like my generation did, but you have to realize the number of parents that did not want their precious child near anyone else that might be infected. My youngest, Adam once made a comment to me how horrible it was to have to be home for school. In a typical mom fashion, I tried cheering him up and letting him know that I completely understood. His response floored me. He looked at me with all seriousness and said, "I am not talking about me, mom. I am talking about the kids that don't have a happy home, and they look forward to going to school to get out of the house and be with their friends. I am fine, I have a happy home and a family that loves me. Not everyone has that." He was right.

If a child who is happy and mentally stable was having a hard time with this, imagine how the less fortunate kids felt. That conversation will forever stick in my mind.

Now, let me introduce you to Black lives Matter, aka, BLM. And, of course, Antifa.

George Floyd, A habitual criminal with a record a mile long, strung out on every drug possible gets detained by a police Officer in Minnesota. The officer was way out of line and knelt on his neck. George Floyd dies.

I am starting to realize now that there was probably more to the story, but yes, it was extremely sad that he died. Everyone with a shred of decency felt that way. I do, however, agree with the fact that it was obvious George was "on something" (I saw the video), and the cops had encounters with him before, so they had to proceed with caution.

The world, the democrats and the news made it racist. I would love to get into stats here about how many whites were killed that shouldn't have been, but I won't. Yes, whites are even killed by cops. Little did I know just how bad the race card was going to be played in the next few months or years.

BLM caused riots everywhere. They tore apart most big cities and went on a destruction and killing spree. They insisted that cops were to be defunded. The democrats backed them up. The Obama wannabes agreed that cops should not be paid. Trump, of course, came out and said that was not going to happen. Oh, dear Lord in heaven, the shit that got stirred up after he said that.

"Trump is racist! Look what he did at the border, he hates foreigners! He hates Blacks! He won't take away police officers' pay checks!!"

I will never understand the ones that accused him of hating foreigners, when he is married to a woman that has an accent thicker my grandmother's mashed potatoes. The number of educated people that bought into all of this baffles me. Trump did more for the African American community than any other sitting President. Yet he hates Blacks also, not just foreigners. People believed it.

The riots went on all summer. The government and the media were turning black against white. Then the notorious BLM parades were created to prove to the world that black lives really do matter. There was one of those parades here in town and so many teeny boppers and twenty-something-year olds– especially females– marched in it. Did they really know what they were doing, or were they just marching because that's what they think they were supposed to do? Most of them marched for self-centered reasons. You know damn well all of them could not wait to take umpteen pictures to post all over the damn place and let's not forget the live videos that were posted. In their little minds, the reason for them marching was" Hey everyone look at me! I am not racist! I am a good person! Look at how cute I look in my marching clothes! Aren't I great!"

While they were posting those posts with such pride, all the other libs heard loud and clear the silent message that was projected. Yes, you are a great person, they succeeded in suckering the libs that were not in attendance. However, to people with common sense, the only silent message they sent was that they were fucking idiots and didn't have a clue about what they were doing.

By marching and being a part of this charade, you are acknowledging that you don't feel *ALL* lives matter. Whether you are white, brown, or black, every life is important. By marching in this parade, you are acknowledging that you are a privileged white person with extra benefits because you are white. Do you have extras because you're white? Do your parents not have to work, not pay taxes, not pay bills and always get the best table at a restaurant because they are white? Did your parents get every single job they ever applied for because they are white? Has anyone in your family been pulled over, got a ticket or maybe even arrested, and did they get out of it 1, 2, 3, because they were white? Whites have had homes foreclosed on, their cars repossessed, and they have been fired from jobs.

Did you, simple minded youngster, have to apply for college just like everyone else, or were you automatically in because you are white? Yea, I am sure the answer is "no" to every single one of those questions. Go ahead and march in an event that you know nothing about, you know, because it makes you look good. None of them took a step back and looked at the existing conditions- ok, I get it, they were teenagers, and their brains are not fully developed yet, that's where parental guidance would have been nice.

I have seen interviews with people in the black community saying that they are not oppressed and have never felt that way. There are also African Americans being interviewed that have stated this whole BLM movement makes them look bad. There you have it, direct from the horse's mouth, as they say, so everyone just needs to chill the fuck out and look past the smoke & mirrors. The kicker is, with all this black slavery bull shit– look it up– in reality, the first slaves were Irish.

Aunt Jemima is gone– Too offensive. A school named after Lincoln is gone. That one confuses me, don't they know he freed the slaves? Several statues are gone. Anything that is offensive to the African American Culture.

Antifa was an organized group that were for hire to riot, destroy businesses and harm people for money. It has been reported that they were funded by the Democrats. Antifa, along with BLM (both funded by the Democrats) were causing much havoc, and the world blamed Trump.

"If it wasn't for Trump, the world would be in peace and harmony. "Trump caused this division and made everyone angry. He is Hitler," they said.

"He is racist," they said.

All not true, and as I will say many times throughout this documentation, it's because they listened to the mainstream media and did not do any of their own research.

When Covid first came out, no kids were getting it. It was attacking the elderly. Then they said anyone 19 and up were getting it. So, this virus has a brain? It knows to avoid children. It flies through the air and thinks "I am going to land on him... no wait, I can't he is only 9."

Really? Viruses don't discriminate by age. They attack all. They later, after several months, said it now affects kids.

About businesses–did the Government play Duck Duck Goose— I mean, umm, you can stay open, you can't; you can have people in your store–you can't. Duck, duck goose. As it turns out, the reason for that was because people will congregate and talk in small mom and pop shops. Big box stores, you're in and out. Look it up, the same thing happened in the President Lincoln era. Anywhere that people might talk to each other were the places that had to shut down for fear of people educating one another. Restaurants were available for carry out only. You couldn't go in, but you could place an order and pick it up curbside. Once you placed order, the cooks then prepared your food— A cook you didn't know and knew nothing about their hygiene habits. They could prepare your food, package it, then hand it to another employee that touched the bag and brought it to your car. You then handed them your money or your card. They then handed you a pen to sign for it. They then handed you your bag of food that had already been touched by a minimum of two people. Then you went home, and your family took out their order and now they touch the products that the employees at the restaurant have touched. You then put that food in your mouth. The Government allowed that. But beware, there was a deadly virus out there and make sure to *not* go into the restaurant, that could kill you.

I really assumed that everyone felt the same way I did. Silly me. To this day, I feel the farce was so obvious. A lot of people though, feared for their life over this and hated people like me. I saw people driving in their cars alone with masks on or walking in the park with a mask. People did not leave their house. No one had visitors over. The statistics on depression and suicide skyrocketed.

Before Covid, people don't even realize it, but we all took precautions with viruses. It was called common courtesy and everyone had it. People forgot that. Governors had to go on TV to tell people if you're sick or have a fever, stay home– no fucking shit. The amount of people that would look at the TV and in a trance like state of mind, nod their head as if saying," Ohhh, ok, Governor, thank you" was incredible.

You dumbasses, you were always like that. You always used common sense during cold and flu season.

Then it came time for the presidential election. It was obvious who was going to win. True, a lot of people hated Trump by now. They got offended by him. Their feelings got hurt. They believed he truly was racist. They believed mainstream media. Even though many people loathed Trump, the amount of his supporters outnumbered that.

Watching the results on November 3$^{rd}$, Biden was killing it. It was Adam that reminded me that Republicans always lose during the day because let's face it, we work. Plain and simple. Once 5 p.m. came around and the working people got off work and went to vote, that's when you saw the votes come in. He was right. Trump votes then poured in, and he was winning by a landslide.

Here is where it gets good and the reason why these notes even exist in the first place:

While I was watching, I noticed something. I am going to make it even numbers to keep it simple.

Georgia:

Trump 300,000

Biden 100,000.

When it scrolled around again:

Georgia:

Trump 100,000

Biden 300,000.

What in the holy hell? Ok, I knew votes could come in, that made sense. But how do you lose votes? I was able to rewind. Sure, as shit, Trump's numbers went down 200k and Biden's went up 200k. Of course, I was in utter confusion, and I kept rewinding the DVR, assuming it was me; I had to have misread. My mom was in the room with me, and she surprisingly agreed with what we were witnessing. I immediately called Ella. I don't know how or why that happened, but we were winning by such a large margin, I figured I would see the comments and results tomorrow. I thought nothing more about it and went to bed excited with anticipation for the next morning.

Woke up and discovered Biden won. Creepy Joe was elected. Even some Biden supporters were in shock. I am sure there are a ton of Biden supporters that truly believed he won.

The Facebook comments and memes were hysterical but frustrating at the same time. President Trump's posts on Facebook were heartbreaking. He claimed from day one that the election was stolen. High Treason was committed, and he stated he would not concede and accept the results. Every Trump supporter knew the election was stolen. It was not just me that saw the changed votes on the TV. That was all over the news. Wait, let me clarify, all over the real news (Newsmax, Fox) and it was on YouTube and the internet, too. While I rewound and played the switching of votes, a lot of viewers rewound, and videotaped it. The video was then uploaded, and it went viral. Right there, in real time, you saw the decreased number of votes for President Trump. You can't lose votes, people.

I watched every hearing for the voter fraud, every single hearing. The Supreme court worked on these seven days a week. One hearing was even on Saturday night. All of this was televised, but not on the mainstream media. Now keep in mind, they had shown high profile crimes on the news before, but not the crime of stealing the election of the Presidency of the United States of America.

What the hell was going on? Not even a 30 second clip of the hearings. I realized at that point that all the oddities and omissions that I noticed over the last couple of years regarding the mainstream media was not my imagination. They were purposely excluding anything Trump.

During this trial, I saw hours of proof. That's right, I said proof.

From blue collar to white collar, redneck to yuppie, 20-year-olds to 98-year-olds. Hundreds and hundreds and hundreds of people were testifying that they saw firsthand fraud. Every person was under oath and every person knew that if they were lying, they would go to jail. Some of them even had short videos on their phone proving what they saw. The elderly testified that they went to vote and were told they couldn't because they already voted. No, they didn't.

Volunteers testified that they were not allowed to view areas they were assigned to, when their job was to view. Residents testified that they were not allowed in because they had a "Trump" t-shirt on. The people that denied them access, however, had a "Biden" t-shirt on. Videos of people scanning Biden votes, five, six, seven times. People shredding Trump votes. Yes, I saw the testimonies and the videos.

As weeks went on, more and more hearings came. Truck drivers testified that they were hired to go to Mexico, get loaded up and bring the load to Pennsylvania. They witnessed them unload the boxes in Pennsylvania and saw pre-printed ballots for Biden in the process.

Forensic scientists testified. They analyzed the paper and discovered they were not ballot papers, it was altered ballots.

Then there was the mother and daughter duo who videotaped how they were volunteers at a voting site and helped cheat on the election. That was brought up, the video was shown, and they confessed.

Most of the crooked volunteers were targeted. They were approached via mail asking them to volunteer. The targeted were from low-income areas– individuals without family, and individuals who were financially struggling. When they got to their designated area, they were told how to manipulate the votes, and they were paid. If they got caught, which they did, no one would believe them because they would be considered non-credible witnesses due to their background or current living situation, and that is exactly why they targeted a certain demographic. "They" meaning the Democrats, of course. All of this was discussed in great detail with pictures and videos during the hearing.

The news you ask? Oh no, they showed none of this.

During the tabulation of votes, they had to shut down. Some states for technical errors, one state for a pipe bursting–which it has been confirmed that there was not a pipe that burst– and other reasons unknown to me. During the "shut down" they sent everyone home and only a select few got to stay. That's when most of the cheating happened. During the shutdown, in the middle of the night, there were multiple videos from security cameras showing suitcase after suitcase being brought in with Biden votes. Truckloads backing in with Biden votes. Videos of a guy bragging and showing the world that he was shredding hundreds and thousands of Trump votes.

In one of the hearings I watched, Judge Roberts sat there and listened. He shook his head in disgust. He had stated," This is obviously a flawed system. Something definitely is not right and needs further investigation into the integrity of our system. I am ashamed of America right now. We need to rectify this."

Yeaaaahhhh!! Finally, justice will come. Five hours later he denies the case. Throws it out.

Now, that made the news! All over the news, it was how President Trump has no proof, and all of his cases were thrown out. At this point, there were 23 cases pending. News said no proof and that all of them were thrown out–untrue. There was proof and only one was thrown out.

I started digging again. At this point, Ella and I both joined forces and tried to seek truth. We discovered that there was now evidence of International Interference. Obama (he was still very much in the picture), the Clintons and Bidens were in an arrangement with China and other foreign countries.

They sent a team of military to recoup the Main Server in Frankfurt, Germany. They were able to retrieve it, however three of our military men were killed in the process. Not sure what happened to Gina Haspel, but rumors were of her being captured or killed. I guess we will find out later. Gina was the head of the CIA.

Three Military men were killed while trying to figure out what happened to our 2020 presidential election. Is it just me or shouldn't that have been on the mainstream media?

They showed it on Fox. They showed it on Newsmax. It was in Norway's paper. It was in the paper in the Netherlands. Pretty much everywhere except the news outlets in America or papers that people watch and read the most–you know, the popular ones with the most viewers.

It is illegal and High Treason to have International Interference from at least one other Country. We had four– China, Syria, Iran and Italy.

The Italian Government crumbled like blue cheese. They confessed to everything on a reel taped confession. Old-fashioned reel film was used so it could not be manipulated. An official from the Italian Government confessed how this was not just a United States take over, this is global. All four Countries injected Biden votes into the Dominion Voting Machines to make sure he won. It was a hostile world take over. Biden, Obama and Clintons were paid big money– billions from China to join forces. China would then own us and ultimately turn us communist.

So now, with the USB from the Germany server, the confession from Italian Government, it was a win-win, can't go wrong, right? Still didn't win. Judge Roberts threw it out again. At this point it is the middle of December. There were more court cases coming up, but it was looking grim.

Could not for the life of me grasp the concept that no one could see through this facade. I am not talking about people around me; I am referring to the Congress and the Supreme Court Justices. How much more proof do they need?

Every time someone posted something on Facebook suggesting voter fraud or anything pro-Trump, it would be taken down. Anything anti-Biden would be taken down.

Ella and I discovered ex-military comrades that had their own sites. Trump had 80 million voters (turns out there was even more), there was no way you were going to keep them silent. And you shouldn't have to, isn't that the beauty of America?

We joined Parlor, where you can see the latest developments from the military, Trump's attorneys and the status of the lawsuits. The mainstream media gave Parlor a bad name. They reported that it was a platform inciting violence. The Liberals were saying they logged on to it to look at it and it was people planning murders and assassinations and calling it a cult. Not true at all. It was lawyers, blue collar, white collar, doctors, engineers, upper class, middle class, lower class–in other words,

"Americans." Most of the people posted inspirational quotes to try to raise people's spirits up from a stolen election. Yep, real killers.

After reading and digging, we came across a lot of information that I probably wouldn't have believed if I did not follow it from day one. Covid now made sense. Stealing of the election made sense. Cases thrown out made sense.

Not showing anything on mainstream media made sense.

Now this is where it gets good, confusing as hell and as a warning, a little out there. First, the Covid was planned and brought here, just like I thought. It was Obama and Gates and mostly funded by Dr. Fauci.

1.) To scare the shit out of people to stay home. This way they would get more mail in ballots. The mail in ballots were the easiest to manipulate.

2.) To see if we would listen; to see if we can be controlled. I will touch more on the control issue later on.

Stealing the election made sense. Greed and control. The court cases are being thrown out because, and I know this sounds crazy, but they were all in it together. The Judges, the congress, Department of Justice, FBI, CIA, DOJ are in China's pocket. They all received high payments.

Mainstream Media:

ABC news' executive producer Ian Cameron is married to Susan Rice, Obama's former National Security Advisor.

CBS President David Rhodes is the brother of Ben Rhodes, Obama's Deputy National Security Advisor for strategic communications.

ABC correspondent Claire Shipman is married to Jay Carney, former Obama White House press secretary.

ABC news and Univision reporter Matthew Jaffe is married to Kate Hogan, Obama's former Deputy Press Secretary.

CNN Vice President Virginia Mosely is married to Tom Nides, Hillary Clinton's former Deputy Secretary.

NBC President Ben Sherwood is the brother of Elizabeth Sherwood, Obama's former Special Advisor.

This deck was stacked, and it was in their favor.

Mainstream media was only reporting what they are told to say, not the real events. There was no such thing as Investigative Journalism anymore, they were all scripted. Much like an actor, the reporters read the script on the teleprompter, that's it.

Turns out there is a name for this group of people, these crooked politicians. And they are not just Democrats. Some are Republican as well.

They are called the Deep State. The Elite. The Cabal. The Illuminati.

Trump knew the election was going to be stolen. It was discovered that Hillary injected 20% more votes than she actually got during the 2016 election. But it wasn't enough. They underestimated Trump; they should have injected more. With Biden, that's why they had to make sure he won. They did not want to underestimate again.

It's the Presidential race and Trump is a billionaire with a lot of connections and his IQ is higher than Einsteins'– yes, that's true look it up. He has a degree in Quantum Physics (also true) and is a master at the art of war. Just saying. He was not going to back down, and rightfully so.

Supposedly, since Trump knew about the election about to be stolen, he prepared for it. What he was not prepared for was the amount of people that were involved in the deep state. Individuals that he thought were honest were not. People he thought were bad people turned out to be good. A lot of infiltration was at work here; people playing both sides, people on Trump's team that were plants by the deep state. As crazy as it all sounds, it can be true. Think of the true crime movies. Snowden– true story about a CIA agent who discovered the government was listening in on normal citizens and he came forward. He had to move to Russia where they have asylum, otherwise he would have been killed. True story, great movie. There are spies in the CIA, that's their job. It is true life.

One of the people that he thought was good, but in realty he wasn't, was Supreme Court Justice Roberts. That explains all the rejected court hearings.

The corruption goes way deeper than just being crooked, deeper than just being greedy and wanting power. The "Elite" is more than the word stands for. In our world, normal middle class, the word *elite* means, fancy, rich, high class. But in the deep state's world there is more to it. There are several in politics and in Hollywood (yes, celebrities are involved too), but they might not be involved in the Elite club. That's a good thing. The Elite club consists of quick social climbing where actors have the best roles, the most movies made, and the most awards. Politicians have the most power and the luxury of only having good things reported about them on the news, but it does not come at a small price.

The Elite is a group who believe in Devil worshipping, sacrificing kids, human trafficking, pedophilia and drug smuggling. There I said it.

I know, I know- I was skeptical at first too. But if you are reading this and you think that's crazy, there is no way, that is a good thing. It means you do not have their way of thinking and find it hard to believe that anyone can be so horrific. Normal or "nice" people will never understand their way of thinking, but the proof is out there.

The Elite, or the Cabal, or the Deep State (they all mean the same), are a group of people that made millions off child trafficking. There are 1,500 miles of underground tunnels used to travel and move kids (and some adults) from place to place. One of the biggest leaders of the Cabal is Obama. Child trafficking was the only reason why Obama created Obama Care, which was health insurance for lower income families. Families applied for this, and the deep state was able to see all children from lower income families and then investigate their family status and demographic. They would then determine if the child would be missed, or an easy target. While the world thought he was amazing for giving health care to lower income families, he was devising a system to take our children. They had to come up with a system that only the deprived children would be targeted. Bam! – The announcement of Obama Care.

Donald Trump was the first President to ever have anything and everything declassified. All files from the Department of Justice (DOJ), Federal Bureau of Investigations (FBI), Central Intelligence Agency (CIA) and Department of Defense (DOD) were released, including files on himself with those departments which proves he has nothing to hide. In those declass drops, there are hundreds of thousands of files. I read transcripts, looked at videos, pictures–the little bit I read through, was enough for me.

Two other Presidents attempted to bring down the Cabal and declassify, President John F. Kennedy and President Ronald Reagan. Well, you know what happened to Kennedy. Lee Harvey Oswald was a scapegoat. Reagan had three assassination attempts, but they only reported one on the news. He finally stopped trying to bring them down for fear of his life.

How do you blackmail the rich? You can't blackmail them with money, because they have enough. So, their form of blackmail was they would make them commit a horrific crime and they would video tape it. If they turned their back on the Cabal, that video would go viral. Judge Roberts was blackmailed. They picked him up, threw a black hood over his head, brought him to a place where there was a 4-year-old waiting. They put a gun to his head made him have sex with her, then he had to kill her. Now do you see why the court cases were thrown out? If he had not thrown them out, that video would have gone viral. And remember, they control the news, so I am sure that would have been mentioned.

Why do you think Democrats were so opposed to the wall and blocking off the border? Because that is how they smuggled in and out most of the victims that were trafficked. Of course, illegal drugs are transported via the border also. Yes, the deep state is involved with the drug cartels also.

Now let me tell you about Adrenochrome. I hope you have a strong stomach.

Many, many years ago, some rich scientist with nothing better to do than looking for the fountain of youth, decided to conduct experiments. He wanted to find a product that made you look and feel like a 20-year-old, no matter what age you are. Since I am not a scientist, I have no idea what his procedure was to find this. But he did. He discovered that children's adrenaline is truly the secret to youth. Think about it, when you are excited about something, a vacation you can't wait to go on, your wedding day or finding out you're pregnant, don't you feel great? Some people might even say you are glowing. That's because your adrenaline is up. He also discovered that the younger the adrenaline is, the more potent. Again, it makes sense. Think about when you are older and you are stressed about something, you look bad then, right? Well, a kid– good adrenaline or bad adrenaline– never looks bad because they are young.

So, this sick twisted person, along with rich, greedy politicians and Hollywood's finest, tested this hypothesis and it worked. That's when this new business started.

Thousands of kids have been kidnapped by them from all over the country. Ghislaine Maxwell, Epstein's partner, was quoted saying "I found this girl barefoot in a trailer park, who cares. No one will even notice her gone."

Once captured, they drew their blood. Apparently, this scientist figured out that certain blood types make better adrenaline. Depending on the blood type, they either were kept, killed, or in waiting. "In waiting" meant they would sell them and just plain traffic them instead of using their adrenaline. If they had the correct blood type and were used for adrenaline purposes, well this is the part where you need a strong stomach. They had to raise the adrenaline. They had to do something so horrific to this child that their adrenaline level is absolutely the highest it can be. Therefore, they would torture, rape and sodomize the child. Sick, I know. Yep, this is all out for public viewing as well.

In a small child, when that trauma occurs, the vessels around the eyes swell and bruise. Now I want you to think really hard and try to remember all the pictures that you have seen over the years of a celebrity with either a black eye or one hand over their eye. There are plenty of pictures out there. I have seen several pictures of stars with black eyes. Of course, they always have a cool, heroic story to back it up, but the truth is, they were showing their dedication to the Elite. Panda eyes also, painting their eyes like a panda's was just as acceptable to show their alliance, advertising that they were a part of the group. Who would know that? No one, other than the Elite themselves– that was their secret code, the mocking of the children's black eyes.

When they decided that the innocent child's unbearable torture was over, they would draw their blood, expel the adrenaline portion and voila, Fountain of Fucking youth is created. It came in injectable or a cream. They injected it like a Vitamin B shot. The injection made them feel like a teenager and helped with their looks and gave them energy. The cream is an anti-aging miracle. It is $2,500.00 for an ounce of the cream with a 10 oz. minimum order. The vial, I believe, was $10,000.00. Judging by the price they charged, you can see why this business was profitable to them and then the missing persons reports got bigger. They then built those underground tunnels to move people around better. Once they realized how they were getting away with it, they expanded. While we were out looking for pedophiles in white vans, the truth was it was more sophisticated. Not every abducted child is a result of this, but many are.

There was a pizza place in California named "Comet" that had ping pong tables in the basement. They would lure children down there and have a "pizza party." Town members grew suspicious, and everyone called them conspiracy theorists. For years, it was ignored and never investigated. Well, they were raided recently, and they are now shut down. One of the biggest child trafficking institutes ever with access to the underground tunnels, not mentioned on the mainstream media. But the proof is out there.

So, knowing how evil they can be, the whole Devil worshipping aspect did not surprise me anymore. Now everything started to make sense. *EVERYTHING.* Trump was not one of them. Trump could not be bought and if he won again, not only would their corruption be shut down, their child trafficking, child abuse, adrenochrome empire and their freedom would be gone. He has been working on bringing them down for years, and they know it. There is a recording going around where you can hear Hillary say, "If he (Trump) wins we will all have a noose around our neck."

It gets better– turns out Trump was not on the good side alone. He has been working on this for years in conjunction with someone else. He decided to not only take down the Cabal, but to take them all down, meaning, Hollywood stars, politicians, central bankers and anyone who is guilty of corruption, pedophilia, human trafficking and crimes against the people. It is a Global take down. If this all goes into play, he will be known as the man that saved the world, literally.

Before I tell you who the other person is that has been working with Trump, please let me clarify something. No one knows the whole truth. Whether you are Republican, Democrat, Conservative or Independent, the truth is only known by a select few. I will say this though, with all the proof (I cannot stress the word proof enough) that we have stumbled upon, there is no doubt that this is a possibility.

The other person that is working with him is John F. Kennedy, Jr. That's right. He faked his own death. Hey, I know this sounds insane, I will be the first to admit it, but I have spent numerous hours watching trusted truthers, ex-military & ex-CIA podcasts to not believe in the possibility of it. Jr. swore he would take down the people that killed his father. It was not Lee Harvey Oswald. One day while boarding his plane, his military bodyguards did a sweep and search on it and discovered a bomb. He called his good friend Trump over and they came up with a plan. They called in a retired Air force pilot that they knew and filled him in on the plan. He flew the plane and when it got to a certain altitude the pilot parachuted out, the plane blew up and Jr. and his wife Caroline have been living in seclusion ever since. Working with Trump, they devised a plan to expose all of the Cabal.

Life as we know it, is not what it should be. The way that bills and loans are processed has been illegal. Taxes and interest were only supposed to be a temporary thing back in the 1700's. They were implemented to get them over the hump of a failing economy. People got used to the taxes and interest, so once they got over the hump, the corrupt politicians just kept making people pay, keeping all our money for 100's of years.

Found out about this time, that from day one the very first day he took office in 2016/2017, Melania was blacklisted from appearing on magazines, just like I noticed. Television stations were advised not to do specials or fun interviews with them. Court trials went nowhere. And now they removed President Trump from all social media. The President of the United States was not allowed to speak. He gave speeches and talks; they were not shown on mainstream media. Surely, the world can see that something is not right, can't they? To Ella and me, everything was so undeniably obvious.

There have been several whistle blowers that came forward. Most were regarding the election fraud. Some were nurses and doctors regarding the virus. When they first came out, pretty much every patient had to be put on a ventilator and then they eventually died. Three nurses came forward. They said that most of the patients did not need a ventilator. They were sick, but their lungs were strong enough. Well guess what happens when you put someone on a vent with healthy lungs? They die.

The insertion of a vent on healthy lungs will hyper inflate them. The nurses mentioned this to the ER doctors. The doctors told them that the higher ups in the hospital had told them they had to vent every patient, so the nurses just needed to listen. Well, one of the nurses was found dead in her apartment. Not sure where the other nurses are. Each hospital received $14,000.00 per patient that was diagnosed with Covid. So, pretty much everyone that went to the hospital in that time frame had the diagnosis of Covid strapped to their name.

In one of those drops of declassified information that I read, there was an interesting video. Meetings are taped all the time, mostly to go back to for reference. Well, many years ago, the three letter agencies never imagined the recordings would be released. I watched a video with Bill Gates, presenting an idea to the CIA in their boardroom. Bill Gates often wondered what made some people "believe" stuff and some people don't? What was the difference in the chemical makeup of their brain? How are some people easily swayed, and some are strong-willed?

Well, after years of figuring it out with a scientist, he found the answer. It's in our DNA/RNA and it's a chemical composure in your brain. He figured out how to alter it. He came up with a serum that once injected, it will alter the chemical make up in your brain, making you more obedient. He was introducing this to the CIA. CIA loved the idea and they manufactured this serum which was later called a vaccine. Now they just needed a reason to inject this into people. They had to create a virus. That's right, people. The Covid vaccine came out before the virus.

Hydroxychloroquine (HCQ). That cures Covid. There is documented proof that Obama stated it is not to be used until he said so—the declassified drops were wonderful! Can someone explain to me why Obama had any say so?

Vitamin D, too–people who take Vitamin D rarely get Covid. Just like people who take Vitamin C rarely get cold or flu. Wouldn't that have been great advice for the American people to hear on the news? 99.7% survival rate. As anticipated, a higher survival rate than any other virus.

They advised us to watch the electoral votes on January 6th. We were hoping that Mike Pence would do the right thing since he saw all the proof of the election fraud. With my mom living here, it's very difficult to watch things like that since she is a Biden supporter and dislikes Trump with every morsel in her soul. I decided it would be best to go to Ella's house to watch it. Right before, something did, in fact, happen, but it's something neither one of us expected. Let's just say that's a day that will go down in history for sure.

"The Storming on Capitol Hill." I won't even elaborate on that because that was shown on the news, and it was in all of the papers. Everything that happened on that day is common knowledge. And of course, they blamed Trump and his supporters and that is the reason it was on the news. When Ella and I saw it start, they turned off the cameras and postponed the electoral votes, transferring the coverage to mainstream media. She and I looked at each other with mouths dropped open and a look that could only mean one thing– What the fuck?

At first, we thought another deep state move to do anything to prevent Pence from not validating the votes. While throwing our hands up in the air and questioning what was next, we heard the commentator state that this storming was Trump supporters, or MAGA as they said. Right away we knew in our heart of hearts that was not Trump supporters. Not a chance in hell. I walked back home while dreading opening my front door and facing my either irate– or thrilled– mother. As expected, my door wasn't even shut behind me when she met me at the foyer screaming that I am insane to support Trump. She did, however, transform her anger into happiness when she realized how bad this makes Trump look. She then proceeded to quote me "facts" from the mainstream media. I knew right then and there, I was speaking upon deaf ears and trying to express how I felt would just be a waste of oxygen on my part. We agreed to disagree and dropped it.

They announced that they would continue with the votes later that night. While I did not go back to Ella's, I went upstairs to watch it alone. Mike Pence did not do the right thing and did not question the votes, and they went to Biden, even though Pence was aware of the fraud. Another day of disappointment and deceit. Another day of wondering what the hell is going on. This is where I would have stopped and threw in the towel had I not been digging and following it. And I think Ella would have stopped here, too.

But since we saw:

1.) The hearings with all the evidence

2.) The proof of Justice Roberts being blackmailed

3.) The proof of the news not showing us anything

4.) The proof of Pizza Gate

5.) The proof of funds transferred from China to Obama, Clintons and Bidens

We could not stop, not now.

That night, I went into my bedroom where Andy immediately woke up and he asked what had happened. I started to tell him in a very Erin Brockovich way, spouting out yet again all the proof of the voter fraud and the election being stolen. I rattled off numbers and stats so quickly that if they had a way of measuring speech, I am sure my mouth was going 10 miles a minute. His response was to give it up, there is nothing that we can do now. Hello? Andy, have you met me? I don't give up.

In fact, this is where we kind of lost our husbands' interest. Whenever electoral votes are counted it's usually a done deal. If truth be told, it was that night that a lot of Trump supporters dropped off. By no means am I referring to them not being Trump supporters anymore, they just gave up on the election fraud. They still believe in Trump but felt there is nothing we could do until the next election in 2024. Ella and I had to plug along. We had to see this through.

There is a difference with this one– big difference. Not just because of fraud, but because of Biden's agenda. It will be worse than Obama. The Democrats' Agenda '21 is online. Again, there are resources out there. You can do your own digging.

First create a virus.

Lock down due to virus

Open borders

Gas prices will rise

Predicted home sales to decrease

Mandatory vaccines

Need vaccine passport to travel

Ban all books that are offensive

Mail a request to homeowners to relinquish guns

Go to homeowners' home to relinquish guns if they do not turn it on their own

Anyone who refuses vaccine must report to FEMA camp.

Crypto currency

You will be chipped

Long term goal, arrest all Trump supporters.

Now this is from a history book on how the Nazi's took over Germany:

1.Banned guns

2.Got rid of God

3.Banned church services

4.Tore down statues

5.Burned the flag

6.Got rid of any and all history they did not agree with

7.Got rid of the public police so only the rich could afford it and put their country in a state of fear

8.Created domestic terrorist organizations that disagreed with the "Brownshirts" aka Hitler's "Bullyboys."

Read above. Then read again. Everything that was done in Germany, before the camps started, has happened here already. Antifa & BLM (organized domestic terrorists) burnt our flag even.

And they have already started to implement vaccine passports.

Yet they call Trump "Hitler." Typical, though. Usually, the guilty party does call and accuse other people of their faults. Hypocrisy at its finest.

They had already been implemented in his first 52 days in office and Ella, and I heard about this agenda in December.

We have come to realize that pretty much all elections have been rigged. It's not an election, it's a selection.

If nothing is done, they will steal every election and all of the above will come true. Hoping that these notes I am typing do not turn into being a second version of Anne Frank's Diary.

Trump's attorneys- Sidney Powell specifically– and General Flynn said there was no way Biden would be inaugurated on the 20th. There is irrefutable proof of election fraud and international involvement. So now they told us to watch the inauguration. The last thing I wanted was to watch the damn Inauguration of a man who did not even win correctly. But I would.

Nothing happened. "Sleepy Joe" was inaugurated successfully. No Swat team swung through the air with the greatest of ease to kick him off the podium.

Nothing. I did see a video where the military had their backs turned to fake Biden and they are refusing to acknowledge him as the real President.

And now Parlor has been taken down. You see, that's what always made us wonder. Why? Why can't we speak? Why can't we listen? Why can't we read articles on that platform?

I mean seriously, I really want to know why that platform was cancelled. Why can't an American citizen have access to everyday articles on that platform? What don't you want us to see?

How do Jack Dorsey and Mark Zuckerberg have the authority to silence the President of the United of States?

Trump had no way of communicating to the outside world. Mainstream media wouldn't allow him to talk to the public, social media gone. He was silenced. Nazis called it control of information. Today, they call it fact-checking. Same thing.

Several podcasts, interviews and videos that we watched alluded to the fact that we were in the biggest military take down in the history of the world. They referred to it as a movie. There was a massive military operation going on to expose the Cabal. Regarding the inauguration, they said it was pre-recorded, and the weather did not match the day, and it was done somewhere else, and the entertainment was actors. At that point I was mentally exhausted and just wanted the show to be over with. Or movie, as they called it.

We found Telegram. Ok, at least we still had a source of information. Not sure how accurate it is, but so far, it's been spot on as far as what has really happened.

With each passing day, we yearn for more information, for something that will just jump out at the world and scream the truth. Then, each night when nothing happens, you get disappointed.

There had been several "drops" is what they called them from a military intelligence called "Q." Not sure who or what that is. It is sent in a form that has to be decoded. I didn't have the time or the energy to do all that. It's a whole numerical system. Ella and I usually let the other followers decode and then we read it. We are not even sure if this is a legit scenario but have decided to keep our minds open to all possibilities. Sometimes, they were correct, sometimes they were wrong.

For instance, the correct ones were the arrests and deaths and suicides that occurred. We would read the decoded message and the next day, or a couple of days later, they would be correct. Like the stock market crashing or escalating or the resignations of many CEOs. A lot of that was actually on the fake news or mainstream media. They told us to be prepared because several CEO'S resigned, and it really meant they were arrested.

The CEO of Disney stepped down.

The CEO of Microsoft stepped down.

The CEO of Hulu stepped down.

The CEO of IBM stepped down

The CEO of LinkedIn stepped down

The CEO of uber eats stepped down.

The CEO of eBay stepped down

The CEO of MGM stepped down.

The CEO of CNN stepped down.

The CEO of Nestle stepped down.

The CEO of Volkswagen stepped down.

The CEO of Mastercard stepped down.

The CEO of Nissan stepped down.

The CEO of Victorias secret and Bath and body works stepped down.

The CEO of Harley Davidson stepped down.

The CEO of Tinder stepped down.

The CEO and family member of the Rothschild's committed suicide.

An extremely influential woman in China jumped off her balcony to her death.

A lot of the resignations were noted on the news, but not all. And not the suicides. Ella and I knew about the resignations days before it happened.

Several Hollywood stars are already gone, either arrested or on house arrest. Actors you would never suspect. The worst was Tom Hanks; he was the leader in the Hollywood circle. The funny thing is that I have stumbled upon a lot of comments and thoughts from everyday people regarding him, making me extremely hopeful that more people know what's going on than I realize.

How many times have we thought we were going to get an EBS. It never came. An EBS is an emergency broadcast system. It is supposed to go off and I believe it will be the military that announces first a scare event, meaning we under attack which will be false. Then, announcing the high treason and the stolen election. Then, there will be seven days of broadcasting the live tribunals and confessions of all involved.

There were several drops that insinuated when it was going to be. But it did not happen. Obviously, or else I wouldn't be writing this. It would be over.

Adam had suggested to me that I should talk to Kenny. Kenny works for Andy. He has been researching and investigating the government for years. I did happen to see Kenny out one day and I told him how I had been following it and explained to him everything that you had already read. He agreed with me completely–except for the end result. He feels they are *ALL* in this together, including Trump. He believes Trump is friends with Biden and Obama and they are all in the middle of a hostile Communistic take over. He says we are all doomed, it's just a matter of time. He says Trump is the leader of the Cabal. They worship the devil, and their devil has breasts and a penis– a hermaphrodite. That explains why all the transgender promotion and wanting to pass a bill stating children can have a sex change. Also, abusing and sacrificing children is their way of honoring their god, the hermaphrodite Devil. While I disagreed that Trump is a part of them, I would stay open minded and research that, just to make sure.

I, of course, instantly went to Ella. While we were shocked by this new revelation that Kenny laid upon us, nothing would have surprised us anymore.

I went down that rabbit hole that night. Research after research. I still felt Trump was good. I do, however, see why Kenny would think that. The art of war is making them believe you are one of them. There are pictures of Trump socializing with the Elites. The Democrats want to do a "Great Reset" where they control our money and us.

Trump has a different "reset." It's called the "Great Awakening." He wants to give the money back to the people. They discovered the Vatican Bank had 327 quin trillion dollars of our money. It took 650 planes loads to get it back to the United States. All our mortgages, car loans, etc., were obtained illegally. This will pay off everyone's loans and put money in people's banks. There will be no more poverty. Now I admit, it sounds too good to be true, but we will see.

So, since both of them have reset plans and Trump has been seen in pictures with the Cabal, I can certainly see why Kenny is entertaining that thought. I do not believe Trump is a "bad guy."

For years, everyone I know says that there is a cure for cancer, but they don't want to release it because it makes them too much money. That is true. Trump is going to expose all big pharmaceutical companies. The med beds, they are beds that you lay in, kind of like having a CT scan. They cure everything.

Misinformation is huge in this movement, that includes both sides, not just the misinformation that the mainstream media feeds, but misinformation on this end as well. They posted recently that several celebrities that have died, are alive. Not sure if that is true, and to be honest, I don't care. Found out that its Michael, not Michelle Obama. Yes, Michelle Obama is a dude. I won't go into too much detail on that because I think everyone knows that already. Real name is Micheal LaVaughn Obama. Joan Rivers said that on national television; the video is still on YouTube, one month later she was dead.

Everyone we see now are actors. Yea, I know that sounds far-fetched. Spoiler alert–pretty much every entry in this wonderful binder of notes will sound far-fetched. Believe me, no one is more interested to see how this ends more than me and Ella.

So, you might be asking yourself, if all this is true, why did it take so long for the public to know and for the truth to come out?

That is exactly what we kept asking, and all other Trump voters who did not throw in the towel.

But now we know why.

Three reasons. They all make sense if you take a step back, breathe and read this.

1.) It's bigger than just a stolen election. When he teamed up with JFK Jr., they decided to bring the whole corrupt world to an end. He has been setting them up for years. The Vatican, the central bankers, Hollywood, politicians, CEOs. Reforming our Banking System. Giving money back to the people and switching current currency over to Rainbow currency. And most importantly saving the trafficked children.

2.) As you can tell by now, Democrats and the news outlets brainwashed so many against Trump. They hated him, they still hate him and quite frankly, they probably hate him more now than ever before. If he were to step in after the stolen election, it would have looked like *he* was the Hitler. Like he "paid" the military or formed a takeover on his own. So many Liberals would have not believed the election was stolen, even with proof. They have been trained not to believe anything Trump says. There was a Coup (government takeover) happening, but it would have been twisted into the Libs thinking he was performing the Coup. Trump had to show the world what it would be like if Biden actually won. He had to show them Biden/Obama's agenda, not just tell them. He has been doing just that.

3.) During his advocacy for this world to be put back in its right mind, he had the United States Corporation dissolved. That's right, it no longer exists. Right now, there is no President. Washington, D.C. has been under silent martial law since January 20th. Why do you think all that wire and fences were up around the White House? It was not to keep people from getting in, it was to keep people from getting out. There was no United States of America Corporation. We are reverting to the original constitution of 1776. When there is High Treason involved in an election, the head of the military is acting President (General Flynn), it then reverts to the original President, which is Trump.

Now do you see why we wanted to get all this documented? Crazy shit going on!

We're not in Kansas anymore, Toto!

Speaking of Biden opening the border, remember in the beginning how the camera crews would come in and zoom in on kids' faces when Trump was President? Yea, well Biden won't even allow reporters and camera crew at the border. Of course, the news outlets listen to him, because, well, he is the Elite and protected. But what is going on is hundreds of illegals are coming over, they are being held in worse conditions, having to use tin foil for a blanket, they are at 1700% capacity (restaurants can only be 25% capacity), kids have died, drug smugglers coming over, more kids missing. But it's out there, the information is out there. Watch Fox, they show it, watch Newsmax, they show it. Those reporters did not listen to him and went into film.

There are quite a few civilians still defending Biden. One posted on social media recently, "Ok, these gas prices suck, but at least he's not racist." Idiot. Others have stated they think they made a mistake, or maybe Trump was right all along. Online, the comments are non-stop with ex-Biden supporters who realize they made a mistake. There is a movement called the "Walk Away" movement. It consists of Democrats/Liberals who voted and supported Biden but have now walked away from him. They see the truth. One of my Liberal friends posted on November 15$^{th}$: "Yes, I voted for Biden, and I wanted him to win. But not like this. I did not want him to steal the election; I wanted him to win fair and square." Ah, that was refreshing. He must have done his research instead of watching mainstream media.

BLM– you know the Democrat funded rioters that you never hear about now that Biden "won?" The news wants everyone to think that the world has peace now. But oh, trust me. Google Portland, Oregon. They are still destroying that area and many others. They just won't show you. In fact, Democrats have created a monster. BLM says they will not stop until Democrats pay them more money–stuff you can only find if you dig.

Covid guidelines are getting more and more comical. Not the virus itself, just the guidelines. You can only eat outdoors. But it's cold out. So, they built tents that you sat under with other people. So, you were indoors, but it's outdoors, so it's ok.

Please kindly go pound sand.

Serious uprise in pneumonia cases. –bacterial pneumonia comes from wearing the mask. Breathing in and out the same air in your confined mask is not healthy. Look up bacteria pictures of your mask after two hours of wearing it. That is what is making everyone sick. But they call it Covid. I have a feeling the CDC, Dr. Fauci and Bill Gates know this already, which is exactly why the masks were mandated. Wait until you find out how much money Fauci was paid to exaggerate the numbers. Mind blowing.

Gotta get the vaccine though. Everyone who believes we must get it, I wonder about. At what point did people forget that we live in America? You do not *HAVE* to inject anything into your body that you don't want to. All the reported deaths that the vaccine has caused and not one word on the news about that. If it doesn't kill you, it alters your brain. Nice.

We have never once questioned the virus itself. We do, however, question the validity of the extreme paranoia caused over it. Everyone will soon find out that this was a political virus, blown to extreme proportions.

They told us to watch for several earthquakes that will be coming up. There was more than any other year. Look it up, you will see. Some of the "earthquakes" even got recognition on the news. Except they were not earthquakes. That is just what they were calling them, but in reality, it was the underground tunnels (DUMBS-Deep Underground Military Bases) being blown up. Under the White House there were DUMBS. We watched the live stream on YouTube for several nights. We saw black suburban's and flashing lights on the night that people got arrested and we watched as they escorted children out. I think the plan is to destroy the White House in D.C. and the new White House will be in Mar-a-Lago Florida. Too much evil in D.C.; Obama held a lot of pedophilia parties there.

But of course, Ella and I will not volunteer any of that information to anyone. We only talk about it amongst ourselves and our families. Never outside of our home. We will be the first to admit, that we sound crazy. If someone is not following this, or they are a Biden supporter, or a Trump supporter who threw in the towel, they would lock us up and throw away the key. When the truth comes out, you can bet your ass we will say we knew *EVERYTHING*, but until then, mum is the word. Technically, that is the wrong thing to do as a patriot. We should be proud and confident about our findings. We should try to educate others (red pill them is the term) about everything we discovered. But we don't.

I tried red pilling my mom again. I didn't just fill her in on Trump and what was going on behind the scenes. I also told her my fear about if I was wrong, how Biden would turn us Communist. She listened, she believed, but then she watched the news and told me I was wrong. You can bring a horse to water, but you can't make them drink.

In the declassified files that were dropped, there are documents that prove UFOs and aliens are real. Now I don't have much info on that because, to be honest, my biggest concern is getting the right President in. Although I must admit, some of the videos were very interesting. John F. Kennedy, Sr. was about to declassify the UFO file and the central banking files before he was executed. Something must be there that they don't want us to see.

Ella and I have our own niche. I look up most of the election fraud and NESARA (new financial system), she looks up the biblical and UFOs/aliens. The two of us make a pretty good team and thank God, we have each other. Believe me, there have been days when I thought, this is bullshit, nothing is going to happen, and she would calm me down and in return, I do the same for her when she is feeling discouraged. Essentially, one of our biggest coping mechanisms is having husbands we can joke with about this; it is our outlet, a great way to tolerate an incredibly horrific situation.

Anyone who knows anything about the Constitution should have a red flag, a huge red flag, raised to them. Apparently, it's in the constitution that the State of the Union address *HAS* to be given in either January or February. It is illegal not to have a State of the Union address within that time frame, a violation of the constitution. Biden did not give one. His first press conference was 53 days after taking office. His questions were pre-planned, and he was horrible. He stated he was in office for 125 years, and how he did not think there would be a Republican party in the future. Ok, that speech had to be staged by Trump. It was that comical and there is no way they would allow that from a "real" president. They would have cut him off. It has been said that since there are a lot of citizens that are fully aware of even the minute details of the constitution, his late delivery of the State of the Union address did alarm many people, causing them to research as to why.

Coming up to the current date, it is March 31st, 2021. There has been so much going on in other countries that the mainstream media is not reporting. Almost another war coming and surely, they are told not to report it since it would make Biden look bad.

Russian hackers stole thousands of U.S. State Department emails.

Russia invades Ukraine.

NATO intercepted Russian planes.

North Korea shot Missiles at Japan.

United States pledged support after Ukrainian soldiers killed by Russians.

United States talked with Australia in response to possible war with China.

Possible mandatory draft in the U.S.

No mention on the mainstream media.

Speaking of 9/11. Bill Clinton arranged it along with Bush. Bill Clinton was not in power at the time of 9/11, but he was the President at the time of the Supreme Court Ruling and had no interest in signing NESARA. On October 10, 2000, under orders from the military generals, the Navy Seals and Delta Force stormed the White House and under gunpoint forced Clinton to sign NESARA into law. Secret Service and White House Security were ordered to stand down. The act would give the money back to the people. He and the Elite would lose a ton of money by not getting our taxes or interest on loans, plus they would lose control of everything. The office that held those signed papers was in the twin towers in New York City. The Elites and CIA arranged for the tower to be taken down. The plane crashed exactly into the floor where the office was located, the office that was holding the signed NESARA papers. Not only was 9/11 one of our biggest catastrophes in history, but innocent lives were also lost, and it was all done so every U.S. citizen would not benefit. Our biggest terrorist attack on U.S. soil was done by our own people, and the reasoning was to prevent helping us. Are you getting pissed yet? If not, please seek help. I am thrilled Trump added execution for Treason to this new government. Death by firing squad, hanging or lethal injection, it all works for me, and they deserve whatever they get.

There was a cargo ship in the Suez Canal. We heard about it first– three days to be exact– before it was on the news. It's part of the plan somehow, not sure exactly why, though. Trump has been wanting us to only use U.S. products and not to get our supplies from another country for years. He always got vetoed. This ship getting stuck was to prove what can happen if you get your supplies from overseas. Now, when we don't get our shipment with our supplies, grocery store shelves can be empty, and our prices go up. Some say there is more to it. The name of the ship's company is called Evergreen Shipping Agency. It is owned by Hillary Clinton. There was speculation that there were children on the ship. Hillary is probably the evilest of all the Elite. When this truth finally shows its ugly head and you have a chance to watch Frazzle drip, do yourself a favor and do not watch it! Some things cannot be unseen.

There is so much, and so much more than we even realize. Since we don't have military security clearance, let's face it, we are not going to have top level information. Hardly seems likely that a military project is going to post their next move online. Whenever Andy asks me why something didn't happen yet, I say, "Well, let me just get out my bat phone and call the big Donald and ask him what the delay is, ok?"

Certainly, they know that it is impossible for us to have the answers, but he is frustrated with the world, like so many others who just want liberty and peace.

Ella and I have a bottle of Tequila waiting on her counter for us. We are doing shots of that bitch once this comes out. Tequila doesn't expire, does it?

There have been several posts from Trump's attorney, Sidney Powell. It looks like they have courts looking at the evidence again and they have the states under scrutiny. Now keep in mind, Sidney Powell is a JAG– a Military Attorney.

It's getting more interesting every day. They are also saying the death of George Floyd was a lark, a game played by the deep state which caused the division and riots with BLM. Some say he is still alive. Not sure about that one. But that would be great if that was true and could be proven. Imagine how that would wake up Dems that voted for Biden and maybe unite everyone.

Finally current! Today is April 1st, 2021.

You are now in real time. I will document what is going on as often as it occurs or, as time will allow me.

The Navy have sent over a medical ship to meet the Evergreen ship that was stuck, which is now loose. Why would they need a medical ship? Were there really kids on there? We are patiently awaiting an update on that situation, and tomorrow, or at least by Monday (today is Thursday). These are supposed to be big days. Supposedly the public will know by Sunday (Easter) or by Monday, at the latest. By next Wednesday, NESARA is supposed to kick in. Now this NESARA thing would be great, but, like I said before it sounds too good to be true. Believe me, we still have mental faculties in place.

April 2nd, 2021

Woke up this morning to news that there were people arrested on the Evergreen ship that was stuck, then released from the canal. Waiting to hear the verification, but they are saying there were bombs on there that were supposed to be detonated if someone came on board. They also found dead bodies and hostages that were alive.

Took my mom for her vaccine today. I told her before that I advise against it and showed her why, but she insisted on getting it. Her reasoning–because all her friends told her too. Well, alrighty then.

I showed the proof that the vaccine was created before the virus. Even if I wasn't following this there's is no way I would get it. Not enough research on it and why would I vaccinate myself for something that has a 99.7 percent survival rate? After all that information, she insisted on getting it.

They are talking more and more about the World War III scare event. Knowing they are not going to discuss the real date on our channels, it always sits subconsciously in the back of our minds. It has crossed my mind before, that this app I am on, Telegram, if Trump is bad, is this their way of seeing who is on here? A part of me wishes I didn't have that discussion with Kenny. Trump being part of the Elite would have never crossed my mind. No, I take that back. I am glad I had that discussion with him. I need to know about all possibilities.

No, I am not losing it, and we don't wear tin foil hats. Ella and I don't do the Army crawl through our yards to get to each other's houses in fear we are being watched. We are nowhere near that point, but you don't have to be a member of Mensa to know that there is something going on. I just want to stay informed. Maybe we wouldn't be so much into this if we didn't have kids. My kids, Jack and Adam are just starting as adults. Ellas's kids, Willow and Mac are at the age of marriage, home ownership and starting a family. Willow already has one child and another on the way. We want them to have a good future.

April 3rd, 2021

There has been more talk and supposedly it has been confirmed that there really were children being trafficked on the Evergreen ship along with dead bodies. The fact that it was confirmed is all of the information we have received so far.

Andy worked with Kenny today. Kenny told him "they" do in fact have everyone's name who is on telegram. Like the Libs are being brainwashed with Covid, vaccines, and hatred for Trump, is the Red being brainwashed with Telegram and Trump's return? Are both sides being played? I hate not knowing. But I always go back to motive. If they are all in this together, why would they have to go to such extremes? They have the money and the power, why not just take us over together? Why would they have to go through the act of a stolen election, Nazi regime, Covid, and all the Supreme Court hearings? Why would they tell us about Adrenochrome, why would they tell us about 9/11, the phony vaccines and why would it be so intense? It doesn't make sense, they would not want us informed.

April 4th, 2021

Easter Sunday.

The weather was absolutely beautiful today! Bright, sunny and warm! Time to put to the side all the hoopla going on in our country, enjoy family and rejoice!

Jack called me and told me about an incident in Tennessee. At a restaurant, they wanted Jack to put on a mask to walk 20 feet to his table. He could see everyone in the restaurant with no mask on, it was only needed to walk to the table. That is the joke going around in the world today.

People say "Whew! I made it to the table before Covid got me!"

It makes absolutely no sense and only the sheep can't figure that out. He stood his ground and informed the hostess that it makes absolutely no sense, especially since she has already been standing there talking to him with no mask on. Didn't his germs already get in there? Tennessee is lifting the mandate in 11 days. I guess they know the virus cannot be caught by anyone 11 days from now, but today you can catch it, so wear a mask.

In the world events–yeah, the world events, the whole purpose of these words being written. Nothing. They tell us not to concentrate on dates but when the code suggests to 80 million viewers a date and strongly suggest something will happen, it is frustrating when it doesn't. They did mention that today fake Joe Biden was taken to the hospital. Not sure why, but that's what they said. They also said the mainstream will not show it yet. Seems like we always get information 48 hours before the mainstream media shows it.

April 5th, 2021

They are insinuating that the world will hear a "BOOM" this week. Ha ha– they have said that many times before.

There have been threatened wars between Russia and Ukraine, between China and Japan, between Iran and Syria, and apparently, they are false, but enough to cause the dramatic World War III that makes Biden look bad, and that was the plan. These "wars" are because of his inability to keep global peace amongst other countries. Countries that Trump made our allies. The Marines changed their website to a red background, which means war.

Then the spec ops Military Intelligence posted "The rain is coming." Trying not to get excited, but with all the hype, it's kind of hard not to. Not going to tell Ella any of this because she has too much on her mind with Willow, who is about to give birth. I am just hoping something happens for the world to see, but I am not banking on it.

Back in the current real world of Andy and myself, I drop initials to him all the time. I will say, "DJT (Donald J. Trump) is not going to let this go," or "FLOTUS (First Lady of the United States) did this or that," or "Everyone in SCOTUS (Supreme Court of the United States) is so corrupt." And trust me, many, many more abbreviations.

He will respond with "Well, what does CB (meaning me) think?" I will look at him sideways and then put two and two together; ah, crazy bitch, that's me! The best was when he asked me, "So what has your intel said today, is it still FITH?"

Again, I look at him and then I figure it out. Ah, yes. "FITH" is fucked in the head! You must laugh.

In all seriousness, this whole situation is far from funny. In fact, whatever the extreme opposite word of funny is, is what it is. So many facts that we have uncovered made us feel sick, it can keep you up for days if you are not strong or able to process correctly. The whole situation is sad and sickening. If we did not have our own little inside jokes, or the support of each other, it could quite possibly drive you to a point of no return. There is a reason why they coined the phrase "Laughter is the best medicine."

April 7th, 2021

Ghislaine Maxwell, the partner of Jeffrey Epstein and the one who coerced young girls to the island, has three million pages of evidence against her. Those pages have all the emails, notes and activities of every politician and celebrity that were on the island.

The Three Gorges dam is supposed to collapse soon. At the end of the damn is the Wuhan lab where they created the Corona Virus and pushed the "plandemic." There is a road called "Yellow Brick Road" and it's the biggest child trafficking route out of the Wuhan to all parts of the world.

They just posted and updated number of attempts on Trump's life. Last was 42, it is now 50. If nothing else, he will go down as the President with the most attempts on his life.

May 18$^{th}$, 2021.

So, imagine that. Urgent warning to anyone considering the injection that there is a deadly nanoparticles ingredient in the vaccine–not advised for human or veterinary use. Issued by a doctor and interviewed by Stew Peters. It's out there. The interview was on Newsmax, online and on YouTube. But of course, taken down. But the article has already gone viral online, and a lot of people did see it. No report of it on the mainstream media. Even if there was a one percent chance this was true, shouldn't the public be made aware of this?

May 21st, 2021

They are mentioning a lot about the game plan with the virus. It was also in their Agenda 21. Once summer came, they were going to open everything up. No more masks, no more lock downs and *EVERYTHING* can open. That, of course, was their plan all along, shut down during election to make Trump look bad. Then open when the fake Biden was in to make him look wonderful– like he saved the world!!! But then, bam! Another shutdown in late summer, an even worse one and they were going to blame the Trump supporters for this for not taking the mask or the vaccine seriously. It will be called Covid 21. It should be interesting to see if this happens.

When this first started, they said there will be a communication blackout. No power and it could possibly be for days. So, for a while Ella and I always made sure we had gas in our car, food in the house, plenty of water and cash. For a world where there is mostly debit and credit cards used, we both went to the bank and withdrew a good-sized sum of cash and kept in a drawer.

The cash is still there.

May 30<sup>th</sup>, 2021

Everything is still quiet. Well, I shouldn't say that– there is stuff that goes on everyday behind the scenes, but to put down everything would be nearly impossible. If I don't state every time someone wants Nancy Pelosi's sanity investigated, or Phony Joe's dementia to be looked at, it's not relevant to list it six times a week. There is this thing called shedding now. They are saying that if someone is vaccinated, the nanoparticles emit from their pores and could possibly contaminate someone next to them. Great. I did my due diligence and decided not to get the vaccine, now I must be careful when standing next to someone that had the vaccine?

There are parents who knew the vaccine was bad, but still had their child vaccinated, because "someday" we will all have to have it. Someday a tornado might hit, are you going to make your kid live in a cellar now? I keep my opinion of that to myself. Those are other people's kids– not my circus, not my monkeys.

This world is so fucked up.

June 4th, 2021

Sensitive? Not sure if that's the word to use. Pussies, maybe? Not sure if that's the word either. All I know is *NO ONE* can joke with anyone anymore. Any slight joke is considered racist, sexual, or some form of offensive material. The jokes when I was young, or hell, even two years ago! The blonde jokes, the Polish jokes, the Mexican jokes, the black jokes– hence the word joke! Nope. Can't do it. Everyone is blaming everything on their race. Employers are literally "afraid" to hire someone that is not of color. They know they will be slapped with a racist complaint.

Let me tell you that in these last few months, there are so many cops that have been shot and killed by a black, no mention on the news. So many good cops that have helped people of all color– no mention on the news. They only mention on the news when a white cop kills a black man. When will people wake up? It is the mainstream media that is making the world racist, who is controlling the mainstream media? The Democrats, why can't people see this? Why do Democrats want to make the cops look bad? Look back in this wonderful book of notes when I recall the Hitler Regime. The agenda 21. Hitler took away all paychecks of the police (defunded) so they would only be available to the rich for pay. When Trump opposed to defunding the police, he was racist. They said he condones white cops killing black men. Seriously? Still baffled to this day how many people cannot see what is happening.

But guess what? There is word that the country might be opening again! It's a miracle! No more Covid! Well, they can't say that, but pretty much that's what it means right? Maybe, just maybe, no more masks but only if your vaccinated–but they won't ask for proof (because they can't). Let me try to get this straight. This virus is so deadly that you insist we get vaccinated, and you insisted we shut down and you insisted we wear masks, but now we can open up and you will trust people to be honest about whether they have been vaccinated and not wear a mask? Open your eyes people. But as frustrating as it is, it's a great time to be alive and witness all this fuckery!

June 27th, 2021

Been shown on the news, yes even mainstream media (for some reason), about the bad effects of the vaccine. Johnson & Johnson is causing blood clots and other brands are showing heart abnormalities in children.

I hear of so many people who got the shot because they "had to." Umm, no you didn't. Their job made them. Get another job. Fake Biden is being ran by Obama and people are getting $600 a week to stay home on unemployment. The unemployment keeps getting extended; therefore, they don't have to go to work. There are plenty of jobs available if you need to switch.

Why do the Democrats keep extending unemployment?

Two reasons:

1.) Because they are for helping the lower class. The unemployed love Phony Biden because they can stay home and get paid. The lower class has been proven to be more obedient if they get stuff for free. They can be controlled.

2.) With all the jobs available, it makes Phony Biden look good. "Look at all the jobs I created!" he says. No, you dumb fuck, there are so many jobs available because no one wants to work! You didn't create shit except for havoc and chaos.

There are signs on gas stations and stores that say: "Had to close early due to not enough staff." Restaurants don't even have enough help.

July 30th, 2021

There was talk that Trump would be back in by August 1st. Not looking good, but we will see. They also stated months ago he would be back by March, then by May, and now it's August 1st. Not sticking to dates. I have absolutely no idea why dates are thrown out there; I will admit it's maddening.

There is a huge symposium coming up on August 10th, 11th, and 12th.

This symposium is being held by Mike Lindell. Let me explain who Mike Lindell is.

Mike Lindell is the creator, single owner and founder of My Pillow. Yep, you guessed it– just a pillow guy. Now, for obvious reasons, we are the laughingstock of non-believers. He is a die-hard patriot. Like so many others, he saw the flipping of votes in real time the night of the election. Since he is highly successful, he has deep pockets and connections with influential people. He started digging and found actual proof of the election fraud. He used his own money and connections to go public. He made several speeches, held many interviews and made a show called "The Absolute Truth." In return, he got death threats, and many major stores cancelled his account. He got banned from Twitter, Facebook, YouTube and other social platforms. Anywhere he talked, they shut it down. And of course, no mention at all about the proof he had.

Why don't they want anyone to hear what he has to say? Whenever someone has irrefutable proof of a crime against the American people, it gets silenced, and death threats occur. Noticing a pattern yet?

Some say that no one can take him seriously because he is just a "pillow salesman." Give me a fucking break. He must have a brain because he is a self-made billionaire that started his business from the ground up.

Doesn't matter what the person does for a living, if they know, they know.

Mike Lindell, along with Trump and many legal experts have put together this symposium. Aired on Right Side Broadcasting, Newsmax and OANN, of course not mainstream media.

August 8$^{th}$, 2021

With all the hype about the symposium on the 10th-12$^{th}$, my question was, "What good is it, if only people that are following this are aware of the symposium?"

I found out that several, Democrats, Republicans, reporters from ALL stations, ALL newspapers and many other outlets were invited. If they attend and don't broadcast or acknowledge in some shape or form, the corrupt election, Mike Lindell will make all their names public with repercussions.

Not sure if that will work, but hey, it's worth a shot.

They are also saying there will be a test EBS (emergency broadcast) on Wednesday the 11th. It will just be a test, nothing of significance, but it will still be interesting to see if that happens.

Covid numbers are still supposedly going up and now it is imminent of another shut down.

Also saying everyone will have to get vaccinated and show their "papers." Just like the Jews.

No problem, I have my blank vaccine card that I will fill out and laminate for everyone in mine and Ella's immediate family. There. We are vaccinated. I still feel it will be unlikely that will happen. Trump will block it.

If all goes as planned for the evil deep state, the vaccine will make people sick within five years, or death. Everyone will respond differently. Some, the vaccine will attack their organs, some will get blood clots, some will just die, maybe in their sleep? Cardiac arrest? Some will not get physically sick, but it will affect their cognitive way of thinking; early onset of dementia, they will lose their sense of humor and common sense. Some will not get sick at all but will never be able to conceive or father a child; it will make them sterile.

Every big pharmaceutical company, for every 5th vial of vaccine, they filled with Saline. Why? Because it would be too obvious if everyone dropped dead or got sick at the same time.

This way, the ones who got the saline (thinking of course it was the real vaccine), will not get sick. The world will have millions of people that say "I got the vaccine, and I was fine! It's a conspiracy theory that the vaccine makes you sick."

Umm, no–you got saline, sweetheart. Please sit your ass down.

One thing I have not touched on yet was all the audits! Yes, real forensic audits!! Arizona's is finished and I believe other states are also.

And of course, Trump won– won by a landslide, but we knew that already.

Things are getting good; I am so glad I have documented this shit.
August 10th, 2021

The symposium was delayed an hour. Mike Lindell came out and stated that their servers were attacked. A hacker got through their fire wall. But they had five other backups. Good thing since they got through three of the firewalls. Anything they can do to prevent the truth from getting out.

This past week, he had a hell of a time even getting there. All the curve balls the deep state threw at him. Including, but not limited to, the airstrip being closed when he was trying to land in South Dakota. He was coming in for a landing and they were told from the control tower that the runway was under construction. True story. He got here and it has started– an hour late.

It's important to him, he stated, because this is the worse crime in U.S. history, meaning the stolen election of course. This is the biggest crimes against humanity case, bigger than Hitler. The vaccine is a mass genocide. A man-made bioweapon (vaccine) that will kill millions.

Mike Lindell is offering 5 million dollars to any cyber genius who can disprove his proof. That is how confident he is.

He also said that tonight there is going to be a big announcement that will change everything. WTF?

Seriously? Is it big, or just getting us hyped up like so many other times before? We will see!

Well, the big announcement was not that big. A big "nothing burger" is what they are calling things that are supposed to come to fruition, but don't. A Nothing Burger.

He came out on stage looking and talking in a frazzled manner. He then introduced three people from Colorado. Now, these three people meant nothing to me, but apparently for the diehards that are following even closer than I am, there was significance. One of them, Tina Peters from Colorado, was on the verge of being set up and arrested. The fact that she was there while they raided her office and were going to arrest her and frame her for many crimes that the Democrats have committed, apparently is huge. Ok, so maybe not a Nothing Burger. I guess Ella and I were just hoping for something more in layman's terms that would show the world some portion of the truth.

Ella and I had Sammy and Andy watch it with us. What were we thinking? They had fun making jokes about the writing at the bottom of the screen promoting Mike Lindell's pillow and advertising your next order can be 66% off if you use the suggested promo code. Mike Lindell is a patriot who is using his own money to get to the truth. Let the poor dude plug his business.

Then, when the big announcement didn't happen– oh boy. Sammy said the big announcement was going to be that he has a "NEW and improved pillow out!"

August 11th, 2021

Now today is the day that we are supposed to be getting an EBS. Not the big one stating everything going on in the world, just a test. It is supposed to come in at 1:20 p.m. this afternoon.

Yep! It came through, as promised, at 1:22 p.m.

They stated the television stations, radio stations and phones that did not comply would be fined.

August 13$^{th}$, 2021

Nothing new, or should I say nothing big, has been advertised. The whole world still does not know anything, and they are now saying that a second or even third booster vaccine will be needed. They did announce a couple of weeks ago that you can still get the Covid while vaccinated and you can still spread it. Then why get it? But of course, people are still running out to get it.

September 24th, 2021.

Well, let me start with Afghanistan.

Thanks to potato Head Joe Biden, the Taliban now has more Black Hawk helicopters than 85% of the countries in the world. They have night vision goggles, body armor, weapons and unbelievably, the Taliban now has biometric devices which have the fingerprints, eye scans and biographical information of all the Afghans who helped us and were on our side over the last 20 years. The U.S. simply abandoned an arsenal of military equipment and weapons. This reportedly includes up to 22,174 Humvee vehicles, nearly 1,000 armored vehicles, 64,363 machine guns, and 42,000 pick-up trucks and SUVs. The list of allegedly abandoned weaponry includes up to 358,530 assault rifles, 126,295 pistols, and nearly 200 artillery units. Oh, and the Taliban will likely inherit state-of-the-art military helicopters, warplanes, and other aircraft from the U.S., too. Eighty-five billion dollars' worth of equipment! We "abandoned" this equipment and "accidentally" left it there? Yeah, ok. To top it off, the current administration has no plans to try to retrieve them.

The Armed forces also left first. Before the American citizens could leave Afghanistan. Huge no-no. That is like the captain abandoning his ship; can't do that. Joe Biden's orders for the military to leave.

Do you really think our Armed Service men would leave 85 billion dollars' worth of equipment? Tell me that wasn't staged. All a part of waking people up. Leaving Americans behind? Also, a part of waking people up. This is exactly what would have happened if Biden was the real president. Now I often wonder if this really is "all for show" is there even a war right now in Afghanistan? Or are Afghans unknowingly part of this movie? What's real? What's not real? If it is real, how on earth would this so-called president still be allowed to be president? He wouldn't, which is why this real-life true crime series always has my attention and intrigues me so intensely. This was an utter embarrassment to America.

World is getting more fucked up by the minute.

Gas is still high, the unemployed are still getting paid to stay home and stores are still closing early.

They went back to the mask mandate, and I will not comply. Think about it, if masks really worked, they would ban them.

Many more people are waking up. They are just now putting certain events together and realize how absolutely nothing is making sense. Their common sense is finally kicking it.

A diehard liberal on Facebook posted:

"I might have been a sheep, and I might have fallen for everything, but at least I know when I die, that when I thought everything was real, I did my best to protect others."

*Thought*? As in past tense? *Might have been*? But if you notice, he never actually said he was wrong. He never said he fell for the mainstream media and all its propaganda. But what he did say was at least he did the right thing. He dances around the subject and points out he is still a good person. I like watching him squirm. It is entertainment for me. When the truth comes out, he will be deleted. I do not believe in deleting someone from Facebook, this isn't middle school, but for him I will make an exception.

I have been thinking about Kenny. His version has crossed my mind several times. Simply because why has nothing been stopped?

It's getting worse, so why haven't the "good guys" done anything. Someone I know, yes, I know them, not a random person that I never met before, they posted a picture of a letter from the bank. The letter stated that the Biden administration wants the banks to keep track of deposits and withdrawals on anything over $600. On those deposits and withdrawals, they want them reported to the IRS.

We are turning communistic. Oh yeah, that's right, they had to show the people. The quote "get your popcorn ready" is running rampant. Fuck your popcorn.

This afternoon is supposed to be the release of the Arizona Forensic Audit. Us patriots have been waiting ten months for this. Please let it be good, or better yet please let it actually go somewhere.

Evening of September 24th, 2021

Watched the whole audit. This audit was on Maricopa County in Arizona only. Watched all three hours of it. They started the audit by mentioning the preliminary got leaked. Of course, the preliminary was not accurate, nor complete. The preliminary showed Biden as still the winner. The mainstream media got wind of that and, you guessed it, it was all over the news.

The truth is Trump won. They showed 17,967 votes were ran through two, three, sometimes four times. And of course, all for Biden.

In addition to multiple votes being run through more than once:

1. Multiple types of paper with various thickness were used in the election, which is against Arizona election law.

2. Over 1,064,746 files related to the election were illegally deleted.

3. Based on the factual results, the election should have never been certified.

4. Machines were connected to the internet. Which is illegal.

5. Nine thousand and forty-one more mail in ballots were returned than sent.

6. Twenty-five percent of early voting came in with duplicate signatures after November 4th, past the cut off.

7. Four thousand and forty-nine voting ballots had blank signatures or unverifiable signatures.

8. Five thousand two hundred and ninety-five were people from other counties.

9. Two hundred and eighty-two dead people– that's just from one county!

During this audit, it was also found out that Trump had 200 extra votes that he shouldn't have gotten. Laughed my ass off at how the camera scanned the room and you saw the reporters from the mainstream scrambling around to record. Then you saw some of them run out of the room with their phone to their ear. Oh, they loved that! Dumb asses. What's 200 votes going to do for you when he won by a landslide? Look at the numbers above.

The final statement given by Karen Fann, Arizona State Senator, was that law enforcement needed to be involved. She also stated she will be writing a letter to the Attorney General for him to do something *NOW*!

She also said this should not have been certified. Ah–, relief. Well, not really. Not until the mainstream media shows it. As expected, it was not shown on mainstream media. Anyone who is reading this and still believes the "news" is a normal, good and honest broadcast, ought to be bitch slapped. Anybody who tuned into this audit, – and yes, a lot of Democrats did because they were curious– but then watched the news the same night has to know how shady this was. It does not take a rocket scientist to figure this out.

So, what now, you ask? Yea, so do we.

September 28th, 2021

At first, they said the "blackout" will last 10 days. But then they said, not all areas. They understand people cannot go on for 10 days with absolutely no power, air, heat, water, internet, etc... It might only go a couple of days with no power. But the internet could be down for 10 days.

When all this first started and we thought the 10 days was going to be "any minute," we were always prepared. Now, with all these delays, we have gotten more laid back. I might need to stock up again, just to be safe since no one knows when it's going to happen.

There are few cryptic things that they say to watch for:

1. Watch the water, supposedly when the gorge breaks in China.

2. Shots will be heard around the world.

3. First arrest will verify action.

The shot will be heard around the world. Well today, Biden got his booster shot. You know, because a booster is needed, and to make matters even more intriguing, Biden never got any of the vaccines. Reports of an ambulance leaving the Capitol after he got it. Some suggested that fake Biden will be reported as dying from the booster. Will that make people see? Is that the "shot will be heard around the world?" Nah, I don't think so. Sounds too simple. First arrest will verify action. Andy, I, Sammy and Ella have a pool on this. Andy says, it will be Biden, Sammy thinks it will be Trump, Ella says the Pope and I say Bin Laden.

Hey, you have to play games to stay sane in this ludicrous world!
October 4th, 2021

Well, today is the day that "something" will happen. Boy, oh boy, here we go again. I tell myself all the time not to listen to dates, yet I do.

While driving, it came across the radio that all social media is out. It is all down. Now to your average person who is not paying attention to what's going on in the world, they probably thought nothing of it except being pissed that they couldn't post their usual "bitching Karen shit", or their lies to make their life look great. But to me and Ella and about 80 million other Americans, we were like "Yes!"

After hearing that, I immediately texted Ella. You see, "A blackout is necessary." We have been hearing this for so long. A blackout does not necessarily mean a total blackout. It does not mean absolutely no power. This is 2021. A blackout could mean no internet, no phones, no social media and yes, no power. It could be a short period of time or for an extended period of time.

They had told us it will be a social media blackout. They said it would be on the fourth of October. It happened.

Facebook and Instagram were out all day.

Facebook employees swiped their cards to get into the building and the cards didn't work. They were denied access.

On the news, they are telling you it was a hack. Some cyber ninja con artist hacked the system. No, my darling, it was the white hats (good guys). It was planned, and Ella and I knew it would happen on October 4th, weeks ago. I have no idea what the purpose of them performing a blackout on social media does; that is privileged information and there is no way they would let the world know their exact game plan.

During the day when Facebook and Instagram were down, Telegram received 50 million more followers! Fifty million! So, yea, people are waking up.

I am overjoyed that the social media blackout happened when they said it would. This gives me hope. Please let this be the start of something!

October 5$^{th}$, 2021

I used to watch WWII documentaries about Germany and ask, "Why didn't those civilians fight back before walking into a gas chamber?" Now I know.

The United States has gone from the land of the free and the home of the brave to: "Show me your vaccine passport or you're fired." The truly disturbing part is that it took only 18 months for Americans to allow their freedoms to erode. Many Americans on the left, happy to be told what to do, welcome the tyranny.

What's coming next? Well, have you seen what's happening in Australia?

Australia has locked their people up.

As reported in The Guardian, "To combat COVID, the nation is literally a police state. No one can leave—literally. You cannot enter the country. You cannot leave the country. You cannot venture out of your own house; you might be arrested for incitement. There are apps that everyone must download which the government pings at random. Those selected have a limited time to take a picture of their location. Refusal to respond leads to the police being dispatched to your residence. This is the 'COVID zero' approach and it's turned the nation into something like North Korea. They locked their people up."

Now anyone who is aware of this and still doesn't believe this whole virus is a control tactic, should be hung right along the side with Biden, Obama, Clinton, Bush and so many others. Yeah, I know that sounds harsh, but seriously how can anybody hear about this and not think otherwise? The only purpose is to control. Hitler started out slowly; he monitored how much jewelry and paintings were allowed to the Jews, then how much food. What's going on here and in other countries has nothing to do with the virus.

Guess what people, all of the above are supposed to be coming to America. Starting with monitoring our money, then it will just progress–first like Australia, then like 1939-1945 Germany.

It has also been determined that Pfizer has been testing their Covid vaccine on orphaned 6-month-old babies. This way when the adverse reaction happens, no one will notice. Hell, if they survive, they are too young to talk; if they die, who cares? They were orphans. Pure evil. An extension of their crimes against humanity.

But guess who is exempt from getting the Covid vaccine?

Members of Congress/Legislative branch

Congressional staff

Judicial Branch

White House staff

Employees of the CDC, FDA, USPS, Pfizer, Moderna, Johnson & Johnson

There you have it. So pretty much, politicians, those in vaccine companies and those in government jobs, do not have to get it. All of those politicians and actors you see on television getting the vaccine–fake.

Wake up people! I cannot stress that enough.

What's funny is the USPS (United States Postal Service) employees do not have to get it. What they are saying is that our mail couriers –who serve millions of homes a day, touch tens of thousands postal items that they then put in your mail box, and they sometimes have to go to your door for a signature, then have to enter into vestibules at condominiums and apartments–they are safe and cannot transmit Covid, so therefore they do not need to be vaccinated? I swear the government thinks we are idiots. Some are.

Now the House Democrats want to impose a Forced Sterilization/ Three Child Limit Bill. Found this out by following Pennsylvania State representative, David Rowe.

If there was any doubt that today's progressive Left have utterly and completely disregarded your personal medical freedom, then let this be the nail in the coffin.

It would limit how many children your family could have, dictate at what ages you could have a family and issue a $10,000 fine for refusing to submit to forced sterilization after having three children. If I am not mistaken, that has been a rule in China for some time now. Well, that fits the agenda of them trying to make America the next China.

I don't think it will pass, but they are trying. Just the fact that they are trying is alarming enough.

October 6th, 2021

They are saying that the five most used words over the coming weeks, months and years, will be *WE TRIED TO TELL YOU*.

Let's hope that is correct. Ella and I do have a t-shirt that says, "I was right." –hoping we can wear them sooner than later.

There have been a lot of storms today. Birmingham, Alabama, storms moving in, so far over 10 inches of rain is reported. Winter storm warning in Sacramento, California (this is only October). And it's supposed to snow in Texas one day this week.

Now, supposedly that is supposed to mean something. Here's the thing I have never touched on this yet in these notes. The government controls the weather. HAARP (High Frequency Active Auroral Research Program) was a little-known, yet critically important U.S. military defense project which generated quite a bit of controversy over its alleged weather control capabilities and much more.

Why did I never touch on this? Simply, because I don't care. Ok, I care, and it's going to be very interesting to learn about, however, let's fix this damn stolen election, first. This is one conspiracy theory (as they call a lot of things that are true, but don't want people to know), that has been proven by NASA and United States Air Force. I never really researched it but given by the notes in this book, don't you think we have enough to worry about?

I remember when Jack Ass Biden was running, I watched one of his speeches. He said, "When I become President, there will be no more floods, no more Tsunamis, no more tornadoes, no more earthquakes." Man, I laughed my ass off. I thought, man, this mother fucker thinks he is God! Well, then NASA and the Air Force admitted they can control the weather through HAARP. So, I was wrong. See, I can admit when I am wrong.

So, Mister (not President) Biden, I thought there would be no more weather disasters? There have been several in the last 11 months, ass wipe.

When the truth came out about the controlled weather, they pulled some stunts to prove it, such as winter 2020 when Texas got an enormous amount of snow. Look it up. It snowed in areas that *NEVER* got snow. It also snowed in the Sahara Desert. Yep, in the Desert. Today's news is mostly about the "weather." Not sure of the relevance, but I am sure it means something.

October 7th, 2021

Oh, dear God in heaven! These Democrats are still blaming Trump for all their wrongdoing. I am telling you, as messed up as this world is, and how scary it is, it's also like a slapstick spoof. If the Twilight Zone was a comedy, it would be the United States right now.

Democrats/liberals are saying, "This horrible economic strain and the out-of-control pandemic is all due to the prior administration and we are still trying to transition smoothly and undo the mistakes the last leader made." There was no economic strain with the last leader. There was peace.

The above quote occurred when they were talking about the food shortage. Yep, food shortage coming up. Even more severe than the last one. I already noticed how shelves are empty.

Food prices are out of control and everyone knows it. Since the pandemic, shopping at a grocery store or eating at a restaurant has become an increasingly expensive experience. So, what's going on? That's right, the previous administration did this.

Someone suggested something on Telegram. They wondered if Telegram was invented to keep us docile. If people feel the truth will come out and it's right around the corner, then they will stay calm and wait. Then when everything is confiscated and stricter rules are in place, that's when we will find out we have been played, proving the Kenny Theory. Something to think about.

There are so many things I have not mentioned here. There is just too much. But trust me, we have been following it all.

I won't get into detail, but a few things we know so much about, and Ella and I have had several conversations concerning the following topics, however, I don't think they were mentioned:

1. Nazi Germany is not what appears to be. Not saying it didn't happen, of course, but it's not as it appears. I am not going to pretend to know what that means, because I don't. No one knows. When the truth is told, the world will be told.

2. Anne Frank wrote her journal 1942-1944. We all know the journal was found and saved. The journal was analyzed many years ago. It was determined that it was written with a ballpoint pen. The ballpoint pen was invented in the summer of 1944. Do the math.

3. Most women you see on television are really men, including the Victoria Secret models.

4. Every big time Cabal leader is related going way back to the Rothchild's and some other names, including Tom Hanks and Ellen DeGeneres. They wanted to keep everyone in the same bloodline.

5. Most you see on television are dead and you are watching actors or hired look-a likes– I think I mentioned that before though.

6. The Biblical side. I know nothing about it. It is written in the bible what is going to happen, however, the Bible that you know, is not the real Bible. It has been changed and altered several times over the years.

7. Aliens. They are among us. They think humans are stupid. They are not wrong.

8. There is a way to "transform" yourself into another being. Like you can literally "float" and be in something else. Not sure.

9. Cloning is real. It is happening.

Then there is the money aspect. The crooked FED, Central Banking, Cabal owned loans, illegal interest and the new money alternatives. The FED and the Central Banking system is all part of the Cabal; I knew Obama was involved with the crash in 2008!

Ella came over today. Something came up and it prompted her to tell mom the truth. She told mom everything we learned for the last year and a half, within 25 minutes. You heard of speed reading? Ella gave mom a speed lesson, if such a thing didn't exist, it does now. Not sure if mom believes it, but she did say to me the other day, "Are we turning communist?"

I am craving for her to realize what the world is turning into.

Mom told Ella that she just saw President Biden on the news today. Ella responds with, "Oh please, he is dead! That's not the President!"

Only Ella can get away with that. My mom's mouth hit the floor. When Ella left, mom said she believed everything except the dead people/ actor part. Ok, I get it. That is a lot to take in, I know it sounds irrational and hell, we ourselves don't even know if it's true! But, hey, baby steps for mom. I will take it.

October 10th, 2021

Today is a Sunday! Great weekend! We went to Amish country, weather was perfect, and the Amish never disappoint. We had fun, good laughs, ate great food, went on a buggy ride and saw a lot of cool Amish ways.

One thing is for sure, the Amish are definitely "Red!" Go Amish! Every craft store we went to, they made birdhouses, yard signs, yard banners, knitted scarves, and so much more all saying "Go Trump." Even some of the horse buggies had "Trump Won" stickers on them. No one wore masks. Ah, who said the Amish were naive? They know more and are wiser than most sheep. Did you know that there are no reports of autistic children in the Amish community? Big coincidence that they do not vaccinate their children and there is no autism.

Nothing is a coincidence.

January 23rd, 2022

We took the plunge and booked a trip– booked with hesitation of course because of the upheavals going on in the world, but we did it and glad we did! Andy, I, Sammy and Ella, went on a much-needed vacation.

The Caribbean was incredible! From the time we got into the car to go to the airport until the time we arrived in our driveway back home, non-stop laughs!

Ella and I were hoping to find another patriot. There are 75% of true patriots that are following this like we are. But to find one is harder than you realize. And even if you do find one, the chances of them "admitting" it and talking about it are slim to none. One day while in the ocean, we came across two couples from England. Ella told them that their Queen was dead. I was dying. They stated they knew she was sick, and Ella responded, "Oh, no, she is not sick. She is already dead." The look on their faces was priceless. They obviously are of the 25% that are not following this!

Nothing as far as public awareness.

Most states now require a vaccine card to get into places. Show me your papers (said in a German accent)! Granted, it is mostly in the blue states, but it still exists. I get really agitated when I hear people caved into the Covid vaccine to get into places. There is no way entering a restaurant, venue, event or concert is that fucking important. I just won't go. But hey, that's me. There have been more jobs lost due to employers saying you "have" to be vaccinated. Even though the Supreme Court just said they cannot mandate it.

They had to wait one year after the fake Inauguration, which was January 20th, 2021. At midnight on January 20th, 2022, which would then turn to January 21st, 2022, we went under martial law. All National Guard have been deployed. It's only evident in large cities.

It has also been confirmed that all Navy Personnel are not allowed any outside communication starting on January 21st, 2022. It is supposed to be 100 days after. New elections, full truth exposed, aired tribunals.

I know, I know, we heard this before.

But I will say this, it's something. It truly is "Good vs. Evil" and we will prevail. Once I think otherwise, I will be the first to document that. I will not go on pretending that Trump is good if I ever find out differently.

I do believe that there will be an EBS, that major pedophilia exists, that there is adrenochrome, that there is human trafficking and that there will be televised military tribunals. I trust the plan still, I just don't know when it's going to make its appearance.

Do I believe with 100% certainty there are actors playing our politicians and the "real ones" are already gone and that John F. Kennedy Jr. is still alive? Not sure. But what I do believe with 100% certainty is that I have seen enough actual proof of what they are capable of– the fraud, the corruption, the trafficking, the child abuse and so much more– to know that there definitely COULD be actors and that John F. Kennedy Jr. could still be alive. 100 % positive of the probability.

As they say, that is my story, and I am sticking to it, for now.

Seventy-two percent of Instagram users have stated they regret getting the vaccine.

Twenty-One thousand deaths

Eleven thousand heart attacks

Thirteen thousand cases of Bell's palsy

Twenty-five thousand plus cases of myocarditis or pericarditis

Nineteen times the expected amount of myocarditis in the 12–15-year-old age group, all from the vaccine. Why are they not stating this on the fake news? Oh yeah, because the mainstream media is governed as to what to say by the deep state. Duh, keep forgetting.

January 24th, 2022

Well, the stock market took a huge hit today. Not sure how far it has to crash for things to start, but it's on the way down, and predicted to go lower.

We were warned that false news will come out bashing General Michael Flynn, and that has happened as well.

Good point was made at an aired symposium today. If Trump and his team (white hats) were not in control, we would still be on a lockdown. Businesses would not have opened, more counties/states would require vaccine passports, you would already see the concentration camps being built in the United States just like in Australia and they would already be confiscating our guns.

A positive thought and a very valid point. Think about it, why hasn't what happened in Australia happened to us yet? Very good point, especially since it was in the Democrats' playbook.

February 24th, 2022

It's been an exciting, disappointing, yet uplifting week so far.

Russia has been threatening to invade Ukraine for weeks. Why?

Vladimir Putin has said he believes the breakup of the Soviet Union was the biggest political tragedy of the 20th century. He has written that Ukrainians and Russians are one people.

Putin made it clear in a speech that he does not believe Ukraine should be a separate state, rather, it is an essential part of the historic, imperial Russia. So, the basic reason for this crisis is that Putin wants to restore what he believes is Moscow's rightful control over the territory of Ukraine. He appears willing to use force to do so, no matter the cost.

Well last night at around 10:30pm our time, he invaded.

Now for the public to see the truth, four things had to happen.

1. It had to be one year after the fake inauguration.
2. World War III had to start.
3. Announcement of Queen's death.
4. Stock market crash.

It is one year after the fake inauguration, World War III is about to start, announcement of Queen's death is supposed to happen soon (they waited two weeks before they announced Phillip's death, yes, we knew about it before the public did) and the stock market just crashed due to the possibility of a new war.

So, 3 things have happened, and one of them is on the horizon.

They have been saying for over a year that the ball will roll fast once a World War starts. They had to have it start to get Biden out of office. The ultimate proof that he sucks and is mentally not right, and illegitimate, to have him removed. This way the sheep cannot accuse Trump of a coup.

Now, what I am not sure of is the fact that they also said it's a false flag. Meaning, they (the white hats) were going to stage the war. The appearance of a war again, to ease the sheep into it. That seems a little hard to swallow. However, a false flag also means that it is really happening, not just for the reasons you think. Now that makes more sense.

The Bidens' ties to Ukraine run deep. They are in bed with Ukraine. Ukraine is a country with one of the biggest human trafficking rings. That ring is tied to the Bidens. Hunter Biden's laptop has emails and evidence of money transfers on it from Ukraine– millions of dollars that Biden sent to Ukraine. Ukraine is deep state.

Remember, a good rule of thumb is whatever the fake news says, think the opposite. They are controlled by the deep state, controlled and paid for by Obama and Clintons.

Fake news says "Putin is bad"- opposite= Putin is good.

Fake news says "Poor Ukrainians" - opposite= Ukrainians are bad.

Ukraine has so much blackmail on the Clintons, Obamas and especially the Bidens. There is so much proof of the corruption that the wonderful United States of America elites are doing, that the mainstream media *HAS* to protect Ukraine on their segments. Otherwise, the Ukrainians would leak all their information on them.

Putin–look how bad the mainstream media speaks of him.

Remember all the stuff they said about Trump? Opposite.

What if, maybe, just maybe, Putin *IS* cleaning out Ukraine? Maybe, just maybe, Putin is a white hat and working with Trump for the better of the whole globe?

Since Ukraine is loaded with the Cabal, children underground, trafficking, drugs, is in cahoots with Biden, and they said this was a global take down from day one, it's definitely a potential scenario.

I wonder if Biden supporters see the fuck up yet. Do they see that when Trump was President, there were no terrorist attacks, and all countries got along? Do they see how horrible we are doing and all the damage that has been done in one year? Do they see that inflation is at its worst in 40 years? Do they see the communistic ways that are happening? I mean that is the purpose of all of this, to wake people up, right?

And if they do see it, will they admit it? No. Not likely.

So many people are putting down Trump for the way he got along with Putin and North Korea's Kim Jong-Un.

Isn't that what a leader is supposed to do? Make peace with other countries?

Instead of being proud of our Commander in Chief for doing something no other President could do–make amends with our enemies– they accused him of being in their pockets.

Well, none of the shit that is going on now would have happened under the Trump Administration and the liberals need to take their asses back to reality and wake the fuck up.

For people like us, the mainstream media is what made us see the truth. The biased newscasts and hatred for Trump was so obvious; their poor acting is what made me seek out the truth.

The European countries of NATO (North Atlantic Treaty Organization), Belgium, Canada, Denmark, France, Iceland, Italy, Luxembourg, the Netherlands, Norway, Portugal, the United Kingdom, and the United States have come out in full support of Ukraine. The U.S. and UK have emerged as the biggest supporters of Ukraine since the beginning of its tensions with Russia.

Of course, the U.S. is supporting Ukraine because they are laundering money for the Bidens. Why wouldn't he help them?

Japan, South Korea, Australia, Canada are also supporting Ukraine and have announced additional sanctions on Russia after it began the invasion of Ukraine.

Did you just read that list of countries? Read again. World War III.

The United States is sending 7,000 troops to Germany to help reassure NATO allies.

They accused Trump of colluding with Russia years ago. It has been proven recently that Clintons were behind that and set him up.

Just this week, they demanded Trump's financial reports. They discovered that all finances were accounted for and in fact... he has more assets than they realized.

The two prosecutors on that case just resigned.

Now anyone that has doubts that something fishy is going on in this world, do you see it now?

Putin has even been quoted. He said, "Anyone who got the vaccine, I do not feel sorry for you. You should have known."

It's all connected; everything going on is interlinked.

Also going on is the trucker strike and convoy. Truckers got together to boycott the mandated covid vaccine and all other tyranny that's been going on. They started in Canada and are now working their way out to the United States, making a visit to Washington, D.C. first. More truckers are joining in and there are more strikes. There will be even less transportation of goods, food and necessities to our local stores.

Some are calling the truckers domestic terrorists.

You see, the Democrats and Liberals are like narcissists. Well, ok, they are identical. They can start shit with you, but if you defend yourself, you're bad.

These truckers are sticking up for their First amendment rights.

First Amendment:

"The First Amendment guarantees freedoms concerning religion, expression, assembly, and the right to petition. It forbids Congress from both promoting one religion over others and also restricting an individual's religious practices. It guarantees freedom of expression by prohibiting Congress from restricting the press or the rights of individuals to speak freely. It also guarantees the right of citizens to assemble peaceably and to petition their government."

So, if they are only exercising their First Amendment rights, how are they domestic terrorists?

Justin Trudeau, Prime Minister of Canada went into hiding when the truckers came to town. Canada has been literally a Nazi Country. The truckers are peaceful protestors, sticking up for their rights. Why do you need to go into hiding? What are you ashamed of? If you feel you are performing for the rights of the people, then why hide?

Locals made lunches for them and greeted them with open arms. After they left, Trudeau declared the country was in a state of emergency, stating it was due to Covid cases on the rise. No, they weren't. Two days after declaring the country in a state of emergency, he then removed it. He has also frozen bank accounts of civilians, is seeking out Trump supporters and calling them domestic terrorists, then fining them. And, fun fact, Justin Trudeau is the son of Fidel Castro. That will be publicly known soon. Everything, Every. Single. Thing. Everything stated in the beginning is starting to come true.

From "wash your hands" to freezing your bank account in just two years. It's been quite a journey to keep us all safe, hasn't it?

Jack is going to Texas. It seems like every time he is getting ready to go away somewhere, something in the world is going on, and of course you know I must mess with him. He is leaving in two days and in my usual sarcasm, of course I have to say," Mayyyybee," meaning maybe you will be going. As always, he rolls his eyes at me, goes along with it, but knows there is a slight chance it could possibly happen.

March 1st, 2022

The night of the fake State of the Union (SOTU) address by the fake president is tonight. Conservative Political Action Conference (CPAC)was last weekend. Trump spoke and many are calling that the actual SOTU. Also, look at the date that Biden is giving the SOTU– March. Remember, it is in the constitution that SOTU must happen in January or February.

But it's useless if the public doesn't hear about it. All these truths are out there, but if mainstream media doesn't show it and the sheep don't hear about it, then what good is it? You will probably hear me say that a lot during this nontraditional documentation.

Also going on today are the results of the Wisconsin hearing to decertify the election. That's right, voter fraud investigation is *STILL* going on. No one knows about that either. It has already been determined that 50 thousand illegal votes were cast, which is more than twice the victory margin.

Well, another audit was ordered, and they discovered it again. There were also 625 thousand dead people, and every nursing home in Wisconsin had a 100% turnout and they voted– the residents. Sixty-four percent of them are either in a coma, or full onset Alzheimer's. But they were supposedly awake and coherent long enough to vote?

The hearing today was asking Wisconsin to decertify the election.

Yes, it's real. I watched it. It was televised. Saw it with my own eyes.

Still waiting on an answer regarding the decertification results.

Also, it was just determined that Mark Zuckerberg's nine million dollars in funding went to five counties in Wisconsin ahead of the 2020 election and that violates the Wisconsin State Election Codes of Bribery. Massive bombshell.

You read that right. Mark Zuckerberg, owner of Facebook. He is a huge player in this world fiasco. Too many people want power in this world. They need to feel important, better than others, they need to be in control and rich; it's the only way they are happy. Zuckerberg is part of the elite. They all want to be a part of the new world order. The great reset.

Why else do you think Trump and anyone else that talked positive about Trump got booted off Facebook? Trump refused to be a part of them. He was banished.

Is it making sense to you yet?

Why didn't that alarm *EVERYONE* in this world? So many people that live amongst us thought there was nothing wrong with banishing the Commander is Chief out of a voice. Every sheep, thought a social media mogul, had the authority to do that. They thought there was nothing wrong with it. Seriously? The sheep saw nothing wrong with a platform like that kicking our President off it while he was still fucking President.

Arizona–Arizona also had proof of voter fraud. That was a couple of weeks ago. I did not watch that hearing. They did say that decertifying one state would not overturn the election, so they were going to wait on all others. Now that Wisconsin is done, maybe two can overturn?

133 MILLION REGISTERED UNITED STATES VOTERS

74 MILLION- TRUMP

81 MILLION-BIDEN

74+81=155 MILLION

DO THE MATH.

I suck at math, I mean I am the ultimate fucktard of math, and even I can see that there are more people that voted than there are actual voters. Hell, you don't even have to do the math, just look at the numbers!

Another thing going on today:

Pfizer had to release their declassified files, and they came out today. Here is what it showed:

1.They made 73 million dollars profit from the vaccine.

2.The serum/recipe for the vaccine was manufactured in 2007.

3.They got the patent for the vaccine in 2017.

But wait, how can all that be? The virus, you know the Covid, did not come out until 2020.

Why were they working on a vaccine for a virus that did not exist yet?

Yep. You heard it here first, folks. Well, not really, you have heard it by now, I just always wanted to use that line.

There are many different theories about Trump and his warp speed vaccine. First, we all know Trump must play along for the sake of the Biden supporters and how they, along with the mainstream media, made most of the world hate him. There is no way he could have said "DON'T TAKE THE VACCINE!" They would have hated him even more. When Trump spoke about taking the vaccine, he had the hopes that people were doing their own research and using their own discernment. Art of War. For appearance reasons, he had to show that he supported it. Anyone following this– or hell, not even following this– anyone with an ounce of common sense could see through that. His supporters are not sheep, even though we are portrayed as a cult, we are far from that. Did not matter who would have endorsed that dreaded vaccine, we would not comply.

Trump lost a lot of supporters when he endorsed the vaccine. They all said if he was good, he would not have endorsed it. Look at the whole picture, people. That is something that Kenny points out as well. Trump endorsing the vaccine was verification for him that Trump is evil.

Also, the vaccine he made was either saline, or injectable hydroxychloroquine, which helps with the symptoms of Covid.

So those two things came out today, the voter fraud proof (again) and the release of Pfizer's records, the same day as the SOTU.

Now, the big question is, will they show any of this on the mainstream media?

I am sure not. Nothing is even reported about the high gas prices, the shutdown pipelines, the price of groceries, the border crisis and nothing negative about the war that just started.

The Obama/Biden leadership invaded seven countries in eight years in the government.

The Trump/Pence leadership signed six peace treaties in four years in the government.

Obama = Nobel Peace Prize.

Trump= Double Impeachment.

Yep, nothing wrong here, folks. Move along.

I really hope that when the truth comes out, that there will be a reporter that comes forward. A reporter that will either give an interview or have a movie made. Is there a reporter out there that said, "Wait a minute. That's not what happened, why do I have report this on tonight's broadcast?"

A reporter that saw the corruption, but there was nothing he or she could do. A reporter that will state they were only able to report a script that was put in front of them. I should probably reword that, I should say I hope there is a reporter that questioned them and is still alive, or not missing; they are the ones I would love to see an interview with.

Tonight, for the SOTU, they have barricades up. You know just like they did after the storming of the Capitol. Supposedly it's for the truckers. The hard-working patriots that supply us with necessities–yea, those domestic terrorists.

It's going to be interesting. I am going to Ella's tonight to watch the SOTU. Usually, the sound of fake Biden's voice sends chills up my spine.

I would rather chew razor blades, but for some reason I do want to watch it tonight. I just want to see how many times he fumbles on his words, or how many times he blames Trump for what's going on in the world. It's always Trumps fault.

Do I secretly wish that the army comes in and arrests fake Biden? You bet your sweet tooting ass I do.

But I know that won't happen.

Jack is in Texas. He absolutely loves it. He said it is so "American" out there.

No masks, no vaccine cards, and everyone gets along. Tons of American flags. Well, this is America, right?

At the concert he was at, a speaker came out beforehand and gave a speech. They ended it with, "Anyone who does not want their freedom, you can get the fuck out of this Auditorium!"

That might sound vulgar for some since everyone has become so sensitive, but seriously, what American does not want their freedom? It was a great statement, and very true. Deal with it. I wish I could have gone with Jack, that would have been amazing to see. Hey, maybe we should plan our next vacation to Texas? Now, that is a great thought.

Patriots have a reputation of being racist. Not true. The Democrats and mainstream media portrayed that of us. Patriots don't like corruption and criminals. If you murder, rape or kill someone, I am going to want to see you hang whether you are white, black, purple or green. And you can't come here illegally. Get the proper paperwork, do what you need to do, then we will welcome you with open arms. Don't sex traffic kids, don't bring your cartel here, honor the constitution. That's it. That's all that patriots want. In fact, patriots are being labeled racists, when in fact, it's just the opposite, they want everyone to just get along and they despise this division.

Shouldn't that be the want of every American?

Folks, I cannot stress this enough, the division that was created is unbearable. As you already read, blacks hating whites, whites angry that blacks are taking the division to such an extreme, Biden voters bashing Trump voters, Trump voters bashing Biden voters, the riots the attacks–just plain massive division. This is not like when I was growing up and one parent voted for one guy and the other parent voted for the other guy, then when the results came out, they were both so calm and planned what to have for dinner and life went on. Oh, it's not like that at all. This is so much different. The deep state is messing with all of us, the sleepers/normies/libs, don't even know it yet, but their hatred towards us is a result of the Cabal's mastermind, it is not fueled by Trump.

People have been disowned by family members over this, friends have lost friends, parents have lost children (and not referring to death due to Covid or the vaccine,) I mean they lost them mentally. Gone. Disowned. The division is astronomical and that is an element that is going on right now, you need to grasp that concept right now, before you read any further.

I did read something that alarmed me. Someone had pointed out that if what I believe is true, something would have been done already. I guess it states somewhere in the Constitution and in the military law book that if a coup occurs it can and must be taken out immediately. The head of the military does not have to wait for court cases, actual proof, etc. So, in other words, just the fact that there were 155 million documented votes with only 133 million registered voters, that would have been enough for the military to step in instantly.

But then I think of all the severity of the corruption. The CIA, FBI, Congressmen, some high up military personnel and so many more were part of the corrupt Cabal. Is that why it couldn't get done? And this is a global problem, not just the United States. The deep state goes as far as Italy at the Vatican, Ukraine, China and a lot of other countries. So that puts me at ease.

While all this is going on, we all still live day to day. The Biden supporters go about everyday sound asleep, thinking every day is grand, however, never missing a moment to mimic Trump. The Trump supporters who are not following this live every day eagerly awaiting the 2024 election, and then there are the die-hard patriots like us who follow this shit. Every. Single. Day.

We check what's going on every day, but don't live by it. Yes, there is a difference. We don't cancel plans if there is a hearing on. I don't rearrange work around a hearing, and I don't stop living. But do we check our news feed every chance we get? You betcha. And we will continue to do so.

71

It is getting a little harder with everyday situations while out and about and with other people. Whenever politics comes up or the vaccine, I politely remove myself from the room. If I am in a situation where I can't remove myself, I act like I am busy responding to an email or text.

If I am invited to an event that is being held at a venue that needs proof of vaccination. I just decline. No explanation needed.

I will end this book of notes once the truth comes out. Truth meaning, no matter what it is. Bad truth or good Truth. If Kenny's way is correct and we are all fucked, maybe this book will end with me going off to the concentration camp. However, I do believe it will be the favorable way, and life will grand! There is definitely a jug of Kool-Aid out there. Question is, is it blue Kool-Aid, or the red?

But either way, this will all go down in history, it will either be how the world was saved by President Donald J. Trump from a grotesque group of people called the Cabal, or it will be the years that President Donald J. Trump had so many people who believed he would save the world.

The truth remains to be seen.

The fake SOTU was actually normal. That's right, I said normal. The comments online were "Did Trump write his speech?"

Those were the comments from the Red. The libs' comments were "Yessss, he is so great! What a wonderful President!!"

I want to throw up.

He literally said everything that Trump has been saying for years! He wants to secure our borders. *NOW?* Now that you let everyone in and condemned Trump for wanting to secure them? But, because it came out of his mouth, the Liberals are ok with it. When Trump said it, Trump was a bad man, a racist.

Biden sounded coherent. He did not slur, did not stumble, nothing!

I was shocked and disappointed all at the same time.

April 1st, 2022

A lot has happened, but nothing at the same time. Yes, we hear shit all the time, and our newsfeed is loaded, but nothing breaking.

So many people (Red people, that is), now also believe Putin is only taking out Biden's bio labs. They are saying that Putin is not hurting civilians. That Putin is a white hat. That Putin is helping Trump clean up the Cabal, the deep state. That would agree with what Ella, and I stumbled upon before. Then again, this all seems unbelievable sometimes.

But for sure it is a possibility. Putin cleaning up the deep state and blowing up the bio labs in Ukraine? Why not? – Weirder shit has happened.

Hunter Biden's laptop is in the news. Yes, the mainstream media! Of course, they are not telling you everything, but it's a start.

How long will it last, or what will come of it, is the question. It probably won't go very far, but just the fact that they are mentioning It on mainstream media is a huge plus.

Boycott Disney is huge! People are blasting all over social media to boycott Disney. Of course, it is mostly the red people boycotting it. It has surfaced about how that place has underground tunnels and it is the largest child trafficking racket.

On top of that, they have turned to the far left and shoving gay rights down patrons' throats.

Those truths are starting to come out. And people are boycotting.

Walt Disney was a satanic pedophile, point blank.

July 12th, 2022

We lost a soldier. Mac is more into Kenny's theory now. He says Trump is bad as well. That scares me because Mac is *REALLY* following this. Mac informed us of this when the two families were together. There is nothing better than hanging out with your adult kids. I take that back, there is something better. Knowing your kids did not grow up to be assholes is the best feeling! Out of our two families, three of them are men, old school men. Their word and their honor are the most important thing to them, a gentlemen's handshake means something, and they will always have your back. They love hard but don't confuse that with weakness. They stand their ground, fight for what they believe in, cannot be swayed, are un-vaxxed, see through the charade of the deep state and they love their country. Willow, while not a male, has the exact same integrity. Life is good. The best part is that no one in our little circle has lost their sense of humor. Seriously, you have no idea how "joking around" has become obsolete. I am so glad that we have not become victims of that. And that is why my circle is small.

The world does not seem as angry. Either people just accepted the fucked-up world, or people just don't care anymore, or people are waking up. I hope it's the latter.

Yes, they are still talking about EBS. Yes, they are still saying there will be 10 days of darkness, yes, they are still saying there will be a new financial system, all of this is a yes, but when is the question. Some say it will be soon. Some say they have following this since 9/11, for 21 years and if it hasn't happened by now, it will never happen. Who knows.

Hunters Biden's lap top hoopla died down. They talked about it on the fake news for a while, they demanded investigations, then nothing.

From the Democratic point of view, Hunter was not the one running for president, and he's not the one who is in office. From the Republican side, if the cameras were turned the other way on the Trump children, would this make bigger news?

It's an interesting conversation to have, but with the laptop being authenticated as Hunter Biden's, it raises the question– what comes next?

Russia and Ukraine, you very rarely hear about that anymore.

Tens of thousands of Ukrainians and Russians got killed since Russia first attacked on February 24th. It was all over the fake news 24/7.

It is still going on but barely any mention. I am not sure what that signifies.

What's even odder, food supply plants are being set on fire, flooded out or somehow destroyed Over 26 plants– too big of a coincidence, how do 26 food supply places have an unforeseen tragedy?

No matter how up to date on this "movie" you may be, there is a situation going on with our food supply that is starting to become alarming. It is not a conspiracy network, but more and more information is coming out, and more and more people are noticing it and talking about it.

Last month, Joe Biden said that food shortages are coming, and they're "going to be real." Jen Psaki (the spokesperson for the White House) at the same time made a contradicting statement, "We're not expecting a food shortage here, at home."

Oh, really? Which one is it?

I don't even want to say it; these food plant fires– there are so many that have happened in such a short span of time– the idea that these disasters are random occurrences is no longer in the equation.

Some believe one of two ways:

1. That Biden and the evil Cabal are doing this to starve us, to bankrupt us with the prices, to get to a point of rationing food like the Jews did, to control us, for population control, or all of the above. There is even a baby formula shortage. There are the moms that were forced to get the vaccine and don't want to breastfeed and now can't get baby formula.

2. Others believe that it was the white hats that destroyed all those food plants because the Cabal was poisoning our food supply.

There are very few that think everything is just an unfortunate coincidence, even the ones that are asleep, and believe me that is very reassuring.

The Libs had a recent meltdown. They overturned the abortion law.

The Supreme Court overturned *Roe v. Wade*, the landmark ruling that established the constitutional right to abortion in the U.S. in 1973.

Libs are saying, "What if someone gets pregnant, but cannot afford the baby?"

Well then, they should have kept their legs closed, sealed off their cooter, used protection, or they can give the baby up for adoption.

There are so many infertile women out there that would love to adopt your baby.

Most states will still allow abortion in the first six weeks for special circumstances, such as rape.

The Biden administration wanted to allow abortions all the way up until the ninth month. Are you kidding me? That is murder, end of story. Oh, my Lord, could you imagine for a minute if Trump suggested that? The Liberals of course are in denial of that. They are screaming that the Biden Administration never said they can abort at up to nine months. Yes, they did, Karen. Look it up. Mainstream Media will not tell you that because that would set off too many alarms. A nine-month-old is a full-blown human.

But now here is the best:

They did interviews with people protesting the overturn.

The real news, that is. The "Red" reporter would walk up to a random patron that was protesting and ask:

"Why are you so upset that this is overturned?"

Lib "Because it's my body, my choice!!!!"

Reporter: "Ok. I see. So, when the vaccine was being pushed, wasn't my body my choice for that also? I mean, you were ok then if people didn't get vaccinated, right? My body, my choice?"

The Lib looked dumbfounded. "Well, umm, umm, that's different."

Reporter: "Why?"

Liberal, "I don't want to have this conversation anymore!"

Then of course, they turned their backs and walked away.

So, while others are waking up, most are still asleep. But for the ones that are waking up, the Democrats, Cabal, and Elite, don't like that. We the people are getting pissed. So, they must have their buddies at the mainstream media distract everyone. They are playing the riot at the Capitol on January 6th all over again.

They tried impeaching Trump for this already. He was acquitted. It's done and over with. But they are bringing it back up again and showing it on mainstream media. Remember, they did not televise any voter fraud hearings. But this, they will cover repeatedly.

When the fake news shows you something, it's usually a distraction to stop you from looking at something else, because we all know it was the Democrats behind the storming of the Capitol.

Possibly a diversion of the 9% inflation hike?

"Don't look here, look over there… "

July 17th, 2022

While sitting at my computer tonight, Adam strolls into my office and rolls his eyes when he realizes I am documenting the latest news, or rather lack of news, going on in the world.

I said to Adam, "Ok, just wait, you will see. You are going to want to read these notes someday."

He says, "Mom, I am not reading that."

Me, "But you are in it."

Adam, "Oh, ok, then I will read it. Did you put in there how I turned into a sexy beast?"

Me, "Um, no, I did not. But you can bet your ass I am going to put this conversation in there!"

So, there you go, I put that conversation in here, as promised.

Ok, so I am very excited about something!

Here's the thing, before *Roe v. Wade* was overturned, one of our truthers told us that it would be. Then, it was announced! We heard about it months before it came out to the public.

The same with the laptop, then it was true.

Well, now it has been told by the same truther, that the Supreme Court overturned the 2020 election!

Do I think it will be exposed tomorrow? Nope. Do I believe it was overturned? Yep.

Those hearings I told you about before, way back when, you know, the ones that weren't televised. Well, supposedly they *HAVE* been doing an ongoing investigation behind closed doors and just recently, it was overturned. The two Supreme Court Justices that turned it over must be hidden. They have to secure them and every member of their family before it can be announced. They are relocating them out of the country.

Once that happens there will be a test EBS. All it will state is everyone is to get to their homes. Now again, this is just shit we are hearing, no one knows the real way it will be done except for them.

After the test one, that's when the real EBS will come. That's when they will play the tribunals. Of course, we don't know the timeline so this could be quick, or it might not be revealed for months or hell, at this point, years.

Remember way back when in the beginning of these notes, I had mentioned that when the truth comes out, the military will make us vote again. That apparently is not the case anymore. Trump never conceded. The reversal of the election will just go back to him. Also, remember, Biden was never the legitimate president anyways. The government was dissolved and put back to the ways of 1776.

NESARA is still talked about. To be honest, we are happy emotionally and life is good. If that doesn't happen, so be it. I have never really banked on that, but for our kids, that would be great. Do I subconsciously hope it's true? You bet your ass. But am I counting on it? Nope. Well, they are saying we can count on it.

In Wisconsin, they have already admitted that the ballot boxes were illegal.

The conservative majority of the Wisconsin Supreme Court ruled on Friday July 8th that ballot drop boxes were illegal in the state, and it didn't take long for right wing election lie evangelists to declare the decision proof of a fraudulent 2020 vote, and even to demand again that the election results be overturned.

The decision regarding drop boxes, a spokesperson for Wisconsin said, "Begs the question: Was it illegal in 2020? I say yes, and there's unfinished business there as well."

The candidate said in a statement that he was "Elated beyond measure" at the decision and added, "Much more to come, buckle up."

Ah, buckle up he says. Trust me, we have been buckled in.

Now, the people that believe Kenny and Mac's way are stating that Trump will either be fake arrested or fake killed. He will still be intact and will be doing evil behind the scenes with the deep state. But those of us following this on Trump's side will be like, "Damn it, if Trump wasn't arrested or killed, he would have saved us!"

According to their channels, that is how Trump will make his exit to us patriots.

I am still thinking positively. I think this will end eventually and Trump will be President again.

I refuse to believe that *EVERY SINGLE* person in politics is the devil. That every single politician wants population control, wants to control us, worships the devil, etc. Man, this shit is even more fucked up than I realized.

Ironically, I am the creator of these notes, yet I don't know the ending.

July 18th, 2022

I noticed little things are being shown. For instance, the fake Joe Biden went to Saudi Arabia. Now everyone knows the President of the United States is treated with the ultimate respect, red carpet and all. Literally, a red carpet when exiting the plane.

Saudi Officials laid out a purple carpet for him. And they showed that on the fake news. No President in the history of the United States, in any country, did not receive a red carpet. He is the exception. I am on the fence if that is necessarily an act of disrespect, or if it signifies something else. Time will tell.

Also, he failed. He went to make a deal with them, and they rejected him. They showed that on the news, too. Oil prices rose, boosted by the failure of President Joe Biden's trip to Saudi Arabia.

"Failure of President Biden."

They said from the beginning "Drip... drip... drip... flood," meaning they will be dropping little tidbits of truth here and there on mainstream media, then hopefully flood us with truth.

If we really are in the house for 10 days, we should have enough food, water and all necessities. Ella is all set. Her basement is like a fallout shelter. She has perfectly organized boxes that are labeled with food supplies and any other items that we might need.

I tell myself I am going to do that. But here I am, this is me, not doing it.

July 29th, 2022

I do know for sure that more people are catching on that things are not right, it's evident in just basic conversations with people on a daily basis. That is not in reference to anything huge that was said, but I hear people saying things like, " Something feels off in the world," or some libs I know don't praise the glorious Biden anymore. My God, you must be an idiot not to pick up on it.

There has been a very interesting documentary that was made called 2000 mules. Yes, of course we watched it.

Per several internet sites:

"Dinesh D'Souza film 2000 Mules. At the very least, the movie makes a compelling case using what appears to be incontrovertible evidence that not only was there massive "ballot stuffing" fraud in the key swing states, but that the fraud literally stole the election from Trump and gave it to President Biden."

"2000 Mules bases its conclusions primarily upon cellphone tracking data provided by carriers and surveillance video of ballot drop boxes provided by multiple state governments. The only way to dismiss the film's conclusion that Biden's victory derived from massive ballot stuffing is to show that the data used to track the cell phones was corrupt, the analysis of the data was flawed or the videos received from the respective governments were doctored. No one has established any such improprieties, yet the mainstream media's knee-jerk reaction is to reject the film and its conclusions and offer absurd suggestions to explain how the data and video evidence is false."

"It has been suggested that the people in the videos are election workers retrieving ballots from the boxes or that the cellphone data is of taxi drivers who happen to pass the ballot boxes. All one must do to reject such nonsense is watch the film."

"In a perfect journalistic world populated by real journalists, this film would indicate a large amount of smoke worthy of investigation. But again, the same super-partisan, leftist media is making zero effort to get to the truth. I challenge any Democrat, Trump hater, any Never Trumper to watch the film and see whether their rock-solid belief in the honesty of Biden'selection remains so afterward."

No of course not. That election was not honest. It was stolen.

Now keep in mind, this movie was/is out there. You could stream it on any major network. It is known about. People were talking about it. Was it mentioned on the fake news? Nope. And that movie was only one third of the fraudulent election. It did not even touch base on the algorithms in the computer, the injected votes into the system via internet, the other countries involved. It was just about the hired "ballot stuffers."

The push for electric cars, the war going on between Taiwan and China, Cadillac has stopped making gas cars– so much is going on!

It's exhausting. It's impossible to document every single thing that the deep state/elite are up to.

But it's all going to be historical, believe me whatever I missed in here, you will be able to find in the real world. Everything will become public knowledge.

August 4th, 2022

As of now, no great big scare event, no military personnel and no superhero with supernatural powers came and swung from the towers to save all of our asses.

Same old shit different day. Same shit meaning we are getting little "drip drips" and not enough "BOOMS!"

Wash, rinse, repeat.

Biden tested positive for Covid, then tested positive again, then again. They are "worried" about him.

He is back in isolation. Supposedly, Biden is fully vaccinated and has all his boosters. I call bullshit. Refer to that list of the ones exempted.

More than likely, they are just trying to keep him out of sight. He is an embarrassment.

Now there is a new virus! It is called Monkeypox. Governors in some states have declared a National Emergency.

It is contracted by men having anal sex. Answer me this, if you had to wear a mask on your face for Covid, do we now have to strap a mask on our assholes? (Asking for a friend.)

The declaration allows the Department of Public Health to utilize resources and funds across the state and quickly distribute vaccines in the prevention and treatment of the virus.

Ah, there it is–another vaccine. Because Covid vaccine didn't get enough people sick or kill enough?

"We have seen this virus disproportionately impact the LGBTQ+ community in its initial spread," said one governor.

So, you're going to tell me that most of your state is LGBTQ? (Lesbian, gay, bisexual, transgender, queer, or sometimes questioning.)

Well, peeps, I have no way of knowing what year you are reading this, but fucking transgender is huge.

Healthy boys playing t-ball have now decided they want to be a girl, beautiful young girls that played with Barbies now decided they want to be boys.

Parents encourage it. They are letting kids as early as five years old determine what sex they want to be.

Straight men turning gay, straight women turning lesbian– a lot of bisexuals.

Anyways, that's Monkeypox. They are talking about locking us down again for this.

Try telling people that they are going to be locked down for a gay man's disease. Oh dick! (No pun intended). Shit will hit the fan. Again, no pun intended.

What seemed like a better world with people's personalities lately, quickly came to a halt. A different vibe this last week. Someone I know who is a Lib, stated that she feels like the whole world is just angry again. She did not elaborate on this, but I am kind of feeling it, too. And for a Lib to notice, it must be bad. Sometimes people just suck. Can't explain it. Just such negative auras. Toxic, dark. It's nothing in particular, just sucky.

It has been claimed that there were a lot more of 5g towers, and also new satellites, that can sometimes affect people's energy. I don't have a clue.

August 8th, 2022

Remember that date!

The FBI raided Trump's home. This day will go down in history. All this bullshit will go down history!

This day, especially. Never, has a past or current President's home ever been raided by the FBI. Never.

No criminal charges have been filed against Trump, and the Department of Justice has remained tight-lipped about its ongoing investigation. Conservatives have said that this unprecedented search was just another "deep state" Democratic stunt to persecute Trump.

Worse, Trump's supporters have speculated, could this all be an elaborate attempt to keep him from running in the 2024 election?

This search was not justifiable.

August 14th, 2022

Joe Biden has passed a bill that is allowing them to hire 87,000 IRS agents. Supposedly they are going after the middle class. For fuck's sake, really? The IRS shouldn't even be a thing. But unfortunately, it is. The IRS is a very sad reality.

Now, some have said that this bill is over a 10-year span. IRS will hire 87,000 new agents over 10 years and the first set of hires will be after he is out of fake office. Ok, so then why was this addressed now? Like there is not enough bullshit going on—Russia with Ukraine, China with Russia, China with Taiwan, grocery shortage, gas prices, baby food shortage. But let's do a behind closed door meeting regarding fucking over the middle class in the next 10 years.

And oh, it will cost the American's $79.6 billion. Yep, a funding boost was granted for the Internal Revenue Service, totaling $79.6 billion.

Trump will be arrested.

I don't know guys. I am getting scared that Kenny, Mac and Adams's way might be right. Yes, I said Adam. We lost another soldier. Adam feels the truth should have come out by now. It hasn't, so therefore he feels it implicates Trump and that he is part of the problem. I explained to him again; this is Global take down and it takes time. That is the same line I tell myself continuously to keep me sane and to remind myself to trust the plan. He, like so many other Americans, is mentally worn down, he did not want to hear it.

Here is the latest on the infamous Trump home raid.

Former U.S. Army prosecutor Glenn Kirschner predicted that former President Donald Trump "will be indicted" asserting that his "days are numbered."

"Donald Trump will be indicted," Kirschner asserted. "I'm not sure which jurisdiction will indict him first, but he will be indicted."

From the Red side:

Two scenarios.

1.) One is that Trump knew of the raid and set them up. If they want to declassify what they found, then go for it. It will incriminate Biden, Obama, the Clintons, Pelosi and all others.

2.) And this one I cannot stand because I am tired of it all, but here it goes:

It is still part of the movie. It's all planned. He will go to jail, but his incarceration somehow will bring up all other documents and take down the Cabal.

They have been saying from day one that "The first arrest will verify action."

This is bigger than us, no matter what people say. It is going to take the military. It is impossible to "fix" anything governmental. They just need to be annihilated.

August 31st, 2022

Dr. Anthony Fauci announced his plan to retire at the end of Joe Biden's term in a new interview published Monday, lamenting Americans were no longer listening to his recommendations on masking or vaccines.

Gee? Ya think? He will retire by the end of Biden's term. Like he has a legit term, or even a choice for that matter.

More and more people are waking up about the vaccines and it is being publicized in more places now how bad the Covid vaccine is.

The sheer number of young, healthy adults dying "suddenly" has become so well-known now, that even the corporate media can no longer ignore these record number of deaths occurring among the working-class ages between 18-years-old and 65.

The correlation between these "sudden deaths" and the roll out of the Covid vaccines is indisputable, but because "correlation does not equal causation," the corporate media and the government health agencies continue to deny that the vaccines are at fault.

Healthy adults, just dying. No reason at all. But all of them had the Covid vaccine.

I still love and respect everyone I know that got the shot, I wish they wouldn't have, but it was their choice. I feel sorry for the elderly who stay in the house and only watch mainstream media and have no access to the outside world or internet. The mainstream media scared them all to the point of no return– of course they frantically decided to get to the nearest vaccination site.

The Supreme Court of the United States (SCOTUS) has overturned the election. It has been verified on every channel.

Yeah, yeah, I know, you heard that before. But remember, everything that is leaked turns out to be true. Since all this bullshit started, not one thing that we heard on our channel, something that got "leaked", not once did it not come to fruition.

And now they are talking about it more. It's out there in the open and they are, of course, debunking it.

London Bridge's falling down......

That is another riddle to this wild ride we're on. We are waiting on that. London falling. The queen died months ago. Yes, it's true, they are just waiting to announce it. They are mentioning London Bridge is falling down more frequently now.

The latest update on Trumps home raid:

Of the "TOP SECRET" government records, seven were found in a container in Trump's office and 11 others were found inside a Mar-a-Lago storage room.

Meanwhile, 17 "SECRET" documents were found in Trump's office and 37 inside the storage room, according to the list.

Trump — and/or members of his team — could potentially face obstruction of justice charges for allegedly concealing the classified documents, according to experts.

The DOJ has not yet said publicly who, if anyone, they believe is guilty of possible crimes in connection with the raid.

So, this man gets raided, and they raided his 16-year-old son Baron's room.

But they never raided Clintons with the Benghazi deal, never raided the Clintons when Frazzle drip came out, never raided Obamas when Pizza Gate came out. And they never raided the Bidens with the Ukraine fiasco and his crack smoking son. Hunter Biden was caught doing deals with China and hookers and drugs, that son never got raided but they raid a good natured 16-year-old boy's room.

Imagine, if that was anyone other than Trump. Someone else's 16-year-old's room being raided unjustly? It would be made out to be horrible, the mainstream media would be portraying that news with such empathy and compassion. Craziness.

September 12th, 2022

Dingdong, the witch is dead! The announcement of Queens Elizabeth's death!

She died on September 8th, 2022. Well, at least that's when they announced it. They announced it 1776 days after the first Q drop– 1776.

They announced it on September 8th, the exact date Princess Dianna was on *Time* magazine, but a different year obviously.

All of these are coincidences, I am sure. Or are they? Oh, that's right, nothing is a coincidence.

While out running errands, I ran into our friend Joe. The first thing he said to me was "The Queen is dead, Sidney! But she has been for a while!"

"Yep, that's right!" I said.

He has been following this too; in fact he warned me not to let anyone know that I am taking notes. I wondered why he would make a statement like that, but then quickly pushed that mystery out of my mind.

History has it that her son, Charles, will now be King.

They said we are waiting on London Bridge to fall down. I'm uncertain if that phrase is a metaphor pertaining to her death or if the bridge will literally fall. Will the Queen's death cause exposure of the truth of the evil antics of the Royal family?

They say the King can only be protected by the Queen. The Queen is dead. No protection for Charles. They announced on the news today that "Trump was not invited to her funeral."

No shit.

He is in the middle of taking them down, why would they want him there?

But of the course the public sees it as "The Royal Family has ousted Trump"– a statement the Libs love and of course run with.

Today, it was noted that late last night, Trump was seen leaving a golf course... in his golf shoes and all, flying to Washington DC.

There are rumors that he had to fly in for his arrest.

But nothing else has been said.

Our channel is telling us that something is going down the 14th -18th then again on the 20th-24th. There have been all kinds of media equipment trucks at the White House. They are also posting a live video regarding NESARA/GESARA on the 16th and concerts all over the world are being cancelled.

When the new financial system hits–maybe on the 16th, but I don't think so– I think it will be start of the switch over, but not actually in full force.

When it does happen, supposedly we are all going to wake up and check our bank accounts and there will be nothing in there, a $0.00 balance. Paper, cash money will be gone. Worthless. It will be a total shock, despair and a horrible feeling to see you have no money in the bank. But behind the scenes they will have what was in everyone's bank account, it is all mirrored and will then switch to the Quantum financial system. You will have the same amount of money, but in a different system. The actual bank building will still be there, but the financial system will just be structured differently.

Per one truther: Naturally, banks and other financial institutions form the primary targets for most cybercrimes. In response to this, many banks have made it a point to update their systems and practices to prevent the occurrence of such crimes. This means that financial institutions have finally begun to embrace emerging technologies that can help meet the expectations of today's consumers.

This is where QFS comes to the rescue. This future-proof system is being extolled as the future of financial transactions as a whole. It was not developed to run on conventional computers but through a quantum computer placed on a satellite. To provide maximum security, the Quantum Financial System is well protected by Secret Space Programs (SSP).

Several experts believe that quantum technology could solve problems related to security, processing power, and data efficiency.

It is an honest system, backed by gold and silver.

Why do we need a new worldwide Quantum Financial System?

Let me explain:

Every country in the world is bankrupt. Even so, they kept printing money out of thin air, which means it isn't backed by gold, silver or precious metals. Every country was in so much debt there was no way they could ever pay it back.

Why were they bankrupt? Because those running the countries were the Cabal who were using all the money for child trafficiking.

Meanwhile, while they were running this despicable racket, we have all suffered from crippling bank fees, rates, taxes, mortgage interest, licenses, fines and much, much more. They robbed countries of all their gold, etc. by charging for every possible thing they could get their hands on.

A different financial system was necessary to put a stop to the evil a.k.a. the new Quantum Financial System.

The Cabal have infiltrated every part of society, skimming as much as they can get for themselves. They believe we "underlings" should be happy with the little left each week for us to somehow get by. In this new system, bankers will not be able to make money on our money as they have done in the past.

There is no end to their wicked and evil ways. They have been tearing countries apart by pitting country against country in despicable wars. You see, they pay for both sides of the war and sit back and laugh as we lose our sons, fathers and husbands, (and our women as well), who believe they have been on the battlefield saving their countries!

For many years, the Worldwide Alliance, the White Hats, have been plotting a plan for us to be rid of these evil monsters. Many years have gone into their meticulous planning, using the best military minds chosen from around the world. Absolute precision was required. When the time was right, the plan went into motion.

President Trump made a tour of the world in 2016, visiting every country and presenting these facts. The Black Hats had been able to turn this world any way they wished. They were all sold out to Satan who directed their evil ways. Many people say they don't believe there is a Satan, but it's not the case with these satanic worshipping, demon possessed, dirty, filthy "people." They know he's real, just as they know he has a thirst for children, the younger the better.

Quantum Financial System removes all their power!

These "people," although they were stock-piling huge amounts of gold, silver and precious metals they had robbed out of all the countries around the world, always had a hunger for more.

So, they planned to put into action a completely new financial system which could not be tampered with in any way. To this end, the QFS (Quantum Financial System) was born. This system tracks every coin, knowing where the coin came from and to whom it is going. Its method prevents all fraudulent business transactions.

This system is clean and pure. Meticulous care was taken to ensure no dirty money is transferred over to it. This system has undergone the most exact testing.

We all have had our bank accounts added to it already. It's so good to know this new system takes away all the power from corrupt politicians, corrupt "royal" households, etc., who were involved in child trafficking and pedophilia, to say the least. With no method of transferring money, they are dead in the water!

Many have no idea of what our politicians have been up to. Virtually every government worldwide is corrupt and wicked. Gradually, it will all be released to the public. Those who want the details earlier will be able to find them; I am one of those people.

Will we ever get to know everything?

I don't know. In fact, with what many of us already know, I don't think we want to know everything. We know enough. Gut-wrenching details most of us can do without, just enough for us to comprehend the enormity of it all. But we will need to be there for the rest of society as they begin to learn just how much they have been duped.

Now, many in society don't even want to know about it. They would rather continue living in their little bubble. Unfortunately, one day very soon, that bubble is going to burst! Then they will need to look at the cold hard facts.

Everything else is a smokescreen, just something to keep minds focused as the White Hats work behind the scenes.

But they have to enforce the NESARA before the Quantum financial system sets in.

Remember in the earlier notes:

NESARA was to be announced at 10 a.m. EDT in October 2001. The attacks occurred on 9/11 to stop NESARA's announcement.

That my dear, is why 9/11 happened.

Posted *EVERYWHERE*, on every channel (our channels) that anyone who lives in Chicago needs to get out now!

Illinois Governor J.B. Pritzker signed the bill into law last year, provisions such as eliminating cash bail will take effect on January 1, 2023. The law makes Illinois the first state in the country to eliminate cash bail.

The Safe-T Act will also restrict who can be arrested, increase eligibility for probation for people convicted of some drug crimes, among other changes to policing and police training. Supporters of the law say it will make the criminal justice system fairer for Black, Latino and minority communities.

Fairer? They did a crime for Christ's sake; it doesn't matter what color or nationality you are.

The Cabal, deep state, and Democrats are all for the criminals. It will make kidnapping, robbery, and some murders non-detainable.

I am telling you; it's getting ugly.

There are actually several other cities that people are being warned that they need to get out of.

It's big cities.

There are 17 cities that they mentioned. Get out!! There is going to be, at some point, total chaos. When Dems get mad, they destroy things. Well, they are too weak to destroy things, so they hire people to destroy things for them, like everyday thugs looking for two minutes of fame, money for drugs, Antifa and BLM.

Plus, if they see their money gone or their cash is useless, yea, not going to be pretty. They said the cities are going to burn.

Zelensky, President of Ukraine has been arrested behind the scenes. Zelensky is very evil! It's over. The only ones hiding the narrative are the mainstream. All the big shots of every news channel have already been arrested.

They have been calling this a game of chess from day one– 3D chess to be exact. I know nothing about chess but apparently in the game of chess, the objective is to get the Queen. Once you have the Queen, it's game over.

They announced that the Queen is dead- game over.

Just heard on a podcast today that Americans will wake up when they see their finances gone, and then they will tell the public what is really in the Covid vaccine.

They said that doctors can reverse the damage that the Covid vaccine has done to people's bodies. The bad news is that it could take up to 5 years.

Biden gave a speech that literally bashed about 80 million Americans:

"We're at a serious moment in our nation's history," Biden said. "The MAGA Republicans don't just threaten our personal rights and economic security, they're a threat to our very democracy. They refuse to accept the will of the people; they embrace political violence."

Seriously? We don't threaten personal rights. We embrace our personal rights– that is his way of saying we don't listen to him. We will not let him turn our country communistic. We won't get the poisons in the vaccine. That is our personal right.

"They embrace political violence," he says. He is more than likely referring to January 6th and showing his anger that Trump has millions at his rallies, his peaceful rallies.

He continues to say: "What's happened is there are not many real Republicans anymore ... I respect conservative Republicans; I don't respect these MAGA Republicans."

MAGA—Let me remind you of what MAGA stands for–Make America Great Again.

So, he basically has no respect for citizens that want to make America Great Again?

Biden's comments — and the latest poll results — are in stark contrast to the vow he gave during his 2021 inauguration speech in which he said he would "unify" the country after the Trump administration.

Even Libs thought he took his "power" too far on that one.

A new movie came out called *My Son Hunter*. It was done in movie form, not a documentary.

Pretty good at showing the hypocrisy and the back door deals. Many platforms showed it, as it was streaming everywhere–over 30 million views on the first night. It shows in detail how the mainstream media helps them cover things up, how the FBI is in on it, how they purposely blamed Trump for everything, how Hunter smokes crack, is involved with China, the CCP, and his dad, Joe Biden, knew everything.

September 23rd or 24th, they are saying that on that day something will happen. Something so huge that you will remember exactly what you were doing when it happened, for years to come. Just like everyone knows what they were doing on the assassination of Kennedy or on September 11th.

I am thinking it will be a bad thing, a nuclear scare or something. Ella thinks it will be a good thing, like announcing the election is overturned.

October 6th, 2022

Nothing. Remember the dates? September 16th Nesara announcement? The 16-18th something will happen? September 24th, something so big will happen that everyone will remember where they were?

Welp, none of that happened.

Not disappointed–it's kind of a "what the fuck" moment– but not disappointed.

As always, strategic events did happen behind the scenes, but we assumed something would happen to show the public. You know what they say about assuming, so that's on us.

For instance, Igor Danchenko was arrested and admitted that he was an FBI informant behind the made-up Russia bullshit on Trump.

Ok, above is not the exciting news, the exciting news is that the FBI hired him to do that–indication of how corrupt our FBI is. And this actually made the fake news.

Per The New York Post: "The Russian analyst charged with lying to the FBI about his role in the infamous "Steele dossier" was allegedly a paid confidential human source for the agency, a newly unsealed court filing revealed Tuesday.

Igor Danchenko became a paid FBI informant in March 2017 — months after the feds started questioning him over his involvement in the dossier on former President Donald Trump, according to the filing by special counsel John Durham.

He pleaded not guilty to five counts of making false statements about some of the information he gave to Christopher Steele, the former British spy who was paid by Democrats during the 2016 presidential campaign."

Even though that made the news, did it wake more people up? Probably not.

And that was announced on the news on September 18th. One of the dates that were given. Now to your average person, that might seem like nothing. There is always a story of corrupt people in the news. But to the people following this, it is something. It wasn't exactly something you will always remember where you were when it was announced, nonetheless it was something big. It showed that the FBI does cover things up, it proved it. And most importantly, the fact that the news showed it, shows the black hats do not have total control anymore. If they did, they would never allow a news segment to show that Trump truly was set up and it was by the FBI.

October 8th, 2022

Remember, numerology is big for what's going on in the world. Don't really understand it, but it's a thing.

The 8th is an important date.

August 8th- Mar-a-Lago (Trump's home) raided.

September 8th- Announcement of Queen's death.

October 8th - (today) Bridge blows up/collapses.

Ukrainian officials have hinted that Ukraine may have sabotaged a crucial bridge linking Russia and the annexed territory of Crimea to spite Russian President Vladimir Putin on his 70th birthday. Not exactly the London Bridge, but it's a bridge.

A fuel tank explosion on Kerch road-and-rail bridge took place at around 6 a.m. on Saturday while a train was crossing it, causing it to collapse, according to Russian officials.

November 8th is the mid-terms.

Not sure what they are saying about December 8th.

I listened to the rally tonight, and the bridge did go down.

To be quite honest, I am tired of the rallies. Same old shit, different day. Trump bitches about what they did to him. I get it. Yes, they did fuck you over. Then he goes on to say how he will "Make America Great Again." Every. Single. Rally. For almost two years now. Enough already. This is the first rally I ever really watched. The other ones, I just watched clips of it when people posted them. I can tell just by the clips and then watching the full one tonight that they are the same damn thing, all the time. I know he drops a lot of hints/comms via his rallies, and for that reason, I do enjoy the decode channels the next day.

I understand the main purpose is to keep things positive and to keep spirits up. My spirits are up; I don't need to watch the same thing over and over again.

Some have been following this for years, and I do mean years. Most people in my chat room have been following this since 9/11. Unfortunately, there are a lot of patriots that have screwed themselves royally, financially. They have not paid income tax in years. Some have posted that they went out and bought a car they couldn't afford because they think NESARA is around the corner, some have posted that they have not paid their mortgage because NESARA will come.

That is pure craziness. What if it takes another 20 years to go into effect? Remember, there is a small chance that our beliefs are wrong.

There is not a chance in hell that I would be able to sleep at night knowing that I had bills that I didn't pay or wondering if I am going to get arrested due to tax evasion. Not a chance! Ella feels the same way. We are still responsible and not relying on anybody or anything.

I think why I am so interested in this is because I love true crime. Always have. Even as a young girl, my friends would want to watch a chick flick and I wanted to watch a true crime movie like Al Capone's biography, the Nazi war, etc.

At one point, I even wanted to be an FBI agent. Good thing I didn't. Now that I know how corrupt they are, I would probably be dead. I would want to be that "good" FBI agent that would be a whistle blower and find myself "suicided" by Hillary.

So yeah, this is very interesting to me. We are living a true-life crime story.

I do feel everything we believe is true and the people that are clueless are so cruel. I want the truth to come out for the diehards that have been following this more intensely than us, so they can be vindicated. Especially the ones that lost family members and friends over this.

October 25th, 2022

Something exciting happened today for us! Ella found out that Darren Bailey will be eating lunch at a local restaurant today. Darren Bailey is the man running for Illinois governor. He is endorsed by Trump. Pretty exciting! Jack was off work today, so he went with us. A man walked in, and we thought for sure he was with them. He asked the bartender about his reservations for a party of six and he asked to be seated somewhere private. We knew for sure then that he was with Darren Bailey. As the man was walking away, he stopped dead in his tracks, looked at Ella with a puzzled looked then asked, "You are Willow's mom, right?" Holy Shit! He knew Ella! His family babysits Ella's grandkids, woot woot! He verified that he was with the Bailey crowd and that Cindy, Darren's wife would only be there. When Cindy walked in, he introduced us, and we talked with Cindy for a while and had our picture taken. It was sensational, and I must disclose, we were temporarily a little star struck.

Cindy Bailey complimented Jack for being so young but knows what is going on. Um, hello, do you know who his mom is? In all fairness, I cannot take credit for that. Both of my boys saw through this charade from day one. Both Cindy and Ella's new friend informed us that there is a possibility that Darren will be at another local venue in two days.

October 27th, 2022

Ella and I found out the establishment where Darren Bailey would be today. Ella texted her new intel, as we call it, and he responded that they will be there at 1:15 p.m. He then sends a second text stating that there will be a rally for Darren coming up with a surprise guest and he sent a picture of Trump! Now of course we were excited, however, when the excitement wore off, we kind of knew better. I mean come on, the chances of little old us meeting Trump, um, yeah, doesn't happen too often.

We drove over there, and Darren was not there again, so we talked more to Cindy and took more pictures.

At that point, our new friend looked at us and told us that it was confirmed. That Trump will be a surprise guest at Darren's rally! We will see.

November 4th, 2022

This is the weekend that is supposed to have the Darren Bailey rally. He has not texted Ella and I am not sure if Ella texted him. I get it, it would be a little awkward. We don't want to appear like stalkers or just a pain in the ass. And again, I don't think either one of us really counted on it anyways.

November 7th, 2022

Today is the day before mid-terms!

Before I tell you about The United States, let me fill you in on Brazil. Remember this is a global thing, not just the United States.

Brazil had their midterms already. The two candidates, Jair Bolsonaro and

Luiz Inacio 'Lula' da Silva were running. Jair Bolsonaro was the conservative, and Luiz da Silva was the democrat. Luis da Silva is also a convicted criminal. Out there, *EVERYONE* was pro Jair Bolsonaro. Well, the democrat won. Impossible. The Brazilians knew it was stolen.

Supposedly, if a Red Wave occurs tomorrow, they will immediately try to impeach Biden. If it gets stolen again, then military will step in.

November 14th, 2022

Well, the red wave did not happen. It was anticipated and projected by everyone, but, nope, didn't happen. Darren Bailey did not win as Governor of Illinois. Chicago is loaded with drug dealers, criminals and blue people. I am not surprised.

Arizona–Kari Lake. She was similar to the republican in Brazil. She is the one *EVERYONE* wanted, and she was the projected winner. By the way, results are not in for Arizona yet. As you see above, the date today is November 14th, and the voting was on the 8th. They are still "counting." Maricopa County. The same county that had the most fraud for the 2020 Presidential election.

They had machines break, they found mail in ballots, and they need to still count, but it is looking like Kari will not win. Texas had signs of voter fraud, Georgia did and so did Maryland. No red wave. The only places that had problems with their counting machines were the counties that were predominately red.

So now hear this, believe me, we are not getting our hopes up, but tomorrow there is supposed to be a big announcement. Like real big, from Trump himself. So, help me God, it better not be just that he is running again in 2024. The amount of hype that is going around about this is mind-boggling. They are saying it will be the biggest announcement in American history. I will say this, this is straight from Trump. Trump announced it himself that he is making a huge announcement.

Some say he will announce that he is Speaker of the House, and he will impeach Biden. I guess that will be good, but we want something even bigger! We want the world to know the truth about everything! Baby steps. Hell, at this point I will take newborn burps. Sometimes we do take little steps, but then the next day, those steps seem to go backwards.

November 15th, 2022

Tonight was the "BIG ANNOUNCEMENT." All day long we checked the newsfeed. It was so pumped up! Trump invited reporters from every country. Every state was invited as well, but every country is huge! All the newsfeed stated that it is *NOT* only that he is running again. It is something more!

We invited Mac, Sammy and Ella over. We ordered pizzas and had a discussion beforehand.

Mac is still on the page that Trump is bad, saying Biden and Trump had lunch together, figuratively speaking. I still have a hard time believing it.

And of course, all kinds of jokes were going around. Some were saying that his speech was going to be he is offering a deal on Mike Lindell's "My Pillow" or that he saved money while bundling with Geico. Well, even if nothing comes with the big announcement, at least we had fun.

We wrote down bets on what was going to be said. Mac put that he was just going to announce that he is running again; Ella put that they will reveal how money was taken from crypto currency; and the best was Sammy's, he said that Trump was going to announce that Melania was pregnant.

The big announcement came and went. It was a fucking glorified rally and all he said was that he was running again in 2024. A disappointment. But par for the course. That's the way it's been going.

He hyped us up. His exact words were "You do not want to miss my announcement. It will be the biggest announcement in 100 years and tonight you will party like its 1776!"

Then nothing. If they truly are trying to keep us docile, does he realize how many diehard patriots that pissed off? They are livid. And it was stated that a lot of patriots are done. Just done.

November 17th, 2022

Getting ready to start my day this morning, while on the phone with Ella, Tina, who is a friend and also following this, beeps in. She is screaming with excitement to hurry up and turn on Fox News!

The news! The actual news that is shown on the TV, broke in to say that Joe Biden is under investigation for money laundering, wire fraud, and then they said HUMAN TRAFFICKING! Joe and Hunter Biden! Repeat, they said human trafficking!

Turns out we did win the House, not a huge red wave, but we won the House, and they started it right away!

The Republican-controlled House of Representatives will investigate Joe Biden for a series of alleged crimes including human trafficking for which extensive documentation already exists, Representatives Jim Jordan of Ohio and James Comer of Kentucky said at a press conference.

Comer, who is set to chair the House Oversight Committee, said whistleblowers have come forward to detail how Hunter Biden and his relatives "flourished and became millionaires simply by offering access to the family."

All members of Congress recently received information on the Biden family's alleged corruption with national security implications from Marco Polo, a research group run by former Trump administration official Garrett Ziegler that documented and indexed the contents of the abandoned Hunter Biden laptop.

Ziegler said, after obtaining a copy of the laptop, Marco Polo investigators had undertaken "what every single law enforcement institution in this country, especially and including the FBI, is not going to do," which is compile and release a detailed historical record of everything contained on the laptop Hunter Biden abandoned at a Delaware computer repair shop in April 2019.

"Was Joe Biden directly involved with Hunter Biden's business deals, and is he compromised? That's our investigation," Comer said.

The Republicans announced that Biden and his family will be investigated for the following violations:

- Conspiracy or defrauding the United States• Wire fraud
- Conspiracy to commit wire fraud
- Violation of the Foreign Agents Registration Act
- Violations of the Foreign Corrupt Practices Act
- Violations of the Victims of Trafficking and Violence Protection Act of 2000
- Tax evasion
- Money laundering
- Conspiracy to commit money laundering

"I want to be clear, this is an investigation of Joe Biden," Comer stated. "The Biden family's business dealings implicate a wide range of criminality from human trafficking to potential violations of the constitution."

The investigation will investigate whether Biden "is compromised or swayed by foreign dollars or influence," Comer added.

Comer noted that Republicans "will pursue all avenues," including those "that have long been ignored."

Jordan, who is set to chair the House Judiciary Committee, criticized senior intelligence analysts and media outlets who insisted that emails obtained from Hunter Biden's "laptop from hell" were part of a Russian disinformation effort, and accused federal officials of working to suppress the story.

"We're going to try to help Representative Comer and the team here at Oversight with our work on Judiciary, but with a specific focus on what the FBI was doing," said Jordan. "There's so many questions that need answers so we can get to the bottom of this."

"This is the focus on the Judiciary Committee, the political nature of the Justice Department and the linkage now to what was happening with the Hunter Biden story," said Jordan.

I almost peed myself! It was so nice to see it on the actual TV! Now there is ABC, CBS, NBC, CNN, MSNBC, FOX AND FOX NEWS. This was shown on FOX News, the only station that has flipped and is telling the truth nowadays, well, as much as they can. But after it was aired, the other stations followed! Yes! Mainstream Media, fake news showed it! Now of course they only showed a small portion of what FOX News showed, but that's ok!

Even if the sheep are still in denial, they can NEVER un-hear human trafficking!

After this came out, it was written that the reason why he hyped up his speech so much, was because the Cabal thought he was going to announce all of that at his speech. He wanted them to think that. They were shitting in their pants! Trump is a fucking genius! Art of War–we were told since the very start that he will have to sometimes disappoint us to throw them off.

February 14th, 2023

After our vacation last year, the four of us decided we are going to go away to somewhere tropical every winter. No better way to recharge your batteries, ground your feet in the sand and just let the ocean air take you away. We tried some place different this year, while it was interesting and beautiful, it was not as nice as the previous destination. But hey, it was still the Caribbean with sunshine, good food, and great company. I felt bad for Ella; she really did not care for it at all. She tried hiding it, but it was still noticeable. She later confessed to me that it was the "feel." We stayed at a resort that is owned by the Pritzker family. He is one of the Cabal and the country we visited is high on the list for trafficking. Her gut would not allow her to enjoy herself. I get it. Once you know what you know, it's impossible to push it to the side. I'm telling you, once you uncover everything, it is utterly out of the question to carry on with life as if you don't know.

Sam Brinkman completely crashed crypto millions of dollars stolen from the American people.

They also have proof that most of this money went through Ukraine's system- they filtered into Bidens personal account.

Per the same article: One of the people who Joe Biden should thank for becoming president is a 28-year-old cryptocurrency zealot who sleeps on an office beanbag chair most nights, believes businesses focus too much on social responsibility, and has, seemingly out of nowhere, become worth $10 billion.

This affected millions of people; millions of people lost money. Just gone. It was laundered through politicians, Ukraine and into the Biden's wallets, while the working Americans lost it. "Oh well," was basically their response.

When all this shit first started, we briefly–and I mean very briefly–thought about buying crypto currency. Damn. Dodged a bullet on that one. That's why we TRUST NO ONE with everything going on.

It has been exposed that Madonna, queen of pop is being investigated for human trafficking.

Per the Daily Telegraph: "US superstar Madonna has been accused of being involved in the human trafficking and sexual exploitation of African children by the charity group Ethiopian World Federation (EWF). EWF petitioned Malawi's President Lazarus Chakwera to investigate a non-profit set up by the 'Queen of Pop' in 2006 called Raising Malawi which reportedly seeks to help orphans in the country. Madonna herself has adopted four Malawian children.

In the petition, the EWF asked the president to restrict her and her associates' "accessibility to Africa and to African children as a precautionary measure until a thorough investigation is done into child trafficking, sex exploitation, sexual slavery, adoption reversal, threat of coercion, fraud, deception and abuse of power or vulnerability."

The group claims that Madonna set up Raising Malawi to "host social experiments on vulnerable African children," suggesting that her decision stems from the "psychology behind her ability to release child pornography, religious imagery, bestiality and vulgar pornography."

Disgusting! But hey, thanks to the people we follow, we knew this already. Madonna is a huge pop star, not a politician, so why wasn't this shown on the mainstream media? Oh, that's right, she is part of the Cabal and Illuminati, she is protected. Allegedly, she has been dealt with already.

The Super Bowl was last Sunday, the 12th. I have never been into football, that is one sport I just don't understand no matter how hard I try. The half time show was satanism at its finest. Before it started, I said to Ella, "Oh, let me guess they will be wearing red. And yep, sure enough they were. Rhianna, with all of her backup singers, had red on, then switched to hazmat suits. Ella, myself and Andy's friend, Rick all said there was a reason for that. There was a reason why they had them wear hazmat suits.

Don't know what it is yet, but there is a reason. Nothing is a coincidence.

For two weeks there was 'balloons" that were flying over sensitive sites to collect information. It was determined that it was Chinese spy balloons. While China denied it and said they were civilian airships, then apologized for the entry into our airspace. Capitol Hill and both chambers of Congress received classified briefings on the incident. The House passes a unanimous resolution condemning China's alleged surveillance of the United States. China hits back with its own balloon allegations, accusing the U.S. of flying its own high-altitude balloons into Chinese airspace without Beijing's permission, on more than 10 occasions since January 2022.

The Biden administration told the American people that it was nothing to worry about.

How did they even get this far into our country? Where was our air security? And they probably would not even have told us if someone from Montana didn't notice it and post a video of it.

On February 3rd, there was train derailment in East Palestine, Ohio.

Norfolk Southern train carrying hazardous materials derailed and sparked a massive days-long blaze. EPA and government officials are telling people the air and water is safe yet all the fish in the lakes are dead.

And guess who has not even once addressed the whole situation? The Biden Administration or the EPA. Not a peep. The townspeople, the mayor, the governor are all begging the government for help.

Do you know who came out? Trump. Trump came and visited and passed out water to the town.

There have been several train derailments carrying toxic fumes. Some make the fake news, some do not. I think right now we are at a total of 17 (you will notice the number 17 a lot in this movement. 17th letter= Q) train derailments and buildings holding toxic materials blowing up and spewing toxic fumes in the air.

In one town, they had to pass out hazmat suits to the residents.

Wait, does that say hazmat suits? Like at the Super Bowl?

The Elite/Illuminati like to do that. They like to flaunt in your face that they know what is coming. They know because they plan it.

It is inconceivable that those hazmat suits in Rihanna's show were not planned.

Nothing is a coincidence.

March 20,2023

Andy and I decided at the last minute to take a road trip to Florida. Our first mistake was going during spring break, but our biggest victory was being able to see Mar-a-Lago. We were able to catch a glimpse of President Donald Trump's residence, a moment I will remember forever. I felt like just driving by wasn't enough and I yearned for more. At one point I joked with Andy to try to pull into the palace. He played along with me while reminding me that we like our lives too much. That's true, I guess we will accept the fact that while it was brief, we were at least able to see it.

April 6th, 2023

It happened guys.

Trump got arrested. Or indicted as they say.

Per the Guardian: "For the first time in U.S. history, a former president surrendered to law enforcement and was placed under arrest.

Donald Trump's arraignment Tuesday thrust the U.S. criminal justice system into dramatically new territory, testing the durability of courtroom rules and legal procedures that apply to all Americans – this time, the 45th chief executive of the nation."

Even some of Trump's biggest critics were quick to question whether Bragg presented enough new information to warrant the charges.

"I believe President Trump's character and conduct make him unfit for office," Sen. Mitt Romney, R-Utah, who voted to remove Trump from office during the ex-president's second impeachment trial, said in a statement. "Even so, I believe the New York prosecutor has stretched to reach felony criminal charges in order to fit a political agenda."

It's a crock of shit! They could not get him on Russian collusion, or January 6th, so they are trying this.

Even the Democrats are saying it's not right!

You know, the people I follow, are still saying, "It's part of the plan, you are watching a movie,"–and yea, you know the rest.

Remember when I told you how they announced even on the fake news about Joe Biden being under investigation, including for human trafficking?

Well, what the hell happened with that? Trump gets indicted, but Biden didn't. They have 37 counts on Trump. More like 537 on Biden, and especially Hunter, but they protect each other. Or do they? Is this to show people how "Elite" they truly are?

I wish our trip to Mar-A-Lago would have been during this time. We were two weeks too early. They showed everyone in front of his house supporting him! You can bet your ass I would have been there.

So much more information coming out also about The Biden Crime Family getting money from China and Ukraine, and nothing being done. Each day, more and more information about his corruption.

We are still at risk with nuclear war threats. China and Russia both want to nuke us. You *NEVER* heard anything like that with Trump in, or hell, any other president. Not even horrible Obama.

April 29th, 2023

Man, I'll tell ya... since I started these notes, things have not been any worse than they are right now.

People's spirits are down more and more with new "laws" that is killing the middle class. A housing crash worse than 2008 is on the horizon. Groceries still high, gas still high, Bidens are still free.

The Biden Crime Family is supposedly still under investigation.

Per James Comer:

"Chairman James Comer and Oversight Committee Republicans are investigating the Biden family's domestic and international business dealings to determine whether these activities compromise U.S. national security and President Biden's ability to lead with impartiality. Members of the Biden family have a pattern of peddling access to the highest levels of government to enrich themselves, often to the detriment of U.S. interests. We are committed to following the Biden family and associates' money trail—consisting of many complex, international transactions worth millions of dollars—and providing answers to the American people. The American people deserve to know whether the President's connections to his family's business deals occurred at the expense of American interests and whether they represent a national security threat."

He continued, "We know that The Big Guy got 10%, but what did the Little Guys get? And how many members of the Biden crime family were involved in Hunter's influence-peddling schemes? We may never know the full story of just how corrupt this superannuated kleptocrat who pretends to be president of the United States and his family really are, but now House Republicans are expanding their investigation of the Biden crime organization — oh, sorry, they call it the Biden "family," you know, like the Gambino "family" — to include more of Old Joe's relatives. At the very least, we should get a glimpse into how "the public service" today is a highly lucrative endeavor for an amoral, unscrupulous liar such as Old Joe. News is leaking out from behind the veil of lies the Democrats and their media allies have shrouded around that at least six more members of the Biden Family have financially benefited from Hunter Biden's many illicit international schemes. This brings the total members of the Biden clan who've been enriched by Hunter's illegal activities to nine."

The real question remains, what about "The Big Guy"?

I am thinking that something will happen. I mean it's all over the news (even the fake news, well kind of), I mean, how can they escape all the above?

Our threat of nuclear war escalates daily.

They rarely talk about this. The threat is real. The media and the Biden Crime Family focus on getting Trump.

And starting May 1st, people with good credit will have to pay higher rates to make up for people with bad credit. You will also get penalized if you put more money down on your loan.

Glad I taught my kids to establish credit, pay their bills on time and to save money in the bank to buy a home. Now, they will get penalized for all three.

The transgender LGBTQ world is endless and overwhelming. So many men are now women and vice versa. They are everywhere and they are protected. Men are even allowed to participate in women's sports. They are allowed to go into women's locker rooms. And there is nothing we can do, because they are protected.

A "real" female athlete had to hide in a room for three hours because she was getting attacked by a group of transgenders. They attacked her because they said she was racist against transgenders. She questioned the results of a swim meet; therefore, she was racist.

When Biden heard about this, he sided with the transgenders; stated he was proud of them for sticking up for themselves. Nothing was said about the female, white, young women who trained her whole life for this event and was attacked and barricaded in a room out of fear. That was not addressed at all by the Biden administration.

They are everywhere, even here to in our little old' county. I had a transgender cashier at a local department store, gas station and the local hotel. Everywhere you go there is a blue haired lesbian bragging about her green haired girlfriend.

So, what, once Biden got in, half the world said, "Hey, I think I am gay! Or hey, I was born a boy, but now I want to be a girl." Let's not forget about the people that feel they are now cats and want to be identified as such. Additionally, they are expected to be treated as such.

I am telling you; I could not make this shit up if I tried.

We have no problem with this, however, why now? Why suddenly are there are so many men wanting to be girls and vice versa? Why are they protected? Why are they being glorified? Well, of course the ones following this know why. I explained it earlier, let me tell you again. It sounds crazy, but hell, everything is crazy. The transgenders and LGBTQ community is being taught and learning that the traditional God does not accept their way of living. So, they are learning about this new God. Who is teaching them this? The Elite. The Illuminati.

That is their God. Their "God" is a hermaphrodite. Half woman, half man. Their God is a devil. Since this new community is following their fucked-up guidance, that is why they are protected, and they are glorified.

Because they now worship this new God, Christians are shit. They are being taught to hate "all others." This is the ultimate reason why they are protected.

Four School shootings recently, all by a transgender. One of them actually admitted that they did it because their God told them to hate and kill all Christians. Small children were killed in that shooting.

That belief, in addition to the hormones that are given to them. Testosterone to women that want to be men, estrogen to men that want to be women. Yeah, they are pretty much mentally unstable.

I still can't figure out what makes a man wake up one day and discover that he wants to wear makeup, grow some tits and walk in high heels. Some have said they are putting estrogen in our food supply chain and that is what's doing it. At this stage in the game, I guess it's possible.

May 9th, 2023

The number of riots, protests and violence in the streets of blue states is unbelievable. It's a combination of the no bond, lack of police– and to be honest, just because they can– because it is a blue state, or city, ran by a blue mayor. The cops are overpowered. These criminals can do the crime and either have no repercussion or if they are arrested, they can be released and sleep in their own bed that same night. These Blue ran states/cities want this. They tell the public that it is because of equality and no discrimination, and they want fair treatment, and we want to help the black community and help criminals get on their feet.

Bull Fucking shit.

You are doing this because you want chaos. You want violence, especially with guns so you can try to ban guns, this way We the People have no way to protect ourselves. You want to blame the Red. You are not doing this for the black community, you are doing this to please your own satanic soul, you want this. You want division. You want cities burnt down and people destroyed. As if you don't have enough power already, you want more.

Shoplifting has become a daily event. It's no big deal at all. You can walk into a store and walk out with stuff without paying and the employees are instructed to not do anything.

The Red states are fine. Not fine, but you know what I mean. They hate the world and what has become of it but are dealing with it. They are hoping for better days, whether it be by prayer or voting or following outlets other than MSM. But they certainly are not destroying towns, killing people and causing chaos.

If these uncontrollable acts are part of the plan, then I guess it makes sense from a conspiracy theorist's point of view –yes, I have officially acknowledged myself as a conspiracy theorist–they had to wake up the sheep in every aspect.

A yuppie, pencil pushing Lib does not want to see violence in the street. They do not want to be afraid to walk to the store. They feel everything should be nicely tucked away in a trans-like atmosphere, while wearing an Oxford linen shirt, where birds sing and unicorns occasionally strut by while they are sitting outside sipping their soy latte. That's why they voted for Biden, right? Because Trump spoke vulgarly, dated hot women, was married three times and was just all around not a nice guy. With Biden, the world will be perfect and beautiful, because he is "nice."

How did that work out for ya?

These towns going to shit is for people like that. It is planned; they need to show the world how fucked up things will get with the Cabal in charge.

Thousands of illegals are coming over the border every day. Drug cartels, rapists, murderers, and some non-criminals also. Thousands, upon thousands.

Then Biden Crime Family and his pals had stolen the election and tore down the wall and let everyone in. Need I say more?

One mall shooting was by an illegal alien. Killed several people. They showed it on Fox, but not on regular mainstream media. It makes the Biden Administration look bad since it was someone that came over the border, so of course they won't show it.

The fake news did show the transgender shootings though. Because remember, they are in a protected class and it's not the transgender's fault, it's the gun. Those damn guns.

Hey, people die in car accidents every day, should we ban cars? People get stabbed, should we ban knives? People get strangled, should we ban rope? Nope, just guns. Deep state is afraid of guns; you can shoot and defend yourself from a distance with a gun. The other objects of potential violence are not a threat to them.

Title 42 is ending in two days. Title 42 was set in place by Trump during Covid.

It allowed border agents to rapidly send migrants crossing the U.S.-Mexico border back to Mexico or other countries. Of course, Democrats didn't abide by that.

To the people from other countries that thought the United States was implementing Title 42, they hesitated to try to come here. Well, now they know it's expiring. So, on top of the few thousands a day coming over here, they are predicting an excess of 5,000 coming over per day.

They are reporting that they are waiting to come in by the bus load.

It's bad guys, really bad.

They have been saying that a big scare event will happen; we thought nuclear scare at first, then money event, now they are saying that it will be that the Drug Cartel will declare war on us, once they are all over here.

Tomorrow, they are supposed to be bringing new information regarding more charges against the Fake Sleepy President, Joseph Biden.

House Oversight Committee Chair Representative James Comer, R-Ky., warned Wednesday will be "judgment day" for the White House as he prepares to unveil additional information surrounding the Biden family's overseas business dealings.

Comer detailed why he believes it will be a "bad day" for the Biden administration during "Fox & Friends First," as House Republicans are expected to make a major announcement on their investigation.

"Tomorrow is going to be a bad day for the White House, and it's going to be interesting to see what Joe Biden has to say," Comer told co-hosts Todd Piro and Ashley Strohmier Tuesday. "He lied about the laptop. He lied about his knowledge of his family's shady business dealings. He lied about his involvement in his family's shady business dealings."

And now today:

A jury found Trump guilty of sexual abuse from the 1990's. And this is not even the charges that he was indicted for–and no, this has nothing to do with Jan 6th– this is something else.

Jury finds Donald Trump sexually abused E. Jean Carroll in civil case while the jury found that Trump sexually abused her, sufficient to hold him liable for battery, the jury did not find that Carroll proved he raped her.

She was awarded 5 million dollars. The Democrats are saying he is not "Presidential material" and won't be able to run. Perfect timing, isn't it?

What about your human trafficking, Joe? What about being in bed with China, Joe? What about being in bed with Ukraine, Joe? What about, what about, what about...

It's only Tuesday and all this shit happened. And more happening tomorrow (Biden charges)! And Thursday (title 42 expiring).

Also, tomorrow night CNN, who is one of the fake news, asked Trump for a live interview! Wow, fake news never wants anything to do with Trump.

And here is just a brief list on what happened last week...

CIA proven to have been involved with 9/11.

Dopey Joe was directly implicated on paper for selling information to our enemies, Hunter was forced to admit in family court in Arkansas that the laptop was his.

Ukraine botched up an attack on Putin's life.

Class action lawsuit against Pfizer because of the poison vaccine.

Sixty-thousand children disappeared from Ukraine and have been trafficked to the West. We are the West.

South Korea and Indonesia joined the list of global powers to divorce the U.S. dollar and currency.

Banks have collapsed.

It was proven that 51 former spies undermined the Commander in Chief's campaign.

I could go on and on.

The only thing we are not winning is the battle with our own minds.

There are just too many fuck ups– too many. If Joe Biden truly was the real president, he would be removed, even by his own people, if there was no darkness going on. The way he stumbles, the way he disappears, the words he messes up, how he cannot complete a sentence, the violence, the economy, the border, the Afghanistan botch up, etc.

This can only happen if it is being done on purpose. The Cabal is not ignorant; they are a lot of things, but uneducated is not one of them. They would never let the world see all these misfortunes. This has to be orchestrated on purpose.

I still trust the plan.

May 16th, 2023

It's a great time to be alive! Yes, the world is ugly, but we are alive and witnessing all of this! And we will survive!

In addition to them announcing all those claims against Biden the other day, the John Durham report came out! We have been waiting four years for this!

John Durham is an American lawyer who served as the United States Attorney for the District of Connecticut from 2018 to 2021. By April 2019, the Trump administration assigned him to investigate the origins of the Federal Bureau of Investigation's investigation into Russian interference in 2016.

You know how Trump was accused of colluding with Russia to win the 2016 election? Well, they hired Durham to investigate it and it took him four years to get this 306-page document out to the public. He says it took so long because there was a lot of investigating and he wanted to get it right. I am sure there is another reason behind the scenes, one we average people will never know.

But it has been proven that not only did the FBI know it was made up by Hillary Clinton, Obamas and Bidens, it was spread and pursued by the FBI also. They had proved that it was made up; they knew it wasn't real, and they helped the deep state charge him.

Durham also discovered that the Hunter Biden laptop was real, and the FBI helped the deep state cover that up too during the 2020 election.

Durham uncovered that the deep state was involved in 2016 election interference and 2020. They never expected Trump to win in 2016 otherwise they would have played more horribly and injected more votes like in the 2020, those that are awake knew this already, but it has been made public.

This is huge!

James Comer and many others are demanding action! Along with Clintons, Obamas and the Bidens, there are approximately 60 other names that he wants arrested.

This is high treason. The border is also high treason, they said. A sitting President is supposed to protect the people and the fact that he is letting drug cartels come over with no problem; they say that is treason against the country and the people.

The truth is coming out, baby!

Comer said on Fox news that every time they have a verifiable witness or a whistle blower, they end up in jail or become missing. Yep! I think we are up to five missing people now. Remember, the Clintons have 87 past employees that either committed suicide, were killed in a "car accident" or are just plain missing.

Comer is catching heat for that comment.

The CNN interview was amazing! Trump killed it! That interviewer tried baiting him, and he gave it right back. Really surprised CNN invited him. Our people say that Trump's friend owns CNN now, and this was just a show. The turn of events never ceases to amaze me.

The interviewer asked him about Russian and Ukraine. He said if he was President, it would never have happened, but if it did, he could end it in 24 hours.

She also asked for his opinion on the situation. He would not answer either way, did not talk ill about Russia or Ukraine. Remember, Russia supposedly is good now, they only attacked Ukraine to take out the bio labs, blow up tunnels used for human trafficking and save the children. He of course, cannot talk about that.

So, Trump is completely exonerated now. They announced he is completely innocent, and their exact words were "He never did anything wrong."

Not only did he not do anything wrong, but they also named the deep state names and announced that they were involved!

Hallelujah!

They also announced how the Democrats paid for the attorney representing the woman that cried rape. Our truthers say that case was copied word for word from a Law-and-Order SVU episode. It's being put right in our faces, the department store in which it so-called happened in, was the same as the one in the episode! Watching a movie...

The truth is coming out about the storming of the Capitol, too.

January 6th will be forever remembered as the day the government set up a staged riot to cover up the fact that they certified a fraudulent election.

And the Durham report proved the left-wing agenda for the past seven years was not only a complete fabrication, but a vast treasonous conspiracy to brainwash the planet and overthrow the sitting POTUS.

If humanity is to flourish, those responsible must pay the ultimate price.

May 18th, 2023

Here we go:

Rep Marjorie Taylor Greene has introduced articles of impeachment against President Joe Biden.

The House member announced her highest-profile impeachment of the week during a press conference today!

"Biden has blatantly violated his constitutional duty, and he is a direct threat to our national security," she said. "Therefore, Jospeh Robinette Biden is unfit to serve as the President of the United States and must be impeached out in the real world where American taxpayers live."

Greene has introduced impeachment articles for several officials this week, including Homeland Security Secretary Alejandro Mayorkas, FBI Director Chris Wray, Washington, D.C., United States Attorney Matthew Graves, and Attorney General Merrick Garland.

Hey, it's a start!

Now, remember this is all a show! The crimes that are being exposed are much more than just impeachment– they are crimes that are punishable by death.

But they have to start out with impeachment, then it will gradually go to more extreme. Then hopefully the military steps in.

This is the latest alleged sequence of events:

1. EBS
2. Disclosure
3. New QFS: NESARA announcement
4. WFB email W/800#
5. Initial KYC Thru regional call centers
6. Redemption Center Appts. Schedule
7. XRP Buyback. Participation will be voluntary
8. Announcement of IRS income Tax Abolishment with Repayment of all taxes and interest paid.
9. Announcement of New Consumption Tax of 14% only on new items, food, clothing, medication excluded.
10. Resorting back to 1955 prices

I have lost hope a few times. When weeks go by and I hear nothing, not even on my channels that I follow. Where every time we checked, we heard the same old bullshit. Meanwhile in the real world, you live with all the bullshit.

The world has gotten so ugly. So much talk about how bad whites are, how racist everyone has turned, how guys want to be girls, the prices, the taxes– It's horrible and to know that all of this does not have to be this way. It's frustrating! But I must admit, I love my life! I love a sunny day and enjoying nature, love laughing with my kids, my husband, and my friends. I appreciate my life and always look at the positive. Thank heavens, because the days that I get down about this shit, it would suck if other aspects of my life sucked as well.

Andy and I run a maintenance company. In this line of work, you meet all kinds of people when trying to acquire new contracts. You already know that I keep my mouth shut no matter what side people are on, although the conversation rarely comes up. My lack of vocalizing my beliefs other than not wanting to be hauled off in a padded wagon, is simple because when you run a small business you cannot take a chance of losing clients. One client started a conversation with me, a conversation I will never forget. He asked me a question about possibly purchasing a five-year maintenance contract through his commercial loan. He then spouted out about the current interest rates and taxes on his building. The look of anger was on his face, and it was obvious he was about to go on a tangent about the banks. He then muttered the word "unbelievable." He then proceeds with "Oh, you have no idea, what's going on." I knew, I just knew he was aware of everything. I paused for a moment, then the Erin Brockovich in me showed its face again, in a very authoritative voice, I said, "Oh, I beg to differ with you sir, but I do know."

I then very rapidly gave a 30 second synopsis on the banking system. I did pull the reigns back and mentally reminded myself that I am working and Erin needs to go back to her holding cell. After my short spiel, his mouth hit the floor, then he yelled out "You are a patriot!" Whew! For those 30 seconds that I lost all my professional self, I was a little worried for a split second that I might have crossed a line. His referring to me as a patriot, was the best compliment I ever received! Needless to say, we secured the contract.

Conversations similar to that have happened several times, not a ton, but enough to make me realize that there are more people that know the truth than you think.

May 19th, 2023

It is spicing up. The Durham report is also shedding light to the public about the Clinton's and Obama's highest plans and treasonous acts.

In fact, Obama is banned from entering Russia. He was put on the no-fly list.

The Durham Report, the FBI bombshell, the new public announcements about the Obamas, Bidens and Clintons and the announcement of the impeachment of Bidens, nothing compared to what is coming out next!

I hope when someone is reading this, that the website of Real Raw News is still up and running. If so, go look it up. It will show all the articles about the tribunals; you will even see the dates. The dates prove that they happened before public knowledge. It will show you about the adrenochrome, the clone labs, the arrests, the trials– it's out there.

Most are at Gitmo (Guantanamo Bay Detention Center). They had to remove the detainees from Gitmo. They moved them to a prison in Guam. Gitmo is only 90 miles from the U.S border, and they feared that the deep state would try to blow it up. There was an attempt already.

They are advising us to take all our money out of the bank. I am not touching my money. I am still at the point where I am not 100% on board with certain people and not completely trusting things. Especially with our money.

Plus, in the beginning and still now, they stated that the new QFS will mirror your money.

I could see taking some out and buying gold or silver, but I am not doing that yet. I might regret it. Or I might change my mind. Not sure at this point.

May 21st, 2023

They have announced that they are going to do a thorough investigation, and make it to the public, regarding the Obamas and Clintons.

They are also now saying that there will be 3 suicides. One famous person, and two other semi-famous people, but the final 2 won't have a huge impact on the public.

June 19th, 2023

Fifty senators were given satellite phones.

The phones were distributed as part of several new security efforts from the Senate Sergeant at Arms and were offered to every senator. It is unclear which senators agreed to take part in the new measure.

In case communication goes down?

And of course, they found something else to charge Trump with. They charged him with having confidential information in his home. This charge came out just hours after they discovered new evidence that the Biden's are still taking money from Ukraine. Go figure. "Don't look at me–look at him," again. Same old shit.

June 24th,2023

A lot has happened today and yesterday.

During the week, five billionaires decide to go down in a submarine to look for *Titanic* remains. They never came up. This whole last week they tugged on everyone's heart strings while doing the countdown until they run out of oxygen. The truth is, they died the Sunday before. Their submarine imploded. The Biden administration told the media not to report it until Thursday and to do a countdown of oxygen. Why? Because on Thursday is when the house voted to impeach Biden, Hunter had a court date and 64 million was reported missing from the Pentagon. He needed a distraction. Everyone in the country concentrated on the countdown and spent their days praying for men in the submarine's safety. He knew that, and on Thursday it was announced they ran out of oxygen, and they were dead. Everyone was crying and was distracted from what was going on with the Biden Crime Family. It was leaked from the Navy Seals that the submarine blew up four days prior.

June 26th, 2023

As I sit here typing these notes, I am feeling pretty good about this week. Did anything happen yet? No.

But looking at the facts, they have more info and damning evidence on The Biden Crime Family, the economy is getting worse, they have proof that he hid the submarine accident for days, and he hired a criminal lawyer.

By the end of the week, they are saying voter fraud should be made public, possibly this week the 10 days of darkness and we will all be celebrating our real independence on the 4th of July! Wouldn't that be nice!

June 30th, 2023

A lot has happened! The truthers and the people I follow had the 27th circled on the calendar. Well, on the 27th, we were hit with an Air Quality Index that was 220. Normal is 0-100. It was the highest it's ever been in the history of the United States. Several states and towns were affected by this. They say it was because of the fires in Canada. Even in the towns that had the fires in Canada, their air quality did not get that high.

The "fog" was so thick you could barely see and the smell! Oh, the smell! It did not smell like fire. It smelled like chemicals or burning electricity. It was horrible. If I was outside even for a short time, my throat would get sore. Andy's eyes would burn.

It is gone now; it only lasted 2 1/2 days.

Several claim it was the white hats blowing up the underground DUMBS, while others say they had to disguise the sky, therefore "fogging" them up so people would not see the military in the air.

But guess what the funny part is, little mention of this on fake mainstream media, they touched base on it for like 3 seconds. "The AQI is high today…" then they went on to the next subject.

No emergency alert from the EPA, no break-ins on the TV at the bottom from the Weather Channel, no governor from any state saying anything and advising people to stay in. Nothing. The only people who knew about it was if they clicked on their own Weather Channel app or experienced it themselves.

That scared me. Anything you see on the news; it's always the opposite.

With no mention of this being "bad" usually means it is bad! Opposite. It got me wondering.

We are still waiting for a definitive answer on what the hell was up in our air. One thing is for sure: it's not from the damn Canada fires.

July 6th, 2023

As I am sure you might have guessed, no extraordinary celebration of our independence, nor anything else. We did, however, have a great 4th of July!

For the first time we hosted a 4th of July celebration. We really had a great crowd with tasty food, great music and a beautiful day in America! The only thing that was missing was the beautiful sound of an ear piercing EBS and the sweet smell of defeat.

Every once and awhile I would look over at Ella and shrug my shoulders, then we would both smile. I approached one of Andy's friends and told him that he needs to check the chats more often, because we are getting so close. He admitted he stopped following everything, so I briefly explained to him what has transpired since he last logged on. He sat there listening intently, all the while knowing he will not log on again. And that's ok. You can still be a die-hard American without immersing yourself balls deep into it.

I wore my "We the People" attire instead of the traditional 4th of July red, white and blue garb.

At the end of the night is when reality set in that we were not going to get the ending today that we so deserve. I still looked up at the sky and smiled. I know that the ending will eventually happen, and I will be here with open arms waiting to embrace it.

September 4th, 2023

On August 25th, Trump surrendered at the Fulton County jail, where he was booked on 13 felony counts related to an alleged scheme to overturn the results of the presidential election in Georgia.

His surrender in Georgia marks the fourth time he has turned himself in after criminal charges were brought against him by federal and state officials, but it's the first time he was subjected to a mug shot. It's also routine for defendants in Fulton County to be fingerprinted and have their eyes scanned for biometric identification.

I seriously don't even know what to say anymore. Yeah, yada, yada, it's part of the plan. They have been telling us since day one that he will be arrested. It just sucks. The sheep are loving this, and the patriots look like fools.

They are also still talking about the Biden Crime Family and Joe Biden getting impeached. But of course, since they are part of the Cabal, it takes longer for them.

Still talking of NESARA. Still saying we are getting closer. They say it's "real" this time. I believe it, I really do but have days where I question whether or not Kenny and Mac's way is accurate. I trust the plan but have decided to look at all sides of the prism just to be safe. Did you notice how I did not say Adam's name in the above? Adam has flipped back, he feels that if Trump is bad, they would have taken us over already and they wouldn't be educating us and exposing all of corruption that has been going on for decades. They would want to keep us in the dark. Makes sense.

September 18th, 2024

They have been saying since day one that China will control us and that they will invade us, but they didn't say how.

Right here in our hometown. The Chinese, not just the Chinese, but the CCP (Chinese Communistic Party) has bought our land.

I am trying to stay on the path. The path I believe is right. The path where this is all a movie, the truth is coming out soon.

But man, I tell you what, when it happens right in your own backyard, it's hard to think that way. The Red in our town is pissed. The blue sleeping people don't have a damn clue. They believe the Democrats have our back while they are scheduling an appointment to get their tenth booster.

Our mayor voted for the CCP purchase of land. So did our trustees. For years they have been referred to as a Mob. I am starting to see why.

The company coming in is not only verified as having allegiance to the CCP, but they are also registered with the Department of Justice as a Chinese foreign principal.

The town held an event for the CCP. I rode with Ella to where it was being held to see what was going on. I made sure to wear large sunglasses and a baseball hat for fear that someone in Andy's line of work would recognize me. In the parking lot, I saw the trustee's cars, the mayor's car, all the police that Andy knows, and others. I told Ella I can't be there. I instantly called Andy and had him come pick me up. When Andy arrived to pick me up and saw a lot of our client's cars there, he was not happy to say the least. Our maintenance company has a contract with the town and all its officials. He warned me not to go there. As fucked up as that is, he was right. I walked to Andy's truck like a puppy with his tail between his legs while continuously looking down at the concrete in case my hat and oversized sunglasses did not fully conceal me.

People protested outside on the street. Only 15 people showed up–15. Why? Well, for three reasons. The first is that a lot of people didn't know about it. All trustees and other officials had to sign a NDA (non-disclosure agreement) stating they would not disclose this crooked deal. Second, the people that did find out about it are afraid to speak up. I am one of those people. I am ashamed to say that, but that is the cold fact. The third reason was simply because people must work. It was held in the morning on a weekday. Doesn't this shit sound like something that goes on in Washington, D.C.? It sure does, but it's in my own town.

More talk of trying to impeach Biden, more talk of the charges they arrested Trump for.

There were huge fires in Hawaii. Just like Canada. Just like California. Awful lot of fires going on. Just like when there were all those train derailments.

This Hawaii incident does have a stranger element about it than the other catastrophes had. There were some buildings and homes that did not get burnt. All the buildings or homes that did not get burnt, were owned by celebrities or other important key players in the deep state, and all non-burnt properties had one thing in common–they all had blue roofs or had something on the property that was blue. That was a smart fire that knew to stay away from anything blue. Now, you might be thinking that it was a fire retardant that the homeowners and building owners added to their properties years ago just in case there was ever a fire, but that is not the case. Oprah's home did not have that weeks prior to the fires. There is a recording out there where someone called Oprah and warned her that there were going to be devastating fires and informed her of the precautions she should take for her home, it was then that the blue roof was added. In the video, you can certainly tell that she was not aware of this plan of fires, however, when warned, she promised she wouldn't say anything, and she thanked the person for letting her know. During that conversation, she did not ask questions as to why or show any concern at all regarding the residents of Hawaii, or the safety of their homes. She was untouched by the fact that this will happen, indicating she is fully aware of the disasters that her group of elite cause. It was like an everyday phone call, no emotion whatsoever; she was completely unaffected. According to a podcast I listened to, Oprah is on house arrest and this recording was done on purpose to show the world how she is a part of all of this. The audio is out there and it's not hard to find at all, not much digging is needed to be able to pull it up, millions have already heard it.

On October 4th, there is supposed to be an EBS and there are several different theories about this.

Per Real Raw News: "The national test will consist of two portions, testing WEA and EAS capabilities. Both tests are scheduled to begin at approximately 2:20 p.m. ET on Wednesday, Oct. 4."

That is what FEMA is saying. But two other theories are going around.

One theory is:

White hats have encouraged their own to temporarily disable cellular phones between 2:00-3:00 p.m. on October 4 when the criminal Federal

Emergency Management Agency is scheduled to conduct a nationwide test of a new Emergency Action System.

The white hats are supposedly taking control of the situation but there is a possibility that the black hats can intervene and send out a message—a fake message that is—using Trumps voice and telling all citizens to "take arms and attack D.C., and to also take back your streets." In other words, invoke a civil war.

Theory two is:

It's a black hat EBS, it will initiate the nano particles of the vaccinated (covid vaccine) and the vaccinated will get sick or drop dead. Also, it could possibly emit an ultrasonic ray that could harm others, including the unvaccinated.

Or it could just be a damn normal test.

"Being awake isn't a blessing, it's a burden. Only the strongest of souls can wake up every day and see the world sleeping around them and still carry on as if it's normal."

September 29th, 2023

Shit is heating up in our small town. More and more people are pissed about the CCP owned land in our town, as they should be. The killer part is people think they have a say so. It is a done deal. Our mob already sold us out. They just don't know it yet. Shit is really going to go down once they realize it. Well, if mine and Ellas's way of thinking is correct, it's not a done deal. It will not happen.

They had a televised town meeting. The mayor literally said at the beginning:

"This is not a Q & A. We will not answer your questions. You only have three minutes to speak. After three minutes, it will go to next person."

Mighty nice of ya. Three minutes to speak your concerns, in America. And how dare the townspeople want to ask questions. Nope, it's not allowed.

Some got up to the microphone and talked calmly. Others were obviously irate.

One man, who only lived here for three years, and is a Lieutenant in the Army, swore to take them all down.

There will be two other meetings this week. Rumor has it that NewsNation is coming to cover it.

October 7th, 2023

EBS happened as stated. Yes, it was just a test.

This morning it was announced that Israel is under attack. They have been saying from day one that "Saving Israel for last."

Of course, no one understood that, and we are not going to. Also, the Dinar (Iraq money), once their currency changes and they have independence, and become a part of the WTO (World Trade Organization), that would be the start of the NESARA.

Speaker of the House Kevin McCarthy was removed. First time they removed someone so suddenly from the Senate since 1910.

Trump just announced today that we are headed for WWIII. Will that be our scare event?

Of course this is exciting for us! We have been hearing about this for almost four years now! I know that sounds twisted, that we were excited about hearing about a war, but if you know, you know.

When I was watching the hearings for the Biden impeachment (which by the way, the normies don't even know that is going on). Jamie Raskin stated that they are only there because Trump wants Biden impeached. He also said that just last week, Trump wanted to stop money being sent to Ukraine.

Hello? If Trump is no longer our CIC, how does he have any say so in having a legitimate President impeached? How does he have any say so in whether the United States sends money to Ukraine?

I see shit like that, and it pulls me right back into the positive thinking. Did anyone catch that? Did the sleeping hear that? Oh wait, only the patriots were able to see that hearing. Mainstream Media did not even tell anyone that Biden was even facing impeachment.

Now Israel. The channels are going nuts. The truther channels that is.

Such huge coincidences.

1. Speaker of House– gone. Talk that Trump might step in.

2. Biden impeachment hearings.

3. Iraq joins WTO

4. Israel attacked

5. Possible WWIII (scare event)

6. EBS test

And I will tell you something, what's another coincidence, our town.

This Chinese thing, the deal they signed with the CCP. Coincidence? I am starting to think not.

They said in the very beginning that "when the truth comes out, they are house cleaning EVERYWHERE. Who knows, your next-door neighbor could be someone that is arrested." That is what they said, to be exact. Corruption everywhere is being cleaned up. Even small towns.

Huge coincidence that all of this is going down in the world, at the exact same time this malfeasance is going in our town.

They could not go back years ago and get them on small shit.

No, they had to get them on something bigger. They dangled money in front of them, and they fell for it, hook, line and sinker, and signed papers with the CCP.

I hope they all get arrested.

Unfortunately, one of people supporting this was "one of us." He used to follow this with me, and he is the one that pointed out to me that the Queen was already dead.

Did he get tired of waiting for the truth to come out?

Did money talk for him?

Not sure.

But we lost another soldier.

When you talk to him, he defends allowing CCP to come in. His defense is that our car parts come from China, and so does everything that we order from Amazon. He repeats it to everyone all the time, in the same mechanical voice.

CaR pArTs R mAdE iN cHyNa…

I responded with…

"Not all whites are KKK, not all blacks are criminals, not all bikers are gang riding killers, not all Hispanics are part of the cartel, etc., etc.,

There are good whites, bad whites, good blacks, bad blacks, and there are good Chinese and bad Chinese."

It has been verified that this company that bought our land, is the bad Chinese, The CCP. They are listed on the Department of Justice most feared list (not that I really trust the DOJ, but you know what I am trying to say). The Chinese that manufacture our car parts, are the hard-working good Chinese. Those Chinese people even hate the CCP.

It's like us hardworking Americans hate the evil Democrats, the Cabal.

There are hardworking Chinese that hate the CCP.

He did not respond to that. And you can tell he was agitated.

Also, our property taxes went up 15%. It's to cover the break that we are giving to the CCP on their taxes. For 30 years, the CCP get a break.

This is going to sound terrible, but if he gets arrested, so be it.

He knew. But because the truth did not come out overnight, he more than likely thought it was bullshit, and he caved in. He helped sell us out.

I like him, I really do. However, I do not trust him anymore.

It kind of baffles me when people give up on this. Nothing happens overnight. Especially something this big.

So, anyone who gave up on this and walked away because "nothing was happening" after 3 1/2 years, they need to take a step back and reevaluate.

This is global, millions– no billions– of people involved. So much bigger than anyone can imagine.

I personally think that what's happened to Joe. Some people feel there is no hope in sight. There is a saying "If you can't beat them, then join them." Now, I don't read minds, but there is a good chance that is the case with him.

October 9th, 2023

Israel escalating–They have put all Military on standby. They are going to send United States Military over to Israel to defend them.

Putin has said that if America gets involved, he will partner with Palestine and bomb the United States.

Trump met with the military in secret.

Biden is nowhere to be found for two days now.

Due to the situation in Israel, they have to pick a new Speaker of the House tomorrow.

They are speculating that it will be Jim Jordan, however, there is talk he could be bad, but I am still thinking he is good.

The channel Newsmax just stated that they recommend Americans need to arm themselves and they are blaming this Israel fiasco on Biden. He released 6 billion to Iran. Iran's goal is to draw the United States into a broader conflict. They have allegedly activated terrorist attacks again in the U.S.A.

Nine Americans have been confirmed dead in Israel. White House goes dark.

White House press conference– no Biden.

This is all scripted!

Do you remember that list of 17 cities? The list that they warned everyone of what cities to get out of? Well, they are posting it again.

But now they are saying "Did you listen to us? We gave you enough notice to get out!" They are advising everyone to relocate now.

There is this "clue" or comm (communication) that has been going around since day one. It's a Mickey Mouse Clock. Yeah, I know it sounds stupid, but Mickey's hands are on 10:10, we have been told it either refers to a date, or a time.

Well, tomorrow is October 10th. We will see.

October 11, 2023

Well, the war in Israel is still rolling along. So many different speculations. They have been telling us from the beginning that this will be a false flag.

People are going nuts. A lot of people (I am referring to the awake) think that when the people we follow call something a false flag, that that means "it's not happening." No that's not it.

We see comments and questions all the time saying things like "I know people that live in Israel They are hearing the bombs! It's not false."

Well, sweetheart, you have not been paying attention. A false flag means yes, it is going on, but it's not for the reason you think. Or the severity that you think.

Yes, it is happening. Yes, there are bombs going off. I have seen videos where they have crisis actors contributing to the propaganda. Yes, I said actors. Most importantly, a false flag is in reference to something started but it is nowhere near what you think is really happening, or why it is happening. It was created to cause a distraction.

Nothing big happened yesterday regarding the Mickey Mouse clock, but that was just a guess. 10:10 could mean a time.

Well, in addition to Newsmax saying that all Americans should be armed, now Fox news is saying it.

They are also warning the 17 cities residents.

October 19th, 2023

Well, it's been a couple of days, but hey, that's ok, you're not going anywhere.

It has been fast and furious. No, no, not with it coming out publicly or the truth revealed, but the war and other things.

Israel, Palestine, Iran, Yemen, all involved now. China, Russia and one other country (forgot who), are about to get involved as well.

The United States Navy just took out a missile that was aimed at them from Yemen.

So now they are saying the United States is under attack. Iran is shooting off stuff by our ships.

The U.S. is loaded with "sleeper cells." A sleeper cell is an immigrant who was graciously welcomed into our country and crossed the border illegally. Not all immigrants are sleeper cells. The sleeper cell refers to an immigrant who was sent here to someday attack us. Once they get the call or the text is when they will be activated to attack or violently protest.

Funny how most immigrants are military aged men. And they are not just from Mexico. Oh, hell no. They are from Iran, Pakistan, Palestine, Egypt, Venezuela, list goes on and on. Sammy told me that they are busing them into our county. They get bussed here, then a car picks them up. Where they go from there, no one knows.

See, as part of the plan, the immigrants can come over because.... once NESARA kicks in, the only way to get your money is to go back to the country that you were born or reside in. That is how Trump will get the immigrants out of here. They will want to go back. They will deport themselves.

I am very confused about the Speaker of the House. They voted, Scalise was in the lead, then he dropped out; they voted again, Jeffries was in the lead; they voted again, Jeffries got the most votes again but that didn't make him the winner. They have to vote again, then Jim Jordan dropped out; now he is back in.

So, we have no Speaker of the House now during a time of war? And Biden is illegitimate.

They issued a worldwide travel caution. Just a caution, but it is worldwide due to all the terrorism.

Terrorism–one word we never had to say when Trump was in office. Just thought I would remind you of that.

They stormed the Capitol yesterday. All the Palestinians who live near Washington, D.C. stormed the Capitol and protested the war. Four Police officers were hurt. No word on mainstream media. You can find it on the internet, Fox news, Newsmax. But not on mainstream. Well, that is until they find a way to blame Trump. Then it will be on mainstream media. That's all they aired when they blamed Trump for the storming of the Capitol on Jan 6th. But this storming– crickets.

Large violent protests in Chicago, too.

It has been three years now. We have been hearing "It had to be done this way," and "They need to wake up," and "We can't tell them, we have to show them."

Is it getting old? Hell, yes. But I get it.

The truth probably could have come out sooner if the zombies weren't so blind and had some common sense.

Think about it.

Covid comes out, deep state and the television freaked people out about it.

Sheep listened.

Stay in your house. You cannot go out to eat. Shut down your business. But you can order carry-out and go to the store.

Sheep listened.

You must wear a mask. Even though breathing in your same oxygen that is trapped in the mask and is a breeding ground for bacteria is more harmful.

Sheep listened.

Facts came out about how it was manmade in China. It was a bioweapon from the deep state. Mainstream media did not show it.

Sheep didn't listen to people who said to research it.

Because of Covid, use mail in votes. Too dangerous to go in person to vote. But you can go to the grocery store with more people there.

Sheep listened.

Live coverage showed Trump winning by a lot. Until the mail in votes was counted. Mail in votes can be manipulated. Biden won fair and square mainstream media said.

Sheep listened.

You must get a vaccine! *YOU HAVE TO*. In America, people thought it was ok that someone told you that you had to do something to your own body.

Sheep listened.

Oh wait, you need two, three, four, five boosters for it to really work.

Sheep listened.

Price of gas went up tremendously.

Sheep thought it was ok.

Price of groceries tripled.

Sheep thought it was ok.

Our borders are completely open. Thousands daily came across. Drug cartels, murderers, rapists, human traffickers, every single one of them breaching the security of our homeland. The television told them it was a good thing. "We are helping others."

Sheep listened.

You can let a child pick his own sex at the age of five. It's ok.

Sheep listened.

We can accept people who think they are cats and put litter boxes in the schools.

Sheep listened.

People can get arrested if they use the wrong pronoun.

Sheep listened.

We need to defund the police. They are no good.

Sheep listened.

It is ok to ban children's books that have been around forever if the deep state felt they should do so.

Sheep listened.

Now there is a war. It is ok that we send millions–no, billions– to the other countries, even though here in the U.S. people are struggling and some donating their blood for grocery money.

Sheep listened.

It is ok that America is now a joke. People laugh at our stumbling, fumbling, dementia fake President. But it's ok. Biden is the best!

Sheep listened.

It is ok that the Biden Crime Family is under investigation. Nothing to see here, folks.

Sheep listened.

So, you see. They are not sleeping. They are in a fucking coma. So, I get now why they say "We had to show them."

Eighty percent of Biden voters did wake up. So, there is still that whopping 20%. How do you wake up someone that is sleeping? Scare the fuck out of them.

So that is what is next. That is the scare event. They need to be hit with, "hey, you could die soon!" type of event to wake them up.

Do I still feel the same way? That Trump is good and there really is a plan? I do.

I agree with Adam. If they were all in it together, they would have just taken us already.

Everything in their playbook that we were made aware of has pretty much been right. The only that has not happened yet was the FEMA camps for Trump supporters.

Trump has prevented that. He is the reason why we are not in FEMA camps. The only bad things that are happening are to wake people up.

They held another meeting in our town. We play it live on a local channel and all of us get together and watch it.

Well, this time they had "actors." Well, not actors, they were actual people from town, but I guarantee you that they were called and asked to go up there.

They were for the CCP company to come in.

The reason why we all think they were called is, well, first, if they were really for it, why are they just now coming out of the woodwork?

Secondly, when someone is passionate about something, they go through the trouble of signing up to talk, then take the time to go to the meeting, then they prepare what they are going to say, and they look forward to speaking their mind.

Three yahoos go up there and calmly said, "My name is so and so, and I vote yes for the Chinese coming in." End of story, then sat down. Really? You expect us to believe that?

One person got up there and said, "Auto parts are made in China, and so is your Amazon products. So, I vote yes."

Same words that Joe tells everyone. Betcha, I know who called that person and told him what to say.

October 21st, 2023

So much shit is going down still. Just like they said it would happen when we are getting close.

Israel war is getting worse.

New information about Biden Crime Family. They found $200,000 more in illegal money.

Proof that Biden paid unaccounted for cash, to purchase his two-million-dollar beach house. And it happened right after Hunter sent a nasty email to China demanding two million more dollars.

James Comer swears to take him down next week.

Nuclear threats.

More Muslim riots. Worse than BLM riots.

More people wanting to kill Jews.

Still no Speaker of the House.

Jim Jordan pulled out again.

Sidney Powell, Trump's attorney that swore to bring down the Kraken, plead guilty to conspiracy to overturn 2020 election–All part of the show.

There is buzz feed every day!

In our town, advocates fighting the CCP has discovered that work emails are public knowledge. The people fighting this got all of them. She will see how far back this goes. How long did they hide it from the townspeople? She put on social media a picture of one of them. It was our town's code enforcer email to one of the CCP. He was so lovey-dovey and gushing over the CCP'S main contact. Man is he being teased for that, everyone is making fun of him. He went on Facebook and changed the name of the town he lives in. Too late. Small town. They all know where you live.

I filled in my family on the latest intel, as they call it, Andy, Jack and Adam listened intently to everything I had to say, and believe me, I can really go on a soap box about this. When I was all done, Andy told the boys, "Hey, take your mom on a drive. Go down the highway, turn right, then another right, and walk in and tell them you want to drop mom off on the 2nd floor." Those were directions to the local hospital's psych ward.

Andy said that story to Sammy and Ella, it was at that point that Ella and I reminded them that we had better have connecting rooms.

This morning, I was going on and on again with Andy while brushing my teeth, foam from the toothpaste spitting everywhere and my inner Erin was kicking in again. He real seriously looked at his phone and said, "Hey Google, how much is a straight jacket?" Then he asked me my size, because he wants me to be comfortable. Thanks babe, at least he is concerned about my comfort level.

After my banter, I went to my office to document. Jack walked into my office while I was working. He says, "Holy shit! That's a lot! Who is going to read all of that?"

I told him, trust me, when the truth comes out, you will want to read this, or if not you, your kids will.

Then he said, "I know why the notes are so long, you must type like you talk."

Love this freedom to speak in my house and with my family, but in the outside world, not so much. There are so many things that can be frustrating on a daily basis.

We have a lot of contractors and their receptionists that are die hard blue liberals. It tests my patience every single time I am with them. One client was so proud of all her vaccines. She was even prouder that she was assigned a QR code for herself so she could be scanned.

Once while trying to secure a rather large contract on an industrial building, the potential client asked me to attend a United Way meeting with them. With massive reluctance, I did. They fully support The United Way, and all of the United Ways woke brainwashing ideology. The meeting I went to was about how women are suppressed in this world, and we need more women power and support women. We are not suppressed. We do not need more women power, at least I don't.

I sat quietly (yes, sometimes I can be quiet), put on a phony smile and counted the minutes until it ended.

This same client loves Taylor Swift, who is the highest priestess in the Cabal, and she loves the Queen of England, who was evil.

Clients who blame everything on MAGA. Little do they know that I am MAGA.

Someone I know that lives in the same town as me, said, "I wish all of these Trumpsters and MAGA people would just shut the fuck up!! They are ruining this country. The plant in our town is a good thing. It is going to bring in so much money and so many jobs! There is nothing wrong with it."

I just listened to her and said," Yes, times are hard. But we got through 2008, and we will get through this."

Never stating what side I am on and then dropping the subject.

The misconception that there will be 2,600 jobs available for this county is simply that, a misconception.

It's been verified that there will only be 260 job openings. And they will not be offered to the locals. CCP is bringing in their own.

But the sleeping doesn't know that. They should, but they don't.

I got a call from someone who found our business online and they wanted me to meet them that instant for a quote on a general mechanical maintenance contract. It was a Sunday. When I informed him that we can schedule to meet during the week, he angrily responded "You work for ME!" I could tell by their voice, they were Asian.

"You work for ME!" Thinking they meant "You, American work for the Chinese" and not so much "I might hire your company, you work for me."

Why? Because we didn't get to that point yet. It was our first conversation. There was no contract secured. So yeah, he meant you, American, work for me. I looked up his phone number and it turns out he was part of the Democratic Party, once ran for Governor of Hawaii and now lives in California. So why do you need a house here in our county?

I said to him," Let's do an experiment. Call another company and let them know that you want to meet right now, on a Sunday. Do that, then call me back and let me know how that worked out for you."

The phone went dead. They are not used to being talked to that way.

My thoughts were confirmed when I spoke with two other engineering companies in the county that they also received calls from Asian people saying the exact same thing. Yep, so my sleeping friends that think this CCP purchase is a good thing? They are going to be in for a rude awakening if they don't wake up soon.

October 23rd, 2023

Well, more interesting things regarding our little town. Our friend, Joe, the one who flipped, and also does subcontracting through the town with his electrical business, told Andy to delete all emails and text messages regarding the plant. Andy knows not to say anything to Joe, so Andy just said "Ok." When Andy got home, he told me about it. Andy then told me that he would not delete anything. He has nothing to hide. As far as text messages go, the only texts he has on his phone are negative ones about the plant. And if he deletes them, won't that make him look guilty? Why would you delete them? So, he is ignoring Joe's advice.

I told Andy that Joe is like the fake news now. Do the opposite of what he tells you. Why does Joe think it's even ok to delete shit like that? I thought you said this was a good thing, Joe, so shouldn't you be proud of your emails and text messages?

And the best part, there was a comment on the Facebook page that was created for people opposing it.

Someone made a comment:

"We have a crooked Mayor just like some board members trying to benefit family members themselves. The main trustee is one of them. He is claiming that this is going to be his retirement account."

Something and someone, that I have not mentioned yet. That "main trustee" that they are referring to is someone we know personally. My whole life I always felt uncomfortable around him, his whole family, couldn't pinpoint as to why, and to be honest, there was no reason back then. I just always just felt "off" when I was around them, can't really explain it. It was not until I was an adult that I figured out about toxic people and narcissists. Andy warned me about them for years, and I always felt "stuck". That is until one-episode years ago at a barbecue and I saw their true colors. Everything happens for a reason, and I believe that one episode was fate's way of waking me up about them. It's not so much what happened, it's how it spiraled out of control and things were flipped to fit his narrative. It instantly hit me like a ton of bricks, and I politely removed myself from that family. I have since always referred to him as the toxic information guy. Silly, I know, but I cannot stomach to say his name, and that is exactly what he does, spills toxic information about everything and everyone like a never-ending spigot.

I told Ella after that whole escapade that "He is so evil, that if he was in Washington DC., he would be part of the Cabal." Never imagining that that statement would become true. Well, there you have it. Now we know, he is part of the Cabal, right here in our hometown.

The guy that posted that comment is part of the advocates for the town's people. He would not post that unless he knew this devil was getting paid. So, this toxic person I know must have either confided in the wrong person who later turned on him, or they found it one of those emails that were gathered.

Joe has been acting different lately. Couldn't figure out why. Joe was following this and knows that from the very start of this, China was projected to try and take us over. Now he is supporting them.

Then one night Me, Andy, Joe and his wife went out to dinner. He blatantly said to me, "To be honest with you, I have no problem with him." "Him" meaning the toxic information guy. Ok, first, I didn't fucking ask. Why are you advertising that without being prompted?

It was eerily weird.

Joe's change towards me was around the same exact time as they all were discussing things about China behind closed doors and him and the toxic information guy must have been bonding.

Gotcha! Now all the pieces of the puzzle are coming together.

I guess the bottom line is never to underestimate a patriot's instinct!

Andy's friend Rick is a patriot, and he fills us in on the happenings of the CCP since we can't be there.

However, Rick is in the group that are diehard Trump supporters and patriots but not following this. He feels we have to wait until the 2024 election. With all this stuff going on in town, I told him that I think they will all get arrested. He laughed and said, "I don't know about all that, but they definitely won't be elected next year." I just shut my mouth then.

Joe told Andy that Rick is spouting off his mouth too much on Facebook. He confessed that the town officials want to start charging him a permit fee for the farmers market that he hosts. They never charged him before.

Those are the kind of games you only hear about in D.C. Or so I thought.

Our town's main player is a man that is really the one pulling the strings. He has ties to Washington, D.C. and Obama. It's as if the mayor is Biden and this other man is Obama.

So, yeah, this CCP thing coming in is a deep state thing.

If it turns out that Kenny and Mac's way is right and this is our new future, governed by the CCP, I will probably be the first one that Joe and that toxic information guy drags out. By my hair, no doubt.

A chance I am willing to take.

News for today is that China, Russia and Iran are Americas biggest threat right now. Christopher Wray of the FBI states that America is in danger from China.

If that's the false flag, I wonder how the elites in our town will act to that? China? A threat?

Speaker of the House has still not been picked. Jim Jordan dropped out again.

A lot of back and forth with that. I am sure there is a reason.

We were told four days ago that" Heart attacks can be fatal. Watch for the cardiac arrest." Remember, they talk in riddles. Comms. Clues.

Well, this morning it is all over the internet and even fake news that Putin had a heart attack last night. He didn't die. But he had a heart attack.

Now the same guy that posted it four days prior is saying, "He did not have a heart attack. It's part of the movie."

Do you remember that suicide of someone famous that was supposed to happen? I mentioned it months ago. Supposedly it happened but it just has not been made public yet.

October 26th, 2023

Holy shit! Our town is exploding. More and more text messages and emails are being posted!

The best part, most of them are from the "toxic information guy!" Hey, a thought, I am tired of typing out "toxic information guy," for now on, let's just call him "Tig."

People are seeing his true colors.

The text message was between him and the mayor. There were pictures attached of people's houses that are against the CCP plant and rude comments about the townspeople. In one of the text messages, he called the townspeople stupid. The ironic part is that his text messages were loaded with misspelled words and wrong punctuation. Of course, the townspeople loved that and asked the question," Who is stupid?"

Someone else also shared something interesting. I never thought of this, but it's a possibility. They feel that one of the guys involved, the same guy that sent that lovestruck email to China, is being set up.

Most of the emails to China are sent through him. He is not on the board; he has no say so. If they get caught–or if they don't get caught and it goes through but it's a failure– he would be their fall guy.

I know a lot of this shit sounds far-fetched and like a crazy movie, but trust me, it's true and its happening. Then again, this whole era is a movie.

They are also taking pictures of everyone's house who talks at the meetings. Will they blow up their house? Of course not. But they will keep it on file and when one of them needs a permit to do work on their home the permit will be delayed, denied or they will have to pay more. They might find themselves getting mysteriously pulled over or messed with in some other fashion.

I tell Ella everything. And Andy tells Sammy everything. But we did not tell them this yet. I admire the fact that Ella speaks what's on her mind and she is not afraid of confrontation, and I wish I was more like her. Those characteristics are part of the reason why we have decided not to tell them yet. If I tell her, I fear that she will contact Joe in some fashion and call him out. Which then in return, Joe will find a way to retaliate against her. So, I had to keep it to myself.

Joe told me and Andy that Sammy voted yes to the plant. That he physically voted "yes." Not true. Sammy is on the committee of the district.

Joe called Andy while I was in the car with him and Andy put it on speaker. It was the day of the event.

Joe: "Was that Ella I had seen at the protest?"

Andy: "Yes, she went up there, why?"

I then jumped in.

Me: "I was there too, but had Andy pick me up"

Joe: "Well she shouldn't be there; she shouldn't be putting shit on Facebook either. Does she know that Sammy voted yes to this?

We didn't believe it. We humored Joe and just said no, we didn't know that.

There is no way I was going to tell him to fuck off and that I didn't believe him. If there is anything I have learned from dealing with people like that is, you can't win. You cannot. It is best to agree with everything they say and then ignore them. That's all you can do.

Plus, Andy and I suspect it's not true.

I asked Sammy that night if the plant was ever mentioned in the district meeting. Never letting him know what I was told. He said that there was one mention of it a while ago at the meeting.

Someone told them how there was a new business coming into town. It will double everyone's home value, it will lower everyone's taxes, and it will employ 2600 employees.

That's it.

Then they asked if anyone was opposed? Everyone just kind of looked at each other, one person said they needed more information.

The guy speaking said they will give them more information when it comes in.

And that was it.

There was no physical voting.

They made it sound like a beautiful thing that is coming in. All roses and fucking begonias. Then no other information was given.

Maybe that is how they got the votes–tricked people?

I feel Ella is going to go ballistic when I tell her, because think about it, who else is Joe spewing these lies to? Sammy is calmer, he might not be as upset, but I will tell them soon.

As I am sure you figured out by now, the deep state is known for throwing out diversions, false flags. You have also figured out that the deep state is right here in our town, and for that reason, the following will not be a shocker to you. A while ago, right when the corrupt politicians in our town were making a back door deal with the CCP, some of the townspeople caught wind of it. Hence, signal the diversion. A well-known and highly respected individual in our town, got arrested for picking up a prostitute. It was a sting operation that the local authorities set up.

We have fentanyl coming in daily into our county, we have a heroin problem, crime on the east end, the world is in shambles, immigrants being bussed in, but they are going to spend money on a sting operation geared towards online prostitution?

He was caught and arrested at the same exact time everyone was meeting behind closed doors, and some learned of it. I think our town had a false flag. Bam, just like that the attention of the possible corruption got thrown to the side and everyone focused their attention on the prostitution bust. It was all over the fake news, in all the papers and that was all the town's people could talk about for months, leaving our little mob to finish the details of the CCP in private.

Don't look here, look over here.

A diversion.

Did I mention that the advocates that are against this called the mainstream media to get it covered and were hung up on? No one will air this.

It was discovered today that the FBI covered up 40 charges of the Biden Crime Family right before election and during election and his presidency.

And the Biden impeachment trials have picked up again.

Also, several countries told Biden to not get involved in the war in the Middle East. If we do, it will have serious consequences to the United States Homeland.

So, guess what Biden did? He just sent over United States troops to the Middle East.

That's a lot of bad shit said about the Bidens, right? Well, enter the false flag!

Shooting in Maine. Ex-military dude who has been in contact with the FBI and Obama just opened fire at a bowling alley and two other places, he is still at large. The sad thing about false flags is that people do get killed.

MK Ultra– it's real, people.

"During the 1950s and '60s, the CIA used brainwashing, hypnosis, and torture on thousands of subjects brutalized by the infamous Project MK-Ultra experiments."

They use people that no one will notice gone. Homeless, drug addicts, convicts.

It is still happening.

Most false flags are done by MK Ultra victims. Look it up. There is all kinds of information out there.

When the deep state needs a diversion, they trigger their "person", and they do the act.

It's looking like this may be the case in Maine. Ex-military? Talking to FBI? Talking to Obama? Bad news comes out about Biden, then this happens?

They found a suicide note written by the shooter before he went on the killing spree. He didn't write that note. He is still at large.

The FBI arranged a stake out at the shooters house after the shootings. Really? All local law enforcement is looking for you, the FBI is looking for you, but you're going to go back home? Nah, don't think so. The FBI arranged the stake out to keep local authorities busy, while they got the shooter somewhere to deprogram or to kill him themselves.

Unfortunately, there still are some deep staters that are still around. Not all shootings are false flags. Truthers say about 50/50.

We also finally got a new Speaker of the House, Mike Johnson.

The whole Jim Jordan will be Speaker of the House, –oh wait, no he won't, oh wait, yes he will, oh, no he won't–all for a reason. We were told that they need Jim Jordan in a different place.

October 27th, 2023

Well last night we bombed Syria! We are officially in World War III!

Fake Biden was told not to enter, not only did he enter, he airstrikes them. Even the fake news says we are in World War III.

Will this be the reason to remove him?

There are enough immigrants here to fill up two states. Two Nebraska's is what they said to be exact.

Only 30% of those were from Mexico. The other 70% are from Syria, Iran and other countries. I only mentioned Syria and Iran again because who did we just bomb? Syria and Iran.

Will that be the false flag? They already said the false flag will be a threat from China, but it can change. Lord knows things are always changing in this crazy movie.

All I know is there are World War III ALERTS everywhere. The Iranian Foreign Minister says, "The buttons had been pressed!"

It seems the conflict in the Middle East has reached the point of no return, is what they said.

The major alert has not been brought to the Americans attention yet; meaning here in the homeland.

We were also told that the impeachment for Biden will not go through, that he will be removed publicly before then.

Hilliary will be arrested publicly soon– Podesta, Obama.

Their body doubles will be arrested. The real ones have already been taken care of. They had their trials already. This is just for the public display. They will be taken out in disgrace, their name forever tarnished.

When the EBS comes out, we were advised to follow instructions. They know everyone will not be home at the exact same time. Follow instructions and we will be fine.

There will also be an EBV event, but only in the big cities. It will take out the power grid and cars will even stop running. It will be short lived and not hurt anyone.

I want so bad to tell people it's all going to be ok. I want to explain in detail how they have been selling our birth certificates on the stock market, gambling on us, making money on us, any income /state income tax you have ever paid, property and vehicle taxes, interest on loans, mortgages, car loans and credit cards. It's all coming back to the people.

But yeah, if I told people that, they would lock me up and mention the 650 plane trips bringing back gold, artifacts and other valuables would no doubt seal my fate for being committed.

We also heard again on a podcast that Princess Diana is alive, and she will show herself, there is also the possibility of Princess Diana actually being Baron Trump's real mother. She also had a daughter, Princess Sarah and Princess Diana is the real Queen of England. Now, listen, I can't give two shits about all of that. I mean, it would be great, but my biggest priority is the truth and being able to live in the world. All the extra gibberish about people being alive that are supposed to be dead would just be an extra bonus.

Ella and I follow 61 people on our channels. Most of them are ex-military, ex-Secret Service members, or have connections in another way. Most of the information in these notes that you are reading is from them. If it was not for truthers like them trying to alert and educate the American people, this world would be devastating. The podcasts, the interviews, the declass documents and all of the information are so interesting and informative.

In live presidential speeches with Fake Biden, they showed the other day his face sagging, it was like a mask was slipping off. He literally had the chin sagging; it looked like two testicles hanging from his chin.

Then in Trump's speech, he made a comment that he would like to punch Biden, but if he did, there would be pieces of plastic all over on the floor! Yep, clues are being dropped left and right.

October 29th, 2023

Well, Matthew Perry died last night. He played Chandler on the episode of *Friends*. The whole *Friends* cast was bad– part of the deep state.

That is going to be an absolute shocker to the world. Americans adore that whole cast.

In the beginning of this, we were told that when it gets closer to look for the name of Rachel Chandler.

She is a huge part of human trafficking and pedophilia. HUGE. She was Epstein and Gislaine Maxwells biggest asset. She worked with them and helped lure the victims in. With the death of Matthew Perry, her name is coming up again.

Her name is made up. They came up with the last name by:

C- is for child. She is a handler, child handler. Hence, the name Chandler.

Some say Rachel is made up, too, it's really a man and his real name is Ray. That has not been verified yet.

So, the name Rachel Chandler was born.

*Friends* was created by the Deep State.

One of the characters in that show had the name of Rachel (Jennifer Aniston), one character had the name of Chandler (Matthew Perry).

Those characters were given those names because if anybody got wind of Rachel Chandler, when they googled her name, it would pop up the cast of *Friends* and not her.

Everyone (that is everyone that is following this) calls Trump "Batman."

Matthew Perry last posts on his Instagram were pictures of Batman.

He also proudly posted how he was fully vaccinated and boosted.

His cause of death was he drowned in his own hot tub.

Since all of the elite were given an ultimatum, either you cooperate and we will let you leave this world in a respected manner, your name will not be tarnished, or you don't cooperate, and the world will see your tribunal and confession and/or your arrest and you will die with a tarnished name.

Looks like Matthew cooperated.

Things are always done for a reason. There is a reason why they had him post on his Instagram the Batman sign and announcing how fully vaccinated he was.

Also, two days before his death, Trump posted on Truth Social.

When Trump drops clues, he misspells words. It's funny because the sleeping probably think he is uneducated, and they are making fun of him, little do they know he is the master at the art of war, and he is sending out clues.

,

He posted:

"This Country is in such bad shape right now; it's like watching a bad Petty Mason episode. This Country is deade."

Misspelled– *Petty* should have been *Perry*. *Deade* should have been *dead*.

Take those two words out–*Perry Dead*.

Matthew Perry died two days later.

And oh, they caught the shooter of the killings in Maine. You know, the ex-military that was talking to the FBI and Obama? Yeah, he committed suicide. They found him with two gunshot wounds to the head. You know, suicide nowadays, you have to shoot yourself twice in the head in case the first one doesn't work.

After talking to Ella last night, she watched a video, not sure who it was, but man does it make sense!

The immigrants–where our research leads us, no one knows. We have no superior intel, obviously. With that being said, there is so much that confuses the living shit out of us. Usually, we can kind of figure it out as weeks go by, but some of this crazy stuff is like what? Other stuff, we feel is obvious.

The one thing that baffled us a little is the immigrants.

At first, we thought it was optics, because letting a bunch of illegals coming into the country is treason, and that will get out Biden.

But nope, not the case. Then we saw people that live near the border tell us that it really is happening.

Then it turned into millions–rapists, drug dealers, cartel, murderers, etc.

Ok wait a minute, if the white hats are in control, then why is this happening? Ella and I had several conversations about this.

But then we remembered the video where these "immigrants" were walking with no shoes and did not even look fatigued. So, they walked for 16 hours with no shoes on and look dapper? Were most crisis actors?

But that video that Ella watched, it said that a lot of the immigrants are being trained by our military. They are being brought in by the bus load and then picked up and brought to nice places but then being trained by the United States military, the good guys. There is not enough military to arrest all the governors, senators, mayors, police, doctors, nurses, and all the corrupt people. There are just too many. So, they pick out the military age people and train them our way!

Two things I wrote earlier. One was that most of them coming across are military age (at the time I thought that was a bad thing and maybe our false flag), second, I wrote about how we are getting bus loads in our county. There is so much corruption in our county that they would need more reinforcements.

That makes a lot of sense! It will be interesting to see if it goes that way.

You know what the most interesting part of the division in the world is right now?

They call us a cult.

Do they know what a cult is?

A cult is a group of people that follow a leader and believe everything they tell you and they do anything the leader says.

Now, let's look at this. When Trump would give speeches and tell people to take the vaccine, no MAGA did. He trusted that we would use our own discernment; he allowed us to use our own common sense. Something a cult leader does not do.

Libs, however, every time Biden or their deep state governor said get the vaccine, they ran out to the nearest facility to get one–maybe two. They said wear a mask; they threw a mask on even if they were in their own car alone. Some people put on two masks.

But we are the cult? Even though they jumped at all the deep state's barking orders.

The hypocrisy is unbearable. Yet with each passing day, they always refer to us as a cult.

November 1st, 2023

Israel expired from the Bafour Corporation.

Which means on October 31$^{st}$, Israel as a corporation will expire.

In fact, if anyone were to look at the China map, you will see they removed Israel completely from there.

One of the reasons why they always said, "Save Israel for last." Israel is a playground for the Cabal. Biggest human trafficking, even bigger than Ukraine. Ukraine is second.

That is why the Biden Crime Family, and his administration wants to send so much money to them. Even my mom said," It almost sounds like Biden is being blackmailed."

And for her to notice that it must be obvious.

They both have so much on him. And China owns him.

Of course, Trump is also speaking that he supports Israel. Speeches like that is what believers like Kenny and Mac think is horrible and it proves to them that Trump is part of the evil.

It's too soon folks… Trump cannot announce that Israel is evil yet. The truth will come out. He is just playing along for now.

A lot of people on my channel are getting fatigued, to say the least. I guess fatigue would be a significant understatement. There was a Trump speech where he said, "We will turn the lights out on Halloween." Yes, we all thought that meant the blackout or EBS. But things have different meanings in the Art of War. Could he have been referring to Israel? The Balfour act? Meaning it expired; they are no longer; they are not a real country anymore; they are bankrupt. Could that have been the reference as to "We turned the lights out?" One can only guess. The fatigue for most set in when they didn't see anything here in America happen on Halloween.

There is going to be a documentary that will blow our minds. Even us followers don't know everything. Of course not, but that is one documentary that I cannot wait to see.

Nothing new on the CCP story in our town.

I will say this, but before I say anything, I must point out that I really don't have a right to say anything about what the townspeople are saying at the meeting. I mean, you don't see my ass going up to the town meetings to talk. These people are giving it their all even if it means losing their job. To these people, I salute them.

However, I wish they would "fight" it a different way at these meetings and on their Facebook pages. When they get up to the podium, they are assuming the board are God-fearing individuals with morals. They are not.

They go to the podium and say a prayer and then ask them to think of the children while they put their heads on their pillow.

They post Bible-thumping quotes on the Facebook page.

People, like members of the board, are laughing at them. You must know your enemy. They are greedy and love money and power. Bible verses will not work on them.

Tell them that they sold us out. Tell them it is Treason. Tell them that all the money they got is useless in prison. Tell them about *THEIR* family. Ask them if they think their kids will miss them when they go to jail? Ask them if their kids will be proud of them for being known as a treasonous prick? Make it all about them in a bad way. Even if the person at the podium doesn't believe they will go to jail (because the only people that believe that is the ones following this), saying that will plant the seed in their head. It will also fuck with them because the meetings are televised, and they will fear than everyone hearing that will spread it around town. Most of them own their own business. I feel if they go about it that way, it will piss the mob off. When people get pissed, they make mistakes, and they fear the world a little more. That's just my two cents, but again, my ass is not going to the podium so I guess I should just shut the fuck up.

I watched an interesting movie last night. Very interesting. Nowadays, I rarely watch regular television and movies. Man, when you stumble upon all this bullshit going on in the world in addition to all of demonic crap we are hearing about celebrities, it makes it hard to watch movies. I will be the first to admit that we do not have 100% proof of any of these things, however, with the stuff we have seen and heard, you can't erase that. It's hard to watch an actor that is accused of so many things and see them in the same light as you used to. On all our channels, they kept talking about a new movie out called *Leave the World Behind* - Ok, I will bite the bait and watch it. Well, holy shit! Let's just say that most things in these notes were mentioned in some sort of way. An ear-piercing worldwide screech (EBS), EMF malfunctions, stories about the Cabal, people scrounging for food and the best was the ending. Throughout the movie the young daughter was obsessed with the show *Friends. Friends*! Of all shows! The ending was just the girl watching the show, then done. The best part is they put Obama's name as a producer. The awake were questioning that and it was explained that they added their names so the sleeping would watch it. If they felt it was produced by the Obamas, they would rush to watch it, no hesitation at all. Their ultimate goal was to have as many people view it as possible. Reviews of the movie were a riot; you could tell who was awake and who wasn't.

Sleeping Beauties reviews:

"What a horrible movie! It made no sense!"

"What the hell kind of ending was that? It left us hanging"

"I can't believe they made a movie like that!"

"What happened? What caused all of that mess?"

"Will there be a sequel, because it had no ending?"

"Why did they end it with the girl watching *Friends*? Did they all survive it?"

Awake Patriot reviews:

"Yep! it's coming!"

"IYKYK." (if you know you know)

"People, there was no ending, because they can't tell you the ending yet."

"There was no ending because Military will not tell you their plan"

"Yesss!!!WWG1WGA!" (where we go one, we go all)

"Buckle up!"

"We are almost there!"

"Great movie"

"Hahahaha… Friends! Perfect!"

"It's coming people!"

There ya have it, someday everyone will understand that movie. The one review that hit it on the head was-" there was no ending because they can't say the ending yet."

For decades, so many movies have been telling us exactly what has been going on. Stanley Kubrick's movies scream with information. Songs, too. Florida Georgia Line blatantly states in its lyrics, "Victoria Secret ain't a secret no more." Find, play, and listen very closely to the song by the same group, "May We All."

November 2nd, 2023

Ok, I am super excited! The amount of comms and the information that is coming out is exhilarating!

Just in case, Ella and I went out and stocked up again.

Trump dropping those hints about Biden's plastic mask, Biden's mask sagging on National TV, the war in Middle East, the start of WWIII, the new Biden proof of money from China, the impeachment trial going on, the immigrants.

Another big clue that was dropped was when they introduced the new Speaker of the House. They said, "I am proud to introduce the 45th speaker of the house, Mike Johnson!"

45th?

But Nancy Pelosi was the 52nd Speaker of the House when she was elected in 2007?

Oh, that's right, the 44th speaker of the house was in 1876, and we are going back to that. LET'S GOOOO! So exciting! And yes, that is true, they did say that. You can pull up old videos of it.

Right now, Washington, D.C. is under the most caution that they had ever been in the history of time–high alert.

An active military site that I follow said that the story about the immigrants being trained from our military, is not true. He said be careful. The sleeper cell story is the true one.

November 3rd, 2023

The protests for the war have gotten worse. Tens of thousands of people are outside the White House right now throwing things at it, knocking down Secret Service agents, smearing paint and getting more violent.

I pulled up the White House live cam and was able to see it on there also, that is correct, I saw it live.

There are also riots in London, France, and at a German airport.

Word is they might blow a bridge up tonight. They said to "watch the sky."

"Remember, remember, the 5th of November" is what they have been saying.

Hoping we are getting closer!!

November 6th, 2023

Ok, so here is the update on the world shit. So exciting!!

"Watch the sky."

While we went through temporary disappointment and yes, checked the sky all day and into dusk only to get a neck cramp and see nothing. Then we saw reports of the sky in Gaza turned bright red, indicating the escalation and all the bombing. They said the war would have to escalate, to a point of terror.

Also, the military in the United States had numerous planes in the air.

Another thing that happened was NESARA has been completed! It will be announced soon, very soon they said. Yesterday, the 5th of November was the day it got finalized.

The new Speaker of the House told the Supreme Court that he "insists" that Biden be removed. There is more than enough evidence that he is corrupt with several different countries and just with the border alone, he committed Treason, he says.

James Comer stated we will see results this week. It's already been done. Just waiting for it to be public now.

On the fake mainstream media–you are not going to believe this– but CNN stated that "Trump might have been right." NBC news mentioned that they never had war with Trump, and they are acknowledging Biden's approval ratings have gone down.

But there are still people out there, I don't know how, but they are still not seeing how bad Biden is. Someone said to me recently, "Trump may be a great businessman, but he sucked as a president!"

I am guessing low gas prices sucked, lowest unemployment rate sucked, low interest rates sucked, no wars sucked, affordable groceries sucked–shall I go on? Of course I did not say that, but you know I was thinking it. How can people still say that with the way the world is now? That is something that I will never understand.

I could not get onto a podcast last night, luckily Ella watched it, and she filled me in! His live was mostly about the NESARA.

I do believe this week is going to be amazing! Some channels have posted that tomorrow is the day that fake Biden will be arrested publicly. They had mentioned that it does not matter if he is publicly arrested before or after the scare event. It's moot at this point.

Banks are crashing. More and more each day. Citizens banks completely collapsed. Customers cannot get to their money. Several mortgage companies have their websites down and people cannot make a payment. All part of the show before NESARA and the new RV kick in.

The scare event, that is a little scary, and we are awake. Meaning, will it be immigrant invasion? Will it be a possible nuclear attack? Will it be boots on the ground attack? Will it be a financial crash? Even though we firmly believe it is part of the plan, and it will be over with within three to ten days, what if it goes to eleven, fifteen or even sixty days? Will I second guess the "plan?" Will I get scared and think, "Oh shit." And how truly bad is it going to get? Will even me and Ella's family be unprepared?

China ramps up aggression towards the U.S.

We are at the greatest risk of consequences on U.S. soil.

During all of this, is Trump's fraud case going on. What a joke. They have a multi-country war going on and they want to keep wasting their time on him. They are showing people how ridiculous they are. Like shouldn't they be working on this war? Kamala Harris is going around giving speeches to the world talking about AI (artificial intelligence). It's all real, well, really going on, I mean. Not exactly real.

Yes, people do notice that. Even the Libs.

Have I ever mentioned that's it's a great time to be alive?

And most people still watch the news. When you have been down so many rabbit holes for more hours than you care to remember, and the person you're talking to says, "If that was true, it would be on the news!"

I think I throw up a little in my mouth when that happens.

The five most used words over the coming months and years will be: "We tried to tell you."

There is another town meeting tonight. Should be interesting because more and more people are getting upset and it's the first meeting since their texts and emails have been posted online.

It has also just been discovered that they have been conversing with a company named JII regarding housing. The problem is the JII is affiliated with Black Rock. Black Rock is a company that Mac warned me and Ella about a couple of years ago. They want to buy everything up, that is all I know, and it is supposedly not good. I honestly do not remember all the details that Mac gave us, but it's bad. They are also the ones that wanted to buy up our farmland.

Back to these notes, remember in the beginning, I had mentioned that Joe told me not to tell anyone that I am taking notes? If I recall, his exact words were that "it could be dangerous to me." I thought it was because so no one from D.C. would hear, yeah, ok like that would happen. But now I know why he said that; he was referring to the people in town.

November 13th, 2023

Well, as you can imagine, no scare event. No EBS, no public awareness, no arrests.

Not getting discouraged, not getting discouraged, not getting discouraged!!!

If I keep telling myself that, maybe I will believe it.

When all of this is over with, I don't ever want to hear another riddle or see another mathematical equation in my life!

So many clues/ comms", so much math. Our brains hurt!

6+1= 7, then subtract JFK's birthday, then add the first date of the solar eclipse divided by todays date = Yes! It's go time!

Ok, totally being facetious above, but seriously that's the formula and the Q drops.

Or the riddles" What makes a canary sing?"; "The 6 o'clock hour can be deadly."; "They won't be able to walk the streets."

`The Julian calendar:

The Julian calendar is a calendar introduced by the authority of Julius Caesar in 46 BC, in which the year consisted of 365 days, every fourth year having 366 days. It was superseded by the Gregorian calendar though it is still used by some Orthodox Churches. Dates in the Julian calendar are sometimes designated "Old Style."

We are supposed to be going back to that. What all that means and why, I don't know. Some rabbit holes are just not worth going down.

A few months ago, I bought a package of sausage at the local grocery store. For the expiration date, they had the regular calendar date and then below it, it said:

"Julian expiration date." That was never there before.

The town's televised meeting was interesting. Three people actually did mention the word Treason. Yeah!

Other than that, nothing new going on with the whole CCP situation. However, much like the world, there is a lot going on behind the scenes. The people that are dedicated to fighting this are working effortlessly with attorneys, state representatives, newspapers and Fox News to fight this. Our town mob has no idea what's in store for them.

In the world, even more information about the Biden Crime Family came out.

They are talking more and more about the med beds. They are getting more details on the healing they can do and also giving instructions about how to make an appointment.

In addition to med beds, there are so many patents for items, from Tesla and others, that were kept secret from the public. Items, devices and inventions created to make people's lives easier. But those patents were suppressed because they wanted the people to count on the government and big Pharma for everything. Those inventions will be made public.

There will be humanitarian projects that you will have to do. I am ok with that, and I am sure everyone else will be. Yeah, no war, wiped out debt, documentaries of the truth, healthier lives and med beds, money back to we the people? I am sure if I have to volunteer to help someone or work a couple of days at a med bed center, I will be A-OK with that. I think it's a good idea.

More and more truth about the vaccines coming out. Marjorie Taylor Greene gave a press conference today on the negative effects on the vaccine.

Babies born with heart problems to vaccinated mothers.

Children with heart disease.

Healthy adults having strokes or suddenly getting cancer.

Healthy adults dropping dead of heart attacks.

For those that do not show any health issues, studies show how it affects your brain and how you process information.

Young couples with infertility issues.

If you check your card for the lot number of the vaccine, if it ends with a #1 that is saline, #2 was the regular flu shot, #3 was the actual Covid vaccine. Number three is the bad one of course. Most that were given ends with a #3. But not all, that would be too obvious. I checked my mom's. She has a #1– saline. That explains why she has had no issues.

The government has just hired four new attorneys to defend them against vaccine injuries. A lot of lawsuits going on already, and we anticipate more coming.

People who only watch mainstream media know none of this.

November 18th, 2023

Why is it so hard to relate anymore to someone who is sleeping? I went to lunch with someone who used to work for us.

Well, let's just say I should have listened to my gut. It was hard for me. After all the rabbit holes I have been down, especially about Hollywood and celebrities, to hear her drool over a star and play videos of their concert, very loudly, in a restaurant, made me contemplate whether or not I should grab the fork and stab my ears so I couldn't hear her anymore. Until the truth comes out, I don't want to hear any celebrity bull shit. I am listening to her talk and all I could think about was the fact that I know she is fully vaccinated, I know who she voted for, she is going on with life like everything in the world is normal, drooling over a celebrity and I just couldn't; I could not talk. I let her do all the talking. I just wanted out of there. I hate being that way. I really do. I guess for me, so much is so obvious to me, and it makes me angry that others don't see it, when it's right in front of their face. It's not that I don't like being with them because they are vaccinated or because they voted for Biden, no, that's not it, I am not that shallow. It's the whole picture, the whole aura and the vibe that is thrown off. I can't explain it.

I survived the lunch and just made a mental note to myself. Never again. If she asks me to lunch again, I will just politely decline.

They traded us or sold us. Not physically of course, but on paper. When we are born, we are given a birth certificate number. There is a red number on the back of our social security cards. If you go to the government bond website, you can check it.

They would look at your demographics, what kind of family you were born to, etc., and they bet on how you would succeed in society. Ok, I am sure there is more to it, I am not the Cabal and do not understand all the logistics of the scheme.

So, of course, Ella and I looked up our families. Yep, it's true. I know that government website is legit, since I have used it several times to check on my kid's savings bonds.

It shows date of issue of the "bond" (meaning our birth certificate), which is our date of birth. It shows how much interest they got on us, and that the bond matured.

Now here is the thing, out of me, Andy, Sammy and Ella, I am the youngest. Why did my bond mature quicker? Why did I have the least amount of money that I was valued at (by a lot, I am not that much younger).

Well, I will tell you why–my bond matured in 1997– 1997, the one and only year that I had horrible credit issues, my credit score tanked. It cleared up in 1998, however, 1997 it tanked. Same year I matured in the bond/Cabal world. If they really do "bet" on us, making bets on how people are going to be as citizens; well, I failed completely in 1997. So, they shut me out? Sold me? I was not a good risk, not a good citizen? They closed my account and took the loss? Big coincidence that the truthers told us about this scheme and then my one and only bad year is the same year they closed me out.

Nothing is a coincidence.

As you see above, today is November 18$^{th}$, but on the Julian Calendar is the 5th of November.

Remember, remember the 5th of November. Ah, love it! That is actually from a movie too. *V for Vendetta*. I need to watch that movie one night.

We have plans to go out tonight. The two families, kids included. It will be fun! Not sure where we are going yet. Wouldn't it be amazing if the scare event happens while we are all out together. What a night to remember that would be.

I know, it's not going to happen, but wishing never hurt anyone.

The January 6th tapes were released! Now the world will see the insurrection was not what they thought.

More Biden Crime Family information. Now they have even more proof that the Biden was blackmailed by the FBI and actually vice versa as well. Wow, this is just unfuckingbelievable.

More Democrats getting arrested for pedophilia or human trafficking. Not the big players, but it's a start. Stacey Abrams' brother-in-law and Podesta's assistant.

November 19th, 2023

What a night! We picked a small local pub to go to, as we wanted somewhere small but fun. During the night we listened to great music, including "Proud to be an American", and "Small town USA,"– perfect songs for the kind of night we wanted to have.

Have you ever been with entertaining people where, you say something… then another person adds to it in an exaggerated fashion, then the next one does, then the next one, and it turns a simple innocent topic into something so ridiculously out there? Yeah, it was one of those kinds of nights.

We did that quite a few times last night and even joked around about starting a reality tv show or making a movie about us. Of course, we would have to figure out who would play us and then we had a thought, "Wait, first we have to get a list of the alive actors–half of Hollywood is either dead or at Gitmo!!

Speaking of exciting, a lot of excitement in the world as well:

Mainstream media, getting slightly better. Not much, but any little bit helps.

Lawyers call for criminal charges against Anthony Fauci.

BLM leader stands behind Trump.

New verification of DNA fragments in Covid-19 MRNA vaccine vials.

The demand for un-vaxxed sperm soars as birth rates continue to decline.

Schools start conducting "sudden cardiac arrest screenings" as heart attacks among children surges.

You guessed it, none of the above is on the mainstream media.

Also, the San Francisco bridge was loaded with protestors the other day.

Yes, the protests are still going on. You know, the "protests." Whereas if it was MAGA people, it would be referred to as a riot or an insurrection.

Our truthers are talking nonstop about bridges still. Bridge, bridge, bridge…

That's got to mean something, right?

November 20th, 2023

Now that the January 6th tapes came out, a lot of the woke companies are pulling their advertising off *X*. Twitter has switched names, and it is now *X*, still owned by Elon Musk.

Everyone knew January 6th was an inside job. It was a typical, textbook perfect deep state, Cabal stunt. They set us up, they set "We the People" up!

They called the election before it was even counted, then hired actors to storm the Capitol posing as MAGA. Then the fake news covered it up, committing treason and tyranny on us. Then they gaslit us, making us feel like we are the problem.

True patriots do not incite violence– they *do*. Now the videos show it. And it is all over the Internet. Did the sleeping watch them? Probably not.

Nancy Pelosi blocked Jim Jordan from investigating January 6th and blocked all questions from being asked, so of course she doesn't want the tapes published.

Elon Musk shot a rocket up to try and break the firmament. Not sure the reason but it has a significance.

After it went up, not much was said. However, they are saying that don't think for a moment that nothing happened with the Rocket. Your TV and NASA lied, we will soon see.

Yesterday, Trump visited the Texas Border. Why would an ex-President visit our border, which is a total catastrophe? Maybe because he is still the CIC? He gave a great speech, and had food served to our Department of Public Safety troopers and National Guardsmen. He took photos and talked with service members. More than the Biden Crime Family did and that cackling goat Kamala Harris.

The same Libs that cried about Trump wanting to build a wall, are the same Libs that are now crying that we are being invaded by immigrants. Wow!

Bye Bye US Corporation–Hello USA!!

The ISO 20022 switch flipped yesterday which means switched to Basel III compliant. Basel III compliant means gold backed assets. Gold, silver and precious metals.

I made sure to check, our bank that my family uses is Basel III compliant. Now that is not something that the public will see, however it does indicate that the Basel III compliant banks are ready for the switch over to the new currency.

I also purchased silver recently. It's 3 1/2 years later and it does appear that the new rainbow currency truly will be backed by gold and silver, so I did break down and buy some. I did not buy more than I could afford and did research on reputable companies to purchase it from. I know if it truly does skyrocket, I will be kicking myself in the ass for not buying more.

Yesterday there were several National Guardsmen at the White House and Capitol. They said they were there for military training exercises. It is speculated that they are there for something big this month. Plus, NYC is a mad house with National Guard everywhere. People said they have been seeing them there for weeks. Raises the question on whether or not something is brewing.

Many have checked the White House Live cam during that time. Witnesses have said that they saw gurneys being carried out of the White House. That wouldn't be the first time, people have seen that before. Just because the public is unaware of something, does not mean nothing is happening.

Oh, but they will. Hard and fast. I swear, when I see people sleeping, I just envision myself holding a stick and they are a piñata, but I will let the real news and tribunals be the real stick.

As of today, US Government bonds are worthless. Global elites will have the rug pulled out from under them as central banks across the globe who were not compliant with ISO 2002 will collapse.

Today on this day, Nuremberg trials began in 1945. Nuremberg Trials were the International Military Tribunals for the defeated Nazi Germany. The Nuremberg trials, the Nazis that were found guilty in 1945, the world thought they were shipped off to prison or executed. Nope, the high up ones, the ones that were masterminds were offered a job with the CIA. Our United States Government wanted them to work for them; they wanted the Nazis to teach them. They were covertly working with the U.S.

There has been reported 17 million deaths caused by the Covid vaccine– 17 million! That is the latest report, up quite a bit since last time I checked, and I am sure it will continue to grow.

Fake Biden met Xi Jinping, the President in China in San Francisco the other day. They cleaned up the streets of San Francisco so nicely and God only knows where they put the homeless people; I am afraid to find out. The streets were adorned with multiple; I mean multiple China flags. Rumor has it that he was there to meet Trump, but of course they had to show the world that it was Biden. They did a press conference with Biden afterwards and I watched it. I wanted to regurgitate afterwards, but I survived. What an embarrassment. He fumbled and mumbled and couldn't even read the damn notes that were preprinted on the cards. He was so proud of himself that he convinced Xi Jinping to slow down on the fentanyl. Slow down? Fentanyl is an illegal drug that is killing Americans, and you were ok with slowing down? Why not demand he stop? Oh, that's right because you are a spineless puppet. Oh wait, he is an actor. I am sure he has an agreement already to stop with Trump. Well, if the fact that fake Biden thought it was ok to just slow it down, or the fact that he ordered all those flags to be put up to honor a Communistic Country, didn't wake more people up to what kind of creature he is, than I don't even know what to say anymore.

There were riots afterwards. Yes, now they are called riots, because it was people that opposed China. They ripped the flags down and they were furious. They lined up in the streets protesting. Oh, I am sorry, they weren't protesting, they were causing an insurrection–or whatever the term of the month is for people who want their freedom. I lose track of the hypocrisy.

Andy asked me last night if nothing happens by January 1st, will I give this up.

Nope. I did not even need to think about it. Absolutely not.

For several reasons:

1. I have come this far.
2. Too much time vested
3. I will always be a patriot.
4. I love my country.
5. Need to stay in the loop, worried about my kids' future.
6. It's been delayed before; I am used to it.
7. I don't back down when I firmly believe in something.
8. I love true crime–we are living one.
9. I know the truth will come out soon.
10. Don't want to be in the dark like the sheep.
11. I still have faith.

Shall I go on? I am sure I can think of other reasons.

Listen, yes, this crap show keeps getting delayed (or maybe it's not delayed, maybe this is the planned timeline) and it can be very trying to say the least.

Do I sometimes still feel like we are getting played? Maybe, but just once in a while. But then I see way too much proof.

Do we get exhausted? Yep.

But I look at it this way. I am still here. I live, I laugh, I breathe. All the burden that I carry regarding this I can handle in the comfort of my own warm home.

The children and adults that were trafficked or sacrificed don't have that luxury.

The vaccinated that died suddenly don't have that luxury.

The Jan 6th people that were wrongfully imprisoned don't have that luxury.

Yes, while this sucks and dammit I wish it was over with, it could be so much worse.

I am sure there is so much that I have already noted that I will find out was wrong.

Or it was correct, until it wasn't.

Meaning things like, I believe now that John F. Kennedy, Jr., is in fact alive, but maybe that day his helicopter went down, was done differently than I had mentioned.

Between misinformation, disinformation, AI generated pictures, fake news, no news, white hats, black hats, photo shops, I am guessing nothing is real until proven otherwise.

IT. NEVER. STOPS.

But it has to at some point. It must, and when the truth gets shot out, I will be ready to catch it.

There is no doubt that:

Democrats held a fake hearing to investigate a fake insurrection in order to cover up the fake election of a fake president.

Judge Clarence Thomas has already overruled the election and it's been verified in Italian courts that it was stolen.

When the timing is right, they will let the world know.

Well, tonight was another televised town meeting. There was an attorney that pointed out how this plant is *DEFINITELY* an organization in the CCP.

Another person got to the podium and pointed out, yet again, how one of the board members sniggers at them when they speak. You guessed it, that board member that they are referring to is Tig.

During the last five minutes, the mayor always asks the board members if they had any other comments. Usually, all board members say "no." Tonight, Tig decided he was going to speak. A decision that I have a feeling he is going to regret tomorrow.

His face was ravaged with irritation. He is pissed, his lips are puckered, his eyes get big, yet slanted at the same time and his face turns red. His voice is calm, but it is a forced calm, shaky voice.

He said he was tired of everyone on the board being attacked by the town residents. They are trying to do what's best for the town, and all they get is disrespected. He stated that if they don't answer a question, it's because they don't have the answer. He mentioned that he has spoken to people in private about attacking the board and how it will get them nowhere, but yet people still come to the meeting and attack them. He wishes this decision was as easy as voting on holiday decorations, but it's not. He then continued to ask the townspeople to behave at the next meeting.

He then reached over with his big, chubby, trembling hand and turned off his microphone.

Please, oh please, let me analyze this.

First, from the townspeople's point of view:

You are tired of being attacked? Aren't you the same guy that had your text messages and emails posted where it showed you calling the townspeople clowns and stupid? Weren't you attacking innocent townspeople who are patriots?

Not an easy decision? Umm, hello, the minute you heard they were CCP would have been a no brainer for every good American citizen. He was right in a sense; it's not an easy decision; it is beyond easy–it is a simple decision. That being "No." There ya go. See how "easy" that was?

You don't have all the answers? Yet you went behind the people's backs, signed a NDA, and kissed the CCP's ass. Do you do that for everything you don't have the answers to? Well then, let me sell you an ocean front beach house in Idaho. I mean, that would be ok, right? You obviously are ok with getting involved with things that you don't have the answers to.

Asking the townspeople to behave at the next meeting? You are kidding, right?

Now that you stabbed everyone in the back, you want to act like an authoritative principal asking the children to behave in a school assembly? I wonder if he had that same look of annoyance when they approached him with this idea and he saw dollar signs? Did that same deranged expression appear when he discovered it was CCP? Did his oversized hand shake when he was negotiating this deal in the very beginning? I am guessing "no", to all the above.

His little speech reminded me of Nancy Pelosi after the Jan 6th "insurrection."

Typical gaslighting.

You want to piss him off? Defend yourself. You are not allowed to defend yourself in his twist-o-fuck world. He thinks– no, he expects– everyone to roll over and play dead to his vial personality.

He, or a member of his family, throws venomous ingredients into a pot, then when the recipients of the nasty recipe respond, he accuses them of stirring the pot and plays the victim.

Last night, that was him playing the victim. People defending themselves–those are all the ingredients that are needed for narcissists to have an internal nuclear explosion. Let him self implode.

Oh yes, they are already making fun of him. I thought he might regret his little banter tomorrow morning, but maybe it will be tonight he regrets it. Karma truly is a bitch.

November 22nd, 2023

In the world…

According to "Survival Tomorrow," it was published that 113 years ago this week, JP Morgan and his banker buddies started a Cartel called the Federal Reserve.

Drip, drip…

Mainstream media reporters and employees are incessantly talking about how afraid they are that Trump will "execute them and send them to camps." He will. He told you. He gave you a chance to come clean. He will imprison; he will execute.

Also announced this morning is the Biden Pentagon official overseeing the department managing elementary schools has been arrested in a human trafficking sting in Georgia.

Why is it all the Biden appointed officials are involved in human trafficking?

December 5th, 2023

Pizza gate is real! You know that conspiracy theory that was going around, spread by MAGA? The one where the political Elite and celebrities would use code words regarding pizza for their child abuse? Yep! That conspiracy! Texas A & M University employee arrested, FBI uncovers use of *pizza* as code word in chats!

According to *USA Today*:

"The FBI just announced this week that 'Pizza gate is real; Pedophiles connected to an elite pedophile ring are actively being pursued and arrested.

"Pizza gate" refers to a conspiracy theory propagated by the far-right conspiracy movement that first emerged ahead of the 2016 presidential election. It asserted Hillary Clinton, and other high-ranking Democrats were involved in a child sex trafficking ring operating out of a pizza restaurant in Washington.

The man was arrested on child pornography charges and used the term *pizza* as a code word for child sexual abuse materials, according to the federal complaint against him.

The FBI is even saying that Seth Rich was more than likely murdered for trying to expose the pedophile ring and that the Washington Post wants to cover it up.

But wait? Now they are verifying that it's true. So, why isn't Hillary being arrested?

They also mentioned the Comet Pizza Parlor that I mentioned previously. But I thought that was also a conspiracy theory?

True definition of a Conspiracy Theorist:

"A Conspiracy Theorist is someone who is smart enough to see the truth before anyone else does." There you go.

Did mainstream media mention this? Nope. A lot of other news outlets did, including Fox. Some norms do watch that. It's all over the internet too. And the above quotes are from *USA Today*, they published it and never really published the truth a couple of years ago. It's a start.

More and more protests going on. The protests are still over the Palestinian/ Israeli war. Still a lot of talk about "Bridges." One of the protests, they overtook the Manhattan Bridge.

The Managing Officer for the CDC, Aaron Aranas, was fatally shot recently when the Marines went to the office to arrest him. He was to be arrested for treason when he and two of his bodyguards exchanged fire with U.S. Marine unit that was sent there to arrest him.

So many arrests still of pedophiles.

Now the immigrant count is up to at least 8 million that invaded our country.

To put into perspective this is equal to the populations of:

Wyoming

Vermont

Alaska

North Dakota

South Dakota

Delaware

Rhode Island

Montana

Maine

Now this is huge–Trump-hating, vaccine loving, liberal talk show host Stephen Colbert, host of *CBS Late Night with Stephen Colbert*, got arrested!

Per Real Raw News:

"White Hats had finished building a crude but hopefully efficient 200-cell prison for mainstream media personalities that, in one way or another, committed treason and defrauded the United States of America."

If all information is accurate, JAG got its first Christmas gift Saturday morning when Navy investigators grabbed Colbert after he stepped off the property of his Montclair, New Jersey, home wearing a blue jogging suit and $60,000 Bulgari Flora sunglasses.

Colbert reportedly blurted, "What the fuck is this?" as investigators subdued him, snapping handcuffs around his trembling wrists. Colbert was informed his new designation was "detainee" and that he had no rights but might earn some with good behavior. Investigators pushed Colbert into their vehicle and brought him to a processing center in advance of a trip to Guam, our source said.

Colbert's chumminess with top Democrats is legendary. In June 2021, he stoked what Joe Rogan called "mass psychosis" for a skit that featured a dance troupe dressed as vaccine syringes and, in October 2022, joined a Fauci body double (the real Fauci was hanged in April 2022) at a Walgreens for fresh booster shots on live television. Since the plandemic's inception, Colbert dedicated over 1,750 show hours advocating for clot shots he had never received.

When they capture people like that, they draw blood first to make sure it is really them. During that process, it was discovered that the son of a bitch is not even vaccinated!

However, Colbert will not stand trial for his political views or vaccine status.

In America, no one is tried or punished for their views. Hence, first amendment. What's important is he is complicit in the fraud—the faux pandemic and pushing lies that Joe Biden won the 2020 election. He took bribes from both the NIH and the DNC. The details will come out at a tribunal.

Why would a multimillionaire accept bribes? Because enough is never enough for these bastards.

The mainstream media and the Colbert family have covered up the arrest by claiming Colbert was hospitalized for appendicitis. Mainstream media again, covering up the truth.

There was a countdown clock posted on every truthers channels. It was a countdown to 7 p.m. tonight. No one knew what it meant, but all were in anticipation of what might happen.

At 7:01 p.m. it was posted everywhere and even on mainstream media that nasty Henry Kissinger died. Good riddance. Planned? I am sure.

Rosalyn Carter died also a couple of days later. I watched the "important" people enter the room at her funeral. Explain to me why Melania was first? The procession to walk in the room Melania was first, then Michelle/Michael Obama, then the Biden's and Kamala Harris last. Was Melania first because she is the real 1st lady?

And oh, how could I forget! There is a new virus! Grab your masks, don't go out, lock up your daughter, lock up your wife, lock up your back door and run for your life! Ah come on, you know you sang that last sentence in AC/DC's T.N.T tone!!!

White Lung syndrome! Yes, from where? You guessed it–China!!! Oh, I just love this!

What we know as of right now, today, is what's happening in China, they are having an increase in some of their respiratory illnesses. They're seeing it in the northern part of their country; they're seeing an uptick in their pediatric population.

Mostly kids and the country is under lockdown, like they did for Covid. There have been reports of some in the US, mostly Ohio, but they have not freaked out yet. They will try. We are a year away from the election, so they will definitely try. Not going to happen.

You know we have been hearing nonstop how everything we learned is a lie and this corruption goes way back.

Most importantly, nothing is a coincidence.

Check this out:

Lincoln was elected to congress in 1846. = Kennedy was elected to congress in 1946.

Lincoln was elected President in 1860. = Kennedy was elected President in 1960.

Lincolns wife lost a child while living in the White House = Kennedys wife lost a child while living in the White House.

Lincoln was directly concerned about Civil Rights. = Kennedy was directly concerned about Civil Rights.

Lincoln had a secretary named Kennedy who told him not to go the theater. = Kennedy had a secretary named Lincoln who told him not to go to Dallas.

Lincoln was shot in the back of his head in the presence of his wife = Kennedy was shot in the back of his head in the presence of his wife.

Lincoln was shot in the Ford Theatre = Kennedy was shot in a Lincoln, made by Ford.

Lincoln was shot on a Friday. = Kennedy was shot on a Friday.

The assassin, John Wilkes Booth, was known by three names, comprised of 15 letters. = The assassin, Lee Harvey Oswald, was known by three names, comprised of 15 letters.

Booth shot Lincoln in a theater and fled to a warehouse = Oswald shot Kennedy from a warehouse and fled to a theater.

Booth was killed before being brought to trial. = Oswald was killed before being brought to trial.

There were theories that Booth was part of a greater conspiracy. = There were theories that Oswald was part of a greater conspiracy.

Lincoln's successor was Andrew Johnson in 1808. = Kennedys successor was Lyndon Johnson, born in 1908.

Notice how the ones with dates are all exactly 100 years apart?

I saw a video before. It showed that John F. Kennedy, Jr.'s father was adopted by Lincoln, making Lincoln, John F. Kennedy, Sr.'s grandfather and great grandfather to John F. Kennedy, Jr.

"Everything is a lie." One of the many sentences we have been hearing nonstop. Way back in the 1900's, they had a fiction writer rewrite history. Remember, the Illuminati started in the 1700's and then grew. That tradition of rewriting history carried on in the years to follow. All our history books are fiction. The events might have really happened, but not the way we think. Some events didn't happen at all. The *Titanic* is not what you think, walking on the moon and the Holocaust, just to name a few. Better sit down for this next sentence–John F. Kennedy... not Jr., the father, the President, knew the Cabal was going to set up Lee Harvey Oswald to assassinate him, it was his body double that got killed. The real John F. Kennedy, Sr. just died in 2021 or 2022. Cause of death, old age. At one of Trump's events in 2020, you see him leaning over to shake the hand of a vet in a wheelchair, the video is still out there, it was John F. Kennedy.

Very interesting.

Focusing back on our town– well, the day after that meeting with the zoning board, Joe talked to Andy. He told Andy that he needs to have a "talk" again with Rick. He said that Rick needs to shut up and informed him that Tig said that he will shut down his farmers market if Rick keeps it up. I guess since threatening with a fee didn't work, now they are going to try to shut him down.

Andy of course, stood up for Rick. He responded with, "Why? He is just standing up for what he believes in. He has the right to exercise his 1st amendment!" Andy said that Joe turned bright red and just walked away. What in the holy fuck?

I seriously cannot believe that this is going on in our hometown.

There have been posts on the website that are against the plant, that they have proof that one of the head guys involved in this received 5 million dollars. They also have emails showing that he is bragging about getting the money. The townspeople's attorney is waiting for the right time to publish it.

The mob is saying now that none of them signed a NDA. Another lie. Well then, Mr. Honest Abe, explain to the people why they published an email and text from you stating that you "couldn't talk about it because you signed a NDA?" Oh, and let's not forget the best part, it's on video. The meeting that was videotaped and put on YouTube from the August 23, 2023, meeting, at the 34.11 mark, you are on there stating that, "I cannot say too much because I signed a NDA, so the less I talk about it the better." Just another form of proof for their continuous lies.

Do they think that if they lie about signing a NDA, that it will make them look better to the people? Um, no. It's worse. Because that would show that you could have talked about it, but you *CHOSE* not to. If the people believed you (which they don't), it would have backfired on you.

January 2, 2024

Wow! It is 2024! Really did not think I would still be writing these notes into 2024, but you know what? It's ok. I mean, it really is ok. It sucks, sometimes frustrating, but all in all, its ok. We no longer get frustrated that public awareness has not happened yet. We know it will, in time. Still trust the plan.

I finally did something. I told Sammy and Ella how Joe made a point to let us know that Sammy voted "yes" to the plant. Sammy was not shocked. He reiterated how they made it sound like a beautiful walk in a flowered lined park. They were lied to. And again, as we already knew, there was no physical vote. When I told Ella and explained it to her, she thanked me for not telling her right away and waiting for the dirt to settle.

As far as Joe goes, he stopped by where Andy and Rick were working on equipment. He had brought up, all on his own, the subject of the plant. He tried telling Rick that it was a good thing and repeated that whole spiel about "car parts are made in China." You know what Joe, you need to give that speech up. Enough already. It's not working. You can keep telling yourself that; whatever lets you sleep at night.

There is another televised meeting tonight for the town. Nothing new has been posted as far as text messages retrieved or emails and it's been really quiet. Maybe the lawyer (for us) advised them to be quiet since there are criminal charges being brought against the board. All of us will still watch the meeting though. It's fun! We love to make fun of everyone sitting up at the tables, and we cheer on the people speaking.

I had another interesting conversation with a client today. She told me how she is always doing her research, she follows different social media platforms and then she proceeds to tell me that the plant is no big deal, that it's a good thing and everyone in town is for it. Well, I would like to know what social media platforms she is following and what search engines she is doing her "research" on because 87% of the town is against it. It is not a good thing, it is CCP for Christ's sake. If this was just a good American business– or hell—, it doesn't even have to be American, if it was an Ally Country and not Communistic, not CCP, it would be a good thing. No one would be fighting it. Who doesn't want their community to grow? Of course everyone would welcome growth. There is *NO* social media platform that states the town is for it. I always thank heaven that these kinds of conversations are on the phone and not in person, this way they can't see my face or my mouth hitting the ground.

Ella and I had a talk this morning. We have the same feeling with the timeline of events; we are more at peace now. This is 2024. Of course, the truth has to come out eventually and when it happens, it happens. No more pressure. In the past, 2020, 2021, 2022, 2023, you anticipate it happening, and when it doesn't, it kicks you in the stomach. We are past that. The fake news is now showing the immigrants coming over, talking about China is about to take us over, mentioning Pizza gate, mentioning corrupt FBI and mentioning all the protests. They said that right before the truth comes out, you will notice the fake news telling more truth. There is so much we don't even know, and I am excited to learn it all. Supposedly, when the truth is exposed, some will literally have a heart attack. A big one is– Christmas. Christmas is not what it should be. It's not the real date and decorating the Christmas tree is really a way of honoring Satan. If that part is true—yeah, all the die-hard religious people will not be able to handle that.

There have also been a lot of articles about flat earth. That's part of the whole "everything you have learned is a lie" theory. Here's the thing– I don't give a shit. Flat, round, oval, oblong, or shaped like Sponge Bob– who cares? That doesn't interest me. Ok, it will prove we have been lied to. Big deal. We know that already. We have learned that there are no such things as nukes. All those threats of nuclear wars? Nukes don't exist.

I went to dinner with two potential clients. Conversations are a little rough still. I will be the first to admit that it's me, not them. I said it once and I will say it again… it is so hard to be awake. Years ago, I would have been able to chime in with the topics that they like to discuss. No problem. But not now. In the past, I would be all for the gossiping about celebrities, who is married to who, how beautiful they are and how much weight they have lost. But I just can't anymore. Most of those celebrities are only beautiful because they applied or injected adrenochrome. Most are only famous because they are part of the Elite, the Cabal. Most are already dead. And big Pharma— huge scam.

One of my sheeple clients started a conversation regarding Ozempic, an injectable weight loss drug. It was originally invented for diabetes. Some evil genius discovered that it can also be used for weight loss. Nondiabetics inject this into themselves to lose weight. Diabetic medicine directly impacts your pancreas. If you take it and you're not diabetic, then what? The side effects are at a high percentage of kidney damage, and it severely upsets your stomach. She goes on to admit that she started taking it and her stomach is "messed up" every day. Big Pharma doesn't care. They are making 3x as much money off it because now they have a bigger demographic, it's not just for diabetes, and everyone wants to lose weight. Jackpot for Big Pharma! In addition, hey, if it destroys your kidneys, pancreas or intestines, cool, they can make more money by prescribing you medicine to fix all of that. If you die, double cool– population control. Then she went on to say how it must be good because Oprah and the Kardashians take it. I wanted to die. I can guarantee you that neither Oprah nor a Kardashian have ever taken that. Big Pharma knew what would sell it. I can feel that my smile in conjunction with my head nodding is so phony, but that is all I can do. I freeze up and I can't speak when I am in situations like that. I just can't. I always make it through the night, but I hunger for the days where I no longer have to "fake it till ya make it."

Now onto world stuff.

The dates– going to have to admit that I thought it would be over–we did not get discouraged in any way when Jan 1st came and went. Turns out, they meant behind the scenes.

And *EVERYTHING* is done. On December 25th & 26th, the military and Trump were up all-night working, and NESARA was softly announced publicly to select media outlets through the Starlink Satellite system which made it legal. NESARA has started between all governments worldwide. NESARA is now liquid under the USN. The money is flowing. Social Security will no longer exist, having been replaced by NESARA.

There were several posts where all the higher ups (white hats) were toasting and drinking champagne. Just a matter of time before we will all be drinking champagne, or in our case, shots of Tequila. Still wondering if Tequila expires.

Today, in New York, there were several bomb explosions. It is being reported as of now that they are not sure of the source. However, we were told that it was the last of the DUMBS–destroying underground tunnels and getting the last of the children out.

Back to dates, not listening, but just letting you know what dates they are saying now. January 7th, something will happen that weekend. Not believing it; I have learned that they are not going to tell the actual date on the internet. But watch, that will be our luck that it happens, two days before our next Caribbean trip. If it cancels due to disclosure of the world, that would be ok. Anyone that knows how intensely we are following this, would probably wonder why in the hell are we leaving the country with all this shit going on.

Here are my thoughts on that:

1. You can't stop living.

2. You cannot rule your life on the "what if's." No one would do anything then.

3. They (the white hats) are not going to let the plane leave, especially to a Caribbean vacation spot if they knew the EBS was about to go off.

4. If it did get to that point, they would have a safeguard in place. Whether it be time to get back home, or safety measures in the other country.

5. My kids are awake, they know what to do and how to take care of my mom if it were to go down while we were gone.

6. How many times have I thought it was going to happen? Remember all those times Jack was traveling, and I would tease him and say, "Maybe you're going, maybe not." Well, if I begged him to cancel all those trips, and he listened, look at the memories he would have missed out on.

And most importantly, it's going to happen when we least expect it and there is nothing we can do about. All the truthers know it's going to happen, and I think we all come to realize that we will never know the dates.

If it was a perfect world, we would return from vacation, time to unpack and unwind, then, bam! Done! Hey, a girl can dream! I joke with Andy that I am going to call Trump to tell him that is the way I want it to go down.

January 4th, 2024

Well, well, well– The Epstein documents were released! First, it proves that Trump was never on the island or at any of Epstein's houses at all! Hah! Take that Dems! Clinton was there 73 times! It is documented how he "liked them young." Such an asshole. So much on there and it is public! Don't worry, by the time you read this you will already know the list. They even mentioned it on the fake news. Of course, they defended Clinton, but the important part is the fact that they mentioned it at all. As recently as three months ago, they wouldn't have.

Also, on the same day, Trump dropped undeniable proof of the 2020 election fraud!

Today is Thursday, and already this week:

1. Trump reveals undeniable 2020 election fraud evidence.

2. TTV gets huge Georgia win,

3. SOS Brad Raffensperger is screwed in Georgia.

4. Epstein docs have dropped.

5. The RV occurred. Sometime today, bond holders have liquidity and Tier 4b should receive notifications to set redemption and exchange appointments. The Iraqi Dinar to - US.

6. Many states trying to remove Trump from ballot in 2024 but are failing. Maine said their reasoning for wanting him removed is because Trump cannot serve three terms and using the 22nd Amendment of the Constitution to support that claim. So, if 2024 would give Trump a third term, wouldn't that mean that you are admitting that Trump is currently serving his second term?

All this week! Almost as if it was–planned?

Damn, I love this! Well, not really, but definitely a great time to be alive!

January 22nd, 2024

We are back from vacation! The weather was extraordinary, that place is paradise! Feet in the sand and soaking up the sunshine was needed.

We met an amazing couple that live in Nova Scotia. When I offered my condolences for them having Trudeau (it was a way of feeling them out from a political point of view), they then responded back with condolences of Joe Biden. They went on to tell us how they felt bad for what our country was going through. I could tell by their tone that they were sincere and knew the travesty that we have been faced with. The husband was also a financial advisor, so he keeps on top of current events in our country as well. His wife told me he follows it nonstop. They were both awake. He told us how he knows our election was stolen and mentioned our inexcusable immigrant situation. Ah, to have someone from another country acknowledge it was a great feeling. Sad, residents of a foreign land can compile those facts, but so many residents reside right here in our homeland, can't.

One night after a glorious day in the sun, he asked me if I knew Russia has written in their books and are teaching their children in school that the 2020 United States election was stolen. I read that recently, but must confess, I did not verify, but thankfully our new friend did. A new textbook for Russian students claims former

President Donald Trump lost the 2020 presidential election due to voter fraud committed by the Democrats. They did not wait for the truth to come out, they did not wait until the alleged November 2024 election, they did not wait until 2025, that is in their books, *NOW*. How is it that another country is teaching our kids about the stolen 2020 election, but not the citizens of the actual country it happened in? That is why, my dear, these notes were so important to us. You will learn about this someday in our country as well.

We let this awake couple become aware of what is happening in our small town. When Andy told him that that CCP bought land in our sweet, Hallmark town and the officials have turned into the Cabal on us, I thought they were going to drop their tall glass of a well-made cocktail. He was aware of the CCP. When encountering them again, he thanked Andy for the information, and he thoroughly enjoyed reading about this. He acknowledged the fact that what is going on in our town is the largest thing going on in our state right now, if not the country. He did his research in his hotel room while watching the Iowa Caucus and he was thrilled that Donald Trump won. This very interesting subject of our town made it a double header for him that night.

We met another couple from Germany. On our channels I have seen several short videos of farmers in Germany blocking the streets and protesting for a better country. Like the Russian books in school, I did not research enough to know if that was true or not. After speaking to them for a few minutes, I asked them about the events that I saw occurring in Germany. This young couple were able to verify that it was, in fact, true. Global.

When my family asks me," How do you know if the people and channels that you are following, how do you know if it's true? Maybe your news is the fake news?"

Well, those two scenarios above pretty much solidify the fact that our channels are correct. You saw none of that on the fake news, so yeah, there ya go.

More comical events going on in the town. They have decided that it is ok to change the rules of the meeting. Because you know, cutting people off after three minutes and not being allowed to ask any questions was not stern or cut- throat enough.

The new rules are:

1. Any person may be expelled from the board room for the remainder of meeting by the chairman or majority vote if they violate any rule provided. For the record, I have watched every meeting. No one ever violated anything. So why was that added? Oh, wait, there was that one time that the trustees felt attacked verbally. So, in other words, if anyone butt hurts the trustees, they can be removed.

2. If there is many speakers, there will no longer be a sign-up sheet. They must line up and then will be called in order.

3. Each speaker is only allowed to speak once. Is there an number of times that you are allowed to speak to the CCP? I am guessing not. Unlimited, I am sure. But don't forget to limit your fellow Americans.

4. Speakers shall refrain from harassing or directing threats or personal attacks to the board members. Ahhh, refer to #1. I knew it!!

5. This one is my favorite. If you go over the three minute mark, they will just turn off your microphone.

Oh, there is more. Plenty more, but those are my favorites! Someone had a great idea. They suggested buying megaphones and when they turn off their microphones, they will just pull out the megaphone! Not sure if they should though, refer to #1 again, will that constitute as violating the rules? Will they be expelled?

They are getting out of hand. Their power trip, that will be short lived, they just don't know it yet; is immensely fueling their already large egos. Speaking of fueling an ego, the mayor could not make it, so they had Tig act as mayor. Yeah, I am sure he loved that. Enjoy your two minutes of fame. He is also the one that was turning off the microphone. The first person he turned the microphone off on was a 82-year-old women. I am sure he went home proudly pounding his chest that night.

I had a very intriguing but very frustrating conversation with one of my clients. The same client that does her research and the CCP is a good thing. Yeah, that one. This conversation was a little more intense.

First, let me start off by saying that I *NEVER* bring up politics to clients. In her case, even if she brings it up, I try my hardest to change the subject. She *ALWAYS* brings it up. Every single conversation. That is so ironic because when she brings it up and gets in her bitching mode, she always mentions that "Trumpers" or "MAGA" all they want to do is talk about Trump and you can't get them to shut the fuck up. The mockery in this world is insufferable.

She proceeds to tell me how all the Trumpers are making this world so hard. She is sick and tired of Trump being a bully and because of him, DeSantis dropped out of the race. Of course, I knew that already, but I played stupid and responded with, "Whaaaaatttt, why did Desantis drop out?"

I wanted to hear her bright response. Her response was beyond reprehensive and all she could give me was because Trump was a bully. He bullied him out of the race. Does that really make sense to her in her head? Did she mention that Desantis is now supporting and endorsing Trump? Oh, I am sure she knows it, but she won't say it, and if she did say it, surely, she would suggest that Trump bullied him into endorsing him.

It was not the time to tell her that Trump and Desantis have always been on the same page. It's a game. A movie. They had Desantis run and tread to the other side to weed out the rest of the bad. He was never going to run all the way for president. It was called "Operation Desanctimonious" and it did reveal a lot of snakes in the grass. "Desanctimonious" is the derogatory name Trump gave him as well, but yes, that is really what the operation was called. Yeah, that would have gone over like a lead balloon.

She then proceeds to ramble on that most of our town are "yahoo Trump supporters."

Well, which one is it? You told me last conversation that most of the town is for the plant. Yahoo Trump supporters are not for plant. So, enlighten me... is most of the town Yahoo Trump supporters or is most of the town for the CCP? Because it can't be both, it has to be one or the other. You are contradicting yourself. Then for whatever reason, she brought up January 6th, 2021, again. She was so irate about how the damn MAGA destroyed our nation's Capital. The intensity in her voice was as if it happened yesterday. Why she lets Trump live rent free in her head, I will never understand.

In all of her superior well-informed research, how has she never stumbled upon all of the evidence of the FBI and Pelosi being behind the storming at the Capitol to make Trump and MAGA look bad? *IT'S ALL OVER THE PLACE!* Online, every social media platform– hell, they even showed a small piece on the fake news! It's on Apple news feed, alerts on phones–everywhere! She then went on to even bring up the burning and destruction of all the buildings downtown and other cities. I pointed out to her that that was BLM and Antifa. She grunted and ignored it. Wait? Does she think that was MAGA? No telling at this point and I am sure her wonderful search engines told her it was MAGA. Figured I shouldn't mention that BLM and Antifa was funded by Democrats. But that is years ago already, so while she was on the subject of bashing every diehard American, I had pointed out about the attacks still going on at the Capitol building and the White House. The Pakistanis and Israelis. They had to call in National Guard again to protect the White House. She did not want to talk about that, she just responded with an aggravated grunt, then went back to complaining about January 6th. Doesn't she know about all the political violence that is still going on? She should, with all the great research she does. Or is she aware of it but doesn't want to talk about it since she can't blame Trump for it?

She also implied that we don't even know if Trump could run for President. He has so many felonies against him, and she says to me. "You know he is on trial right now for so many things." Um, yes sweetie, I am aware of everything. Unlike you. Of course, I could not say that. Does she not see anywhere all the proof of Biden Crime Family? Most of their crimes were even mentioned briefly on the fake news? Again, where does she do her research? She then proceeds to keep chattering about how despicable it is that the more they bring up charges on Trump, the more people want to vote for him. Could it be that they are using common sense and thinking to themselves, "Wait a minute. Why do they want him out of the way so bad?"

Nope. Believe me, I have had enough conversations with her to know that with certainty. However, she does notice that more and more people are flipping to him; did she ever wonder why? Oh yeah, that's right, maybe everyone is bullied into supporting him, you know, kind of like Desantis was bullied.

I believe my most entertaining moment from that conversation was when she spent quite a few minutes lecturing me on how stupid Trump is. The man with an IQ higher than Einstein and has been playing 5D chess with the Cabal and child traffickers (and winning) is stupid. The man behind a global take down and is always for "we the people," is stupid.

Her biggest reason for not liking Trump is his big mouth. Well, then go vote for The Miss America Contest and leave the voting of the presidential elections for the grown-ups. You chose a president who has the countries best interest at heart, not who is the friendliest and makes the best tea and crumpets. Grow a pair.

Lastly, she had mentioned that everyone is taking their 1st amendment too far. She feels that everyone in the world is speaking too much and everyone can just say whatever is on their mind and it's making the world ugly. Does she live under a rock? People still get banned on Facebook if they post the "wrong thing." No one can joke around anymore because everyone gets offended. Everyone is afraid to say anything anymore because it might be incorrect. You cannot call a "he" a "she" or vice versa if they are a trans. Some states have made it illegal to use the wrong pronoun. Schools cannot scold the kids anymore. You cannot say this when you are there or that when you are here. Seriously, where is she getting her information from? I really want to know! Well, one thing is for sure, she ought to be thankful that I can keep my mouth shut.

During this wonderful phone rampage, I was sitting in my office leaning back in my chair, feet up on my desk and smiling away. The smile was to represent a loud laugh that I, for obvious reasons, could not let happen. I think a few times I even made the hand gesture of a man beating off and might have even thrown a middle finger out here and there. The certainty in her voice was a classic. She was stating her research results with such confidence. Because you know, she is the Master of Research. She was very proud of herself for educating me on these little fun facts.

I read somewhere:

"Trying to help people understand what's going on right now is like going back into a burning building to pull someone out, only to have them keep punching you in the face and demand evidence that the building is on fire, even after they admit they can see the flames. "

Man is that the truth.

During this conversation, I tried changing the subject twice and she still wouldn't simmer down. Remind me again how its MAGA that doesn't shut up?

Texas has decided to take matters in their own hands. Enough already with this unsecured border!

Per the Office of the Texas Governor: "Governor Greg Abbott, the Texas Department of Public Safety (DPS), and the Texas National Guard continue to work together to secure the border; stop the smuggling of drugs, weapons, and people into Texas; and prevent, detect, and interdict transnational criminal activity between ports of entry.

Since the launch of Operation Lone Star, the multi-agency effort has led to over 496,000 illegal immigrant apprehensions and more than 38,500 criminal arrests, with more than 34,900 felony charges. In the fight against the fentanyl crisis, Texas law enforcement has seized over 453 million lethal doses of fentanyl during this border mission.

Operation Lone Star continues to fill the dangerous gaps created by the Biden Administration's refusal to secure the border. Every individual who is apprehended or arrested and every ounce of drugs seized would have otherwise made their way into communities across Texas and the nation due to President Joe Biden's open border policies."

They have added extra barbed wire to help reduce the illegals coming over.

Sounds great right?

Well, the Biden Administration put the kibosh on it. They are making Texas take down the wire, and they are stating they can no longer arrest people coming over the border. Their claim to fame is that it makes the border patrol job harder.

You don't mess with Texas.

It feels like a small-scale civil war is going to be coming at the Texas border.

Then Biden goes on record to say that he now believes massive changes are needed at the border because it is not secure and he is ready to act.

Which one is it?

See, all these relentless screw ups are what woke up so many. But not all.

Great news, in a way–JAG and Army CID investigators have arrested nearly 100 media criminals in the last two months. It's not the reporters that you see on TV, however it is the editors and the ones that tell the reporters what to report. Editing and giving someone information to relay on the news is not a crime. However, once their investigation showed that they were paid to do that by the people challenging Trump to withhold the truth; well, now it turns into bribery.

A top spokesperson for MSNBC has been put on record as saying, "A lot of us joke darkly that in a Trump second term, a lot of us will end up in orange jumpsuits in Guantanamo Bay."

Another one has said," I don't like Trump, but think how we the media has attacked him, there must be something that they are hiding." Ding, ding, ding! Took you long enough to realize that. Welcome to the real world.

Trump, the genius that he is, is not stupid. Tricked the media. He went to several magazines and told them that Nikki Haley (one of the Republican candidates for presidency) was the one behind the storming of Jan 6th at the Capitol. Now, he knew they would run with it; they would try to make it look like he was losing his mind, so of course they would print it. It was printed in five newspapers/magazines, *Rolling Stones* being one of them. Why did he do that?

Well, the media had so much joy making fun of him; they had to make it look like he was losing his mind. Well, how can that make it look like he was losing his mind? The only way is to correct him.

They reported:

"Trump is confused! He confused Nikki Haley with Nancy Pelosi!"

And there you have it. Drop Mic. He got the mainstream media to admit that Nancy Pelosi was behind January 6th.

They are putting it right in everyone's face–DAMN, what a great time to be alive! I cannot say that enough!!

January 26th, 2024

Trump won New Hampshire and South Carolina. The other runner Nikki Haley–well that is an interesting story line. All her funding is backed by the deep state even though she is a Republican (RINO). That truth has come out along with several affairs she had with people while married to her husband. Also, the fact that her real name is Nimarata (Nikki) Randhawa. She gave 197 acres of free land to the CCP. They have also broadcasted (even on fake news) that she wants to raise the age of social security. She feels 65 is too young to retire. No wonder why her numbers are so low.

Just like the Super Bowl when they had the dancers in the hazmat suits, now it's the white hats' turn. The last few public appearances, Nikki was wearing a jumpsuit, the color of prison orange.

Mom had a doctor appointment yesterday. Low and behold the masks are back. Wow! Where have I heard this before? Where have I heard that masks are mandatory in the month of January almost February in the year of an election?

There is another disease coming over from China. It is called Disease X. This disease has a 100% fatality rate in humanized mice by infecting the nervous system. Wow, I just had another déjà vu–where did I hear about a new disease coming in the month of January, almost February, in the year of an election?

New reports have been published that the Covid vaccine was the deadliest drug ever in the history of medicine. Dr. James Thorpe alerted the Massachusetts Legislature to the astonishing estimate that over half of a billion were injured by the vaccine worldwide.

At what point will people apprehend the fact that all conspiracy theories have been proven correct?

And now, unvaccinated blood is like gold. To those of us that never gave in, we are the true heroes. Pure Bloods. Don't even care if that sounds self-centered.

They turned us all against each other to distract us from turning against them. Libs have obeyed the deep states' wishes, without even realizing it. They hate MAGA with a passion and that was their goal all along. For that reason, I am totally ok if I sound a little self-centered.

The Texas border is intensifying. After the Biden Administration gave Texas 24 hours to remove the barbed wire and their men, Texas pretty much told them to eat shit. They will not comply. Along with it being called Operation Lone Star, they are also calling it Operation Take Our Border back. Millions upon millions have entered by now. Registered felons, drug lords, thugs, child traffickers, human traffickers.

Who benefits from open boarders?

-Democrats, shipping millions of new voters

-Human traffickers, shipping in sex slaves they can sell to U.S. Buyers

-Terrorists, infiltrating the U.S.

There is no logical reason to advocate for open borders other than criminality.

Do any Libs out there ask why they want the border open so bad? Or have they all been brainwashed into thinking you shouldn't question them. Look over there, look what Trump is doing!

Maybe there wouldn't be so many conspiracy theories if there were not so many conspiracies.

Back to immigrants…

One Texan who was working the border had an immigrant say to him, "I have big plans, and you will all know who I am very soon."

As people did research, they discovered that he had quite a long history. Something is being planned. Something big is coming to this country and it's going to start in Texas. Families are having discussions as to what to do because the husbands are being asked to join a riot force to help secure the border.

Multiple states are coming out in support of Governor Abbott of Texas saying they will help in any way possible to help secure the border.

States sending in NG and people over with the Texas Border:

Florida

Virginia

Georgia

North Dakota

South Dakota

Tennessee

Alabama

Montana

Idaho

Utah

West Virginia

Oklahoma

Louisiana

That's just to name a few, there are 25 total. Several of these states have also previously sent physical help, State Troopers, etc.

House Speaker Mike Johnson also announced he will support Texas. Former FBI (the good ones) have already warned Mike Johnson that the U.S. is being invaded and more than likely have Terror Cells on the interior already.

A Convoy was spotted coming in from Oklahoma. the convoy now has over 2,500 vehicles, raised over 1.5 million and that's just from Oklahoma.

Resources have said that the Canadian truckers are coming as well.

Now get this: TRUMP CALLS FOR ALL WILLING STATES TO DEPLOY NATIONAL GUARD TO TEXAS AMID BORDER FEUD.

It was at that moment that the 25 states sent their people.

But wait, how does Trump have authority?

You know damn well that the mainstream media is going to spin this as he is causing "another" insurrection. Undoubtedly, some people will get brainwashed into that mind frame. They won't be proud that someone is finally defending our country, they will say those damn Trumpers are always so violent. Well, queen bees, maybe if our country was secure, it wouldn't have had to come to this. Do they ever think of the causes of the problems? Suck it up pansies, someone had to do something.

Or maybe it will flip the other way, maybe they all will acknowledge the fact of these immigrants coming over but still blame Trump. I say that because just this morning, MSNBC said that "Trump doesn't want to the fix border and that it is Donald Trump that is keeping the border open." I guess when you are backed into a corner, you get desperate enough to say anything.

Two things with that above statement from MSNBC if anyone asleep hears that and believes it:

1. They pretty must just admitted that Donald Trump is the one in charge.

2. Don't you remember how he wanted the wall? Remember how the fake news zoomed in on the children's faces and said how horrible Trump was for tearing these families apart?

Yeah, so if people believe it, they are more deranged than I thought.

Desantis actually dropped a truth bomb on Fox the other night.

He had referred to Trump as a "de facto incumbent President."

Let's break this down:

*De Facto:* means in fact, or in effect, whether by right or not

*Incumbent;*

means the holder of an office for post.

Sounds like he just said President Trump is still the President.

We have to look at the whole picture though, just not one spot on the canvas. As history proves, there is always a, "Don't look here–Look over there." So, while I am keeping on top on the border, I am paying attention to other things as well to make sure this isn't a distraction.

For instance, it was verified for a second time that the CCP was involved in our U.S. Election in 2020. Of course, Trump would never let China buy up our land; makes sense that they wanted him gone.

Saudi Arabia lifts its liquor ban after 72 years, signifying that the residents are becoming more independent and not so much an absolute monarchy.

It is all intertwined.

Remember all the chemical spills?

Remember the 17 cities to be avoided?

Remember the UN troops being spotted in cities?

Remember the emergency phones given to Congress?

Remember the power grid blackout warning?

See all the policies being pushed to the side:

Domestic Security policy?

Immigration policy?

Intelligence Operations?

Border Security Policy?

Foreign Policy?

Many are waiting for mass arrests.

Many are waiting for Military Tribunals.

Many are still waiting for the full Epstein list.

But no one knows what comes first.

We are all damn ready for the fallout that is about to take place and anything that will accompany it.

When it does come, I know it will be fast and furious.

This whole EV cars is a joke too. It's a fad. It's not going to last. So many car dealers have already put a halt on production of the making of electric vehicles.

Lithium price plunges, miners scaling back production on slowing demand in China for EV.

There was just a huge cold snap everywhere. Everywhere that is ever cold, everyone got it across the whole world at the same time. Ella had a great thought, was it to prove that electric vehicles cannot handle the cold? None of the EV's were able to run.

As far as the weather goes. Yes, lots of scatter going on about how that was strange that the whole world got brutally cold temperatures, snow and ice on the exact same weekend. It is the first time it ever happened. More than likely, it was HAARP, and Ella's thoughts of it being done to destroy the reputation of the EV is very justifiable. With this movement, there are so many avenues you can stroll down. Weather is one where I rarely go down. The fact that it was extremely cold everywhere on the weekend January 13th, 2024, will not affect the future.

February 6th, 2024

I really wish I could find the time to document every day, but unfortunately it is much easier said than done. I must admit though, I am thoroughly starting to enjoy these documenting sessions that I am able to squeeze in. In the beginning, I was sitting at this laptop out of annoyance and the immense feeling of importance to jot everything down for our future descendants. I have now come to enjoy it. Something about being able to express everything going on with no one else around, and pounding it out on the keyboard, is kind of freeing. I have noticed that the days I am not able to do so, I miss it.

As far as January 6th, 2021, goes, they are just now reporting that they found a pipe bomb that day. Now get this, that pipe bomb was found within yards of where Kamala Harris was sitting. Even after it was discovered, Kamala remained yards away. Funny how they blasted all over the fake mainstream media about MAGA, but they never mentioned that there was a pipe bomb? It is just now being released that a man with a backpack placed a pipe bomb, who they later found out was a plain clothes police officer and they did not remove the Vice President. No mention of this on fake news. Nothing to see here folks. Let me guess, they never mentioned it because they couldn't pin it in on MAGA.

The Super Bowl is this Sunday. They are saying to enjoy it because it will be the last Super Bowl as we remember it. No idea what that means. I want to see if there is any comms this year as well.

Even the sleeping seems to feel that something will happen at the Super Bowl this year. Kind of odd, considering the world right now. However, I feel their feelings of concern for something happening are merely based on Hollywood Drama. They have really been hyping up pop singer, Taylor Swift. She is dating someone on the 49ers' team and the way they ramped her up this football season is something to be seen. Too much hype–something is up with that. The hype that surrounded her made everyone aware of who she is. Everyone of all ages. Makes me wonder because they always said the first arrest will signify the start of justice and it will be someone that everyone will know who it is. Everyone suddenly knows who she is, and arresting America's sweetheart pop star would shock the world. Wait until they find out the truth about her.

For whatever reason, fake Biden will not be speaking this year at the Super Bowl. Jesse Waters on Fox had joked that Trump should speak since he is the real President. Man, I wish more people watched Fox, they drop hints like that all the time. A lot of truthers still don't trust Fox because they don't reveal the whole truth. Hell, I look at it this way–they can't. They cannot report yet that Biden is wearing a mask. Trump is still the President; this is all a movie. They tell as much truth as they can.

It was announced today that Trump does not have presidential immunity from prosecution. While the Liberals are probably laughing their ass off about this, the joke is on them. If it has been determined that a past President has no presidential immunity, well, that means all of them.

Enjoy the show.

Tucker Carlson, a highly respected conservative reporter, has been interviewing Vladimir Putin, the President of Russia. There has only been one interview so far, but even during that one and only interview it appears that he is not the devil that the world thought. The goal of these interviews is to wake people up regarding the war against Russia and Ukraine. You are not going to hear that on the news, not even Fox. What people are about to learn will shock them to the core.

More election fraud has been proven. FOIA (Freedom of Information Act) that the FBI and DOJ were made aware of election fraud in Detroit and they decided to cover it up. Not that that was needed though, election has already been overturned, just waiting for the military to announce it.

They are still trying to remove Trump's name from the ballots for the 2024 election, yet he remains on them.

February 8th, 2024

As recent history has proven, a lot of interesting things happen on the 8th of the month.

Today was a SCOTUS hearing regarding removing Trump from the ballot in Colorado. You know, because of the insurrection that occurred on January 6$^{th}$, the incident that he was found not guilty of. How is this even real? Oh, wait, I need to practice what I preach, it's just a movie. He was found not guilty for the insurrection, yet they want to remove him from the ballot because of the insurrection? For whatever reason, it does make sense to them.

It was just announced Trump had to pay Jean Carroll $83.3 million.

Well, guess what? $83.3. 8+3=11. 11.3

11.3 in the Military War Manual means the end of belligerent occupation. Martial law.

Go time.

Nothing is a coincidence.

Tonight is also the drop of the Tucker Carlson interview with Putin. Ella and I are trying to figure out how to get it to play on our TV. Sad, isn't it? Shouldn't this be aired all over news outlets or every channel? We must figure out a way to access it. It is only being shown on Twitter, Tucker's website and maybe some Telegram channels. She is making homemade ham and bean soup, and I will be making wings. Well, at least you know we are going to eat well.

After looking it up online, talking to our tech savvy boys, we were finally able to get the Tucker- Putin interview. We ended up having a full house. Everyone from both families was able to be here except for Jack. I enjoy our watch parties, and the disappointment of the eagerly awaited programs make it much easier with others around.

Not disappointed though. The first part was extremely boring as Putin felt it necessary to give us a history lesson on the countries of Russia and Ukraine. I am sure there is a valid reason for that.

Three things stood out to me during this interview:

1. Putin had mentioned that he had requested to join NATO years ago, only to be shot down by our country.

2. Tucker asked him if he was the one that blew up the Nordstrom Pipeline. Putin responded with "No, you did." Tucker chuckled and then said he didn't. Putin quickly said, "You have an alibi, but the CIA doesn't."

3. Putin made a comment about our border situation.

Now those are huge truth bombs, but like always it was not aired on any channel that the sleepers watch. Not even a five second clip on the fake mainstream media. The sleeping does not even know it happened. I was so delighted when the fake news appeared to be showing a little bit of the truth, then it goes right back to concealing important information.

February 18, 2024

There is a reason for what has transpired recently. As if our fake President wasn't fumbling his words enough, he has said twice within a few days of each other, that he had conversations with dead people. He didn't say that he talks to dead people, he stated that he had conversations with them as if they were still alive. The first one, he confused Francois Mitterrand, the former French president who died in 1996, for French President Emmanuel Macron.

The second one he claimed to have talked to, was German Chancellor Helmut, "a few weeks ago." Chancellor Helmut died in 2017. That, my dears, was on live TV. I am sure the mainstream media edited that out somehow, but that is ok, quite a few people heard it, and it is all over social media. In a normal democracy, that would have caused major concern for all, politicians and civilians. However, this is not a normal democracy, so move along folks, nothing to see here.

We also have the wonderful discovery that they will not pursue charges on Joe Biden. All those documents that were stored in his home, garage, car and the proof of money laundering were dismissed. Per Special Counsel Robert Hur, "There is evidence that Biden willfully retained and disclosed classified materials, but he will not be charged."

On the fake mainstream media, they explained that the reason why is because, well, quite simply, they did not have enough evidence. The real News stations, however, stated the above quote from Robert Hur and then added that the reason was because he would not be mentally fit to withstand trial.

You are basically telling us that a man who claims to have talked to dead people and is not mentally stable enough to withstand trial, is however, capable of handling a nuclear football? Don't the sleepers see how they are insulting our intelligence? Even the dead asleep ones, it is an insult to their intellect. But then again, the shots have dismantled their frontal cortex where reasoning and common sense are.

The good news is that they are discussing invoking the 26th amendment on Biden. A plan we heard about from day one, which makes sense with all the fumbles and jumbles that's been going on.

The West Virginia AG has called on VP Harris to invoke the 25th amendment. Some are squirming at the fact that that would normally mean that the VP would step in and become the new President, and no one wants cackling hyena Kamala in. Relax people, it's all for show.

They have voted to impeach Mayorkas. The head of Homeland Security for the border. He is the first cabinet official in nearly 150 years to be impeached by the house. Kevin McCarthy stated, "Our country may never recover from his dereliction of duty."

The Democrat election playbook that I stumbled upon during one of my many diggings, explained a nine-step plan to blame Trump for the border crisis and they certainly love alluding to that in several of their speeches. They are on record of saying at press conferences that they are trying to clean up the mess at the border from the previous Administration. I could not imagine living through the last three to four years and still not being the least bit suspicious.

The world will change drastically. In a few years, or sooner, you more than likely will not even recognize it. In a good way, that is. Not because of Armageddon or massive destruction. All the suppressed technologies and completely new financial and government structures. Are you ready? I am.

The Super Bowl. What can I say? It's football. I am sure you know by now why I watch it.

The halftime show. Comms of good vs. evil. Alicia Keys wore all red and played her satanic looking bright red piano. Usher wore a white suit with a Phoenix on it. Rise of the Phoenix. Renewal & Regeneration. And did you hear me? He was wearing a white suit.

It was super bowl 58. 5+8=13

February 11th. 2=11=13

Vs 49ers. 4=9=13

Halftime score 10-3. 10=3=13

Chiefs 2023 wins with Kelce. 13

Plays on game winning drive. 13

Satanic number of 13 everywhere. Nothing is a coincidence.

The final score was 25-22. 25+22= 47.

47= Trump, the 47th president.

Now I am not on Twitter (*X*), but someone posted on my channel that on fake dead Biden's account a picture of himself with red eyes and a caption that said, "Just like we drew it up."

I do take everything I read with extreme caution. I do not believe everything I read, because like with any station, there is disinformation, misinformation and to be frank, just plain rumors that can get started. However, someone I know is on *X* and she verified it. She saw it with her own eyes.

Let's be entertained by this display, shall we?

Three years ago, whistleblower David Wilcox said everything will happen fast and furious and the marker will be when the KC Chiefs beat the SF 49ers in the Super Bowl. It is a signal of the cabal defeat and victory to light. Chiefs meaning indigenous rightful owner of the land beating the'S.W.I.F.T" system. Get it? Swift–huge coincidence that is Taylor's last name. Oh wait, there are no coincidences. Did you catch the part that I stumbled upon that three years ago? Kind of signifies this truly is a planned movie.

I am sure the sleepers are absolutely devastated that Taylor did not get proposed to that night. I am also pretty sure they will be alright.

This is interesting, a new podcast dropped stating that the new world will be named "Gloria." The individual letters stand for something, just happens that it spells out Gloria. This intrigues me because at every single one of Trump's rallies he plays the song "Gloria" by Laura Branigan which came out in 1982. I often wondered, out of all the patriotic songs in the world, why would he pick that one? Time goes by and you forget about it, then this podcast comes out. Explains the reason for that song. I get more and more intrigued with every passing day. Speaking of songs, turns out that the reason why he plays "YMCA" at the end of all of his rallies is because prior to Guantanamo Bay (GITMO) being built, it was, in fact, a YMCA. He is taunting the remaining deep state.

Everything has a reason.

They are on a hunt for a "secret binder." It is missing and it shows the CIA under Obama set up the Russia Collusion Hoax on Trump. Is that why they raided Trumps home? The binder also ties Ukraine to spying on Trump. So where is it? They recently posted a picture of Trump on his plane, holding a binder.

They posted an alert late one evening. The evening before the Super Bowl parade. It was a warning from the Parliament stating that we have never been under more of a threat than we are now. Between Russia, China and the Middle East, the United States is under more of a threat now more so than even weeks or months ago when FBI Director Christopher Wray stated so. They are demanding that Biden declassify now. It was all over the internet and shown on Fox, Newsmax and some other select few channels, not mainstream media. This, in conjunction with they want to start the proceedings for the 25th amendment, leads to chaos for the deep state.

An Ex-military intel that I follow, posted: "False Flag alert. It will happen soon."

Welp, they called it. Big false flag.

Shooting at the Super Bowl parade. Now, tell me this. Why wasn't Taylor Swift there, when she had originally planned on going? What made her change her mind? Could it be she was told to stay away? I think so. Taylor Swift is a demonic bitch, and Travis Kelce is no better. He is the one that kneeled during the anthem, he is a vaccine spokesman, and anti-gun spokesman. He is also producing a movie paid for by the Biden Administration with funds from the American taxpayers.

As recent past history would prove, all news stations, podcasts and newspapers only spoke about the parade shooting, totally obliterating the fact that we were on the highest alert ever due to the incompetence of the current administration and also the 25th amendment being activated.

Trump supporters are the brunt again of everyone's joke. Trump was told by a New York City Judge that he must pay $350 million in fraud charges– a civil case alleging Trump fraudulently misrepresented financial figures to get cheaper loans and other benefits. In addition, he is not allowed to do business in New York City. A lot of deeper, devious, evil, human abuse charges against Biden, but they won't pursue them? And low and behold, wouldn't you know it, they broke into *ALL* TV stations to tell everyone this. Never a peep about Biden but this they break in to inform the citizens of the United States.

The truckers are now in talks to refuse delivering loads in New York City due to the outcome of the courts regarding Trumps "fraud" case. Residents of New York are being advised to stock up on water, food and other essentials for the possibility of shortages coming. This could also mean billions of dollars of lost revenue for New York City.

I have been hearing recently, loudly in my own home, the wrenching sound of the fake mainstream media, coming from my mom's bedroom. Days that I work from home, I am forever thankful for my earbuds. I simply insert them, block out the noise protruding from her halfway closed door, drift away and go about my business.

She says to me that night, "You are going to want watch your News Station tonight, bad news for Trump."

Now of course I already knew what transpired and I also knew the mainstream media gloated about this and the cabal owned stations made a point of breaking in and broadcasting this for the world to hear. This would also explain why I heard a giddy laugh from her earlier in the day. Out of habit, she turns on the fake mainstream media, every day and night. Every. Single. Day. And. Night. Man, the hypnotic feature that the mainstream media possesses for the sheep is intense. It really works for someone who has zero insight, and it pulls her right back into the fake world, making her forget everything she has already seen regarding the Biden Crime Family.

I callously responded with," Yes, mom I heard."

She then goes on to lecture me how terrible it is that Trump lied to get loans.

I felt my adrenaline level begin to rise. It took every ounce of energy to not go on a tangent. I can't. Sometimes I do, but I must learn to stop. She is my mom. Everything going on in the world is way too intense for her.

I calmly responded with a response that mostly contained questions.

"Mom," I took a deep breath before I continued in a very slow, calm voice. "Does this seem odd to you? Do you remember that video I showed you that was live from Fox News with Jim Jordan stating that they have more than enough evidence that the Biden Crime family is involved with money laundering, doing business with a foreign Communistic Country and human trafficking? Do you remember watching Fox news with me and seeing the cancelled checks that they showed to and from foreign Countries? Do you remember all of the millions of illegals that have come across our border? Don't you think it's funny that all of that never went anywhere? Don't you think it's funny that not a single Jeffery Epstein client was arrested? Don't you think it's a little odd that they thought Trump was guilty of fraud for years, but they are just now bringing it up in the year of the election?"

She thought about it and said, in the same tone of voice I addressed her in, (touché), "Sidney, don't you think lying to get a lower interest rate is bad?"

Second adrenaline rush occurs.

"Mom, if that is true, which it is not, Trump has more assets, do you think that is worse than human trafficking? This is not red vs. blue, democrat vs. republicans, this is good vs. evil."

She quickly reacted in a very proud voice," But they never even mentioned any of that on the news."

Continuing in my calm voice, I proceeded. "That should be another red flag to you about the mainstream news that you watch. Why didn't they show that?"

She evaded every question that was referenced and then repeated," But you didn't answer me, don't you think lying to get a lower interest rate is bad?"

I glanced over at Andy who was standing in the hallway and positioned where I could see him, but she couldn't. He made the hand motion going back and forth across his throat, indicating to me to stop, then with the same hand he waves it over his head while making a quiet airplane noise. His silent message was not wrong. I need to stop talking because this is way over her head.

At that point I just agreed with her. "Yes, mom, lying to get lower interest rates is bad." I then pressed my ear buds to get them to start playing my happy country songs and removed myself from the room.

Something interesting is going on in town. Some board members are posting on the website, not the big player board members, some board members that are not key assets, they are apologizing. They are explaining themselves how they were "tricked" and not told the whole truth while in the voting process for the CCP to come in. They went on to explain that the CCP was never mentioned– hell, even the word "Chinese" was never mentioned, the 30 million tax break given to the CCP was never mentioned, in fact, they were made to believe that it was going to be an amazing establishment coming in that would lower our taxes and raise our home values. So of course they voted yes. Every good American wants to see their hometown prosper.

My first reaction was yeah right, you just got caught speeding as they say, and now you are trying to back pedal because you know the townspeople want to see each and every one of you behind bars.

But then I thought about it. I don't know this person that posted it. What sealed the deal for me was when I dug a little more and discovered that the people fighting this, have verified that they were all lied to. There were only a select few that knew the whole truth. Their own little Elite. Of course, Tig was one of them.

February 20th, 2024

Brock Purdy. Quarterback for the 49ers. Not much to say except for I am lost. They have been mentioning him a lot, a couple of times before the Super Bowl, and even now afterwards. I am clueless, but I know at some point it will mean something. They kept saying to "watch him." The exact wording by a trusted truther, after posting a picture of him was "This is the face of LFG. Study his face. Remember his face."

Keep in mind that *LFG* means "let's fucking go," a common abbreviation in this movement. It will be interesting to see what comes of this.

There is also an overabundance of whale comms. A lot of truthers are mentioning whales, Trump mentioned whales in his last rally, Robert Kennedy posted about someone whale watching, a truther got a tattoo of a whale and there are commercials with whales. They mentioned that "currency whales" have started getting their appointments for currency exchanges, posts about happy whale month, and almost every channel has some sort of picture of whale. After some digging, I realized whale is a term used in our new financial world–whales are the name of those on the top financially. Once the whales are moving, then public awareness. I guess that explains the statement that I read stating that more whales have signed a NDA, and it's moving.

As I stated before, I will be right, until I am not. As my grandfather used to say, "Right church, wrong pew." That's ok, we will be like a sponge absorbing all of the information that they will give us. At least we will be a lot closer than the sleepers are. We feel proud knowing that all the money that the deep state and mainstream media spent on brainwashing did not work on us.

Allow me to throw one more date out there for you, even though I swore I would never listen to dates again. I did not hear this at first, not for lack of caring, mostly because I don't listen to many Trump rallies. Five months ago, at a Trump rally, he had said that he would be back in five months. After I saw someone comment that, I did log on to see the replay of the rally in question, and yep, he said it. There are a lot of people counting on that date of February 25th, 2024, which is in five days. Do I think it will happen? Probably not, but anything is possible. I do feel bad for people that are totally relying on this date. Yes, listen to it but take it with a grain of salt. I would love nothing more for it to end soon, very soon; five days would be great. The saddest part is the amount of people saying they are going to throw in the towel if nothing happens by then.

Please don't.

When I hear things like that, I can't help but think of a joke I heard when I was younger:

There was a blonde in a sinking boat out in the middle of the ocean. She could either stay on the sinking boat which will get her nowhere, or she can try to swim to shore. She decided to try to swim to shore. She gets halfway to shore and says, "Fuck it, I am too tired," so she turns around and swims back to the sinking boat.

Cute and funny joke, and with this movement, it comes in quite handy. We have come too far to give up now. Don't go back to the sinking boat. We are halfway there, hang on and keep on swimming (more like the doggy paddle in this case), but the safety of the shore is coming! No one knows when it will happen, but we cannot give up! Oh crap, I just realized I documented a blonde joke. To all blondes out there, please don't be offended. Had to throw in that generic apology, because now a days, everyone gets offended.

Had a discussion with Adam this morning and he had a great point. This new disease that is possibly headed our way, just in time for elections, he asked if it was possible that it is called disease "X"–same name as the new Twitter for a reason? Were they showing us before it happened? They are known to do that, both white hats and black hats. Even though I have not seen any info information pointing to that, it is plausible.

The World Health Organization (WHO) is already issuing warnings about it. See, they had to throw monkeypox and white lung virus in there throughout the past couple of years because just having a brand-new virus all the sudden out of the blue, right before an election would be too obvious.

I must admit, I am kind of disappointed that the monkeypox didn't take off further, I would have loved to have seen if the Liberals tried strapping a mask to their ass.

March 11th, 2024

In England, several videos have been posted showing three horses— two black horses and one white horse trotting down the street near the palace. Nothing was announced and the locals had no idea why the horsemen were riding the horses down the street. According to locals, it is not a usual thing. They have different customs and everything means something. This adventure perplexed everyone in the UK. There is no doubt a reason.

Most importantly, Jacob Rothschild died. Not on the 25th, but on the 26th, one day off is nothing, it might as well be the same date. To be precise, he died a long time ago, November 17, 2017 (notice all the 17's), they just decided to announce it on the 26th. Rothschild, Rockefeller and the globalist elites created the U.S. Federal Reserve system. In so many of the Q drops, they mention save Israel for last and the day they announced his passing, I noticed a drop of saying this:

Man #1: "What is your name?"

Man #2: "Jacob."

Man #1: "From now on, your name will no longer be Jacob. You will be called Israel."

Save Israel for last? I do know the announcement of his death has a huge significance. Also, he was 87 (not really). 87 on the drops = Justice.

Those above historical events happened on the 25th & 26th. The same date that was calculated at Trump's last rally. Ok, so he said he would be back in five months, and he is not technically "back", but let's face it, he never left either. The death of Rothschild was a very relevant marker. That, along with the cryptic horse display in the UK, yes, Trump threw that date out at this rally for a reason. I am really hoping that the die-hards that stated that they are going to give up if nothing happened publicly by the 25th, saw all the proof stating that so much did happen. I am sure they were just words of anger, we all have days like that and more than likely, they are still hanging on.

In this movement, it has become evident that any date that is thrown out there is not necessarily the date that shit will come out, however, they are still dates where something memorable is going to happen.

There is word, not sure if it has been verified or not so I am documenting this lightly, that we are getting a hydrogen water plant in town. Even though it's not verified, I do know that hydrogen water engines are already being made. In fact, Toyota received authorization form the Japanese government to test a car that will run on water.

One of the many, many, patents that were suppressed are cars that run on water. There is a story out there, and even a video, you don't even have to look hard, it is still currently on Google (surprisingly, since they scrub a lot off their websites.) It is a story about a man in the late 1970's, he started working on perfecting a car that could run on water. After 20 years of research, this man was able to get a patent, he arranged a meeting with his brother and two Belgian investors. They were clinking their glasses and celebrating while out for lunch. After this new inventor took a sip, he instantly grabbed his throat and ran outside. When his brother ran out to check on him, he saw his choking brother vomiting while on his knees. However, in his final moments he was able to look up at his brother and say, "I was poisoned." His brother insisted he was murdered even though the cause of death on his death certificate states he died of a cerebral aneurysm. Cerebral aneurysms do not cause burning in your throat, nor do they cause you to jump up and run out of a restaurant. When the brother investigated this for three years, it obviously went nowhere, and it was chalked up as a conspiracy theory. Now here we are in 2024, and they are talking about hydrogen water engines, using the same process and technique that this intelligent inventor died for in 1998. The Belgian investors surely were part of the worldwide Cabal, and this poisoning was undoubtedly part of their plan from the minute they first heard of this invention. The deep state makes too much money off us when we pay for gas, not to mention a water car would benefit us, so that invention had to be squashed. At some point, very soon, people will realize that every conspiracy theory is a major truth being covered up by the elite. The comeback of this ingenious masterminding is a part of the NESARA. To implement all suppressed patents, there are 6000. The gentleman's name that this story refers to is Stanley Meyer.

Bringing my focus back to our town, that would make sense. If the white hats truly are in control and they are setting things up for the future, building hydrogen water plants would not be unheard of. No surprise that one of the towers would be in our town, the same town that got set up with the CCP deal. That adds up.

Trump posted Article 1, Section 10 Clause 1, directly from the constitution.congress.gov website. It states:

"No state shall enter into any Treaty, Alliance or confederation; grant letter of Marque and Reprisal; coin money; emit Bills of Credit; make anything but gold and silver coin a tender in payment of debts; pass any bill of attainder, ex post facto law, or law impairing the Obligations of Contracts, or grant any Title of Notability.

A bill of attainder is legislation that imposes punishment on a specific person or group of people without judicial trial. The constitution includes two separate clauses respectively banning enactment of bills of attainder by the federal government and the states. The Supreme Court has interpreted the federal and state bill of attainder prohibitions as having the same steps."

Yep, that is our boy Trump dropping evidence of the QFS. Tell me who the real CIC is! This is on the actual website right now. The evidence is written on the wall in so many places if people would just look. Let's read that part again about money being backed by gold and silver, shall we?

On the same channel, Trump also posted:

"I understand the path God put me on will not end well for me. But it will bring the best possible outcome for Our people. AND THAT'S ALL THAT MATTERS!!!"

What in the holy fuck does that even mean? Evidently, he knows more, a lot more and sadly, it's the mysterious statements like that, that fuel my energy.

Welcome to the most illustrious military sting operations of all time!

Now that the election is getting closer, every politician is looking for bonus points. All a show of course, but Potato Head Biden decided to visit our Texas Border. The amusing part is that Trump went the same day. Of course, Biden went to an area that was not the main section of the intrusion while our Superior Real CIC went to the most hectic area. When the fake mainstream media reported Biden at the Border, in the background it looked like nothing. The bumbling idiot did his usual rambling about how we need to secure the border and trying to act concerned and coherent at the same time, which is not easy for him. I'll tell ya what, whatever actor (or multiple actors) is playing him, they sure are doing a great job of making him look like an idiot. They did not show Trump at the border. They did not show his amazing, commanding talk that he gave while there. Trump issued a serious warning to Potato Head Biden:

"Close the borders now! This is not sustainable for our Country! This is not sustainable for our cities! Our Country is under siege! This is a violent thing you've done, and many people are dying!"

Not surprisingly, it wasn't aired but between the internet, other outlets and platforms, the majority of people knew he was there and what he said.

The Texas Attorney General, Ken Paxton, said that Biden is clearly in partnership with human trafficking and the Cartel.

He spoke at CPAC and stated, "It is all designed by our own government. We are at war with the cartels, the Chinese importing Fentanyl, and our own President against the United States and my state."

Tell me this isn't a movie? If it wasn't, his bony, adrenochrome deprived, scrawny, ice cream sucking ass would have been removed already. Time to pop more popcorn.

It's official! Trump will stay on all states' ballots! The U.S. Supreme Court reverses Colorado's decision: he will remain on the ballot; the justices ruled in a 9-0 decision. I wish I could tell you the numbers meant something, but they don't, at least not that I know of. This SCOTUS decision means that all other states that are attempting to remove him, are null and void.

AT & T had an outage. Several people could not make calls, receive calls or even text. For a small percentage of people, Verizon was also affected. The outage did not last long although I am sure for the people that it affected, it probably felt like a lifetime. Later that evening during my usual catching up and looking for more intel, it was reported that it was for a reason. An employee who works at AT&T told his family to buckle up because something bigger is coming. He claimed the outage was done intentionally and that small outage was only the tip of the iceberg. Strange coincidence, this supposed cyberattack happened the same day Julian Assange's decision was due. Oh, that's right, nothing is a coincidence. Julian Assange is bigger than we think, he is one of Trump's "Trump cards."

Just when you think things couldn't get any more unhinged, you should see the IRS website. Yes, this is posted on the Government, IRS website.

It reads this:

"Illegal Activities: income from illegal activities, such as money from dealing illegal drugs, must be included in your income schedule 1 (form 1040), line 8z, or on a schedule C (form 1040) if from yourself employment activity."

Stolen Property: if you steal property, you must report its fair market value in your income in the year you steal it unless you return it to its rightful owner in the same year."

Another thing I stumbled upon was that, now, and always, filing taxes is optional. Listened to many podcasts on this and have read several articles. If you look, it is posted in small print, that it is optional. I know it sounds crazy, but doesn't everything sound ludicrous? Please let me explain-filing is optional. If you file and you owe money and don't pay, you are in deep shit. If you cheat on your taxes and get audited, you are in deep shit. If you file, you are allowing them to claim the money that you owe and you are allowing them to audit you. But if you don't file at all– they can't touch you. We know someone that decided to stop filling in the 80's. We are now in 2024, and he got his life put together and he filed for the first time since the 80's. Everything went well. No questions as to where he has been for the past 40 years, no questions asked, and he got a refund. However, they got people by the balls because think about it, when you apply for a mortgage, they ask for your last year's tax records, if you don't have them, no loan is granted, therefore, forcing people who want the "American Dream" of homeownership, to file. See how it all comes together for them? Damn, they knew exactly what they were doing.

There are so many tell-tale indicators in this world, but you can't have a lethargic way of thinking. Of course, no one ever says, "Hey, I am bored today, I am going to go check the IRS website." Of course not. However, if people would wake up to the more visible things that are happening right in front of their eyes, it would lead the way for real information.

The Covid vaccine and Covid, it's official and even broadcasted on the fake news, that we can treat Covid like the flu. That new revelation to the sleepers is per the CDC, you know, the "trust the science" people. Sounds to me that conspiracy theorists were right from the start. It has been a year now since Dr. Fauci confessed that Covid vaccines could never have worked. He has been MIA ever since. Shouldn't that be another alarm to the sleepers that he is nowhere to be found? If I, and the people in my circle, believed the mainstream media and they succeeded to brainwash us to get vaccinated, we would be pissed if they are now calling it the flu and the asshole that told us to trust the science is now MIA.

All the big-name families and Presidents and CEOs are selling all of their stock from their own companies. The Walton family sold 4.5 billion of Walmart stock, Jeff Bazo of Amazon sold 8.5 billion, Jamie Dimon sold 150 millions of JP Morgan, Zuckerberg sold 400 million, and Buffet is selling everything. Should we question why so many successful businessmen would sell stock in their own company? Kind of would make you wonder, wouldn't it?

Our immigrant invasion is growing by the day. I believe we are past 7.6 million. To top it off, Mr. Potato Head admitted to flying over 320,000 migrants secretly into the U.S. to reduce the number of crossings at the border. Flew them in so it would appear as if there were not as many at the border. The horrible acts the immigrants are achieving– murder, rape, drugs and robbery. Laken Riley, a young 22-year-old nursing student, brutally raped and murdered in Georgia. She was beaten mercilessly by an illegal immigrant, resulting in her skull being crushed in.

Laken was young, Caucasian, U.S. citizen women and not one Liberal has gone ballistic over that. The same Liberals that are worried about their "women's rights" if Trump gets back into office. Let that sink in.

I do know that the immigrants themselves coming over, that is real. There is no doubt. We have seen them dropped off by the bus loads, right here in our own county. Two people that I know personally have had an encounter with them. One of them was at our local store. She was approached by a woman who barely knew any English asking her to buy all the baby clothes that were in her cart. When my friend politely told her that she was not in a financial position to help her, the lady walked away. A few moments later, two migrant men were looking at her. She looked to her left and there was a third man. She walked a few aisles over and now all three men were staring at her. She turned around and found a store security guard. While she was talking to the guard, she looked over at the three men who were now in a different location, but still in her sight. As their eyes met, the three men then turned and ran out of the store.

Immigrants are a fact. That is not CGI, that is not a false flag. It's real, the question that remains is what is the real reason why they are here? The word *real* being the key factor.

A lot of truthers are speculating, again, that there will *NOT* be an actual scare event. That we are living the scare event right now. You have the people that lost their job because they did not take the clot shot, you have people that did take the shot and are now paying the price, you have the people that took the shot–they might not have any repercussions yet, but they are worried they might, you have the immigrant invasion, you have people being evicted, vehicle repossessions, people seeing their savings and retirement going down, people awake still have the discouragement of the election that was stolen, wondering if this really is a movie, people fearing China taking us over, feeling the inflation and family members who have disowned others. These all are side effects that could not be stopped. Whether you are awake, sleeping or semi-drowsy, there is some sort of pain being felt by all. Everyone in the Country has one thing in common, we are all victims of a fraudulent system. Some see it, some don't, but we are all being victimized.

Telegram now has 900 million users. Keep in mind, the United States population as of 2024 is 341,273,133. Making a difference of 559,786,867 from other countries, and that is of course if every American was on Telegram, which is not the case. Huge numbers and it's refreshing to see how much the number of users has grown. They posted at 6 a.m. one morning that there was going to be a social media blackout. About 9:30 a.m., they were correct. Facebook, TikTok, Instagram, and Snapchat all went down. Do you know what didn't go down? Telegram, Truth Social (Trump's platform) and X- formerly Twitter, owned by Elon Musk. All white hat, conservative platforms did not go down. Andy came home for his break, and he proudly informed me that all social media is down. When I told him I knew that was going to happen at 6 a.m. this morning, he looked at me, perplexed. I then reached over for my phone and contently showed him the screenshot that I captured on my phone saying that it was going to go down, hours before it happened. We both looked at each other and grinned. Not sure exactly what the platforms going down signified, all I know is it happened like they said it would.

A couple of other events that we were told about months before they happened:

1. Boeing. Our treasured intel told us months ago to keep an eye on Boeing. Flights were grounded. However, more recently, more flights grounded and several incidents. Wheels falling off, window issues and most importantly, a whistleblower, John Barnett, came forward and just like that, suddenly, he commits suicide, so they say. One shot to the head. At least this one only needed one shot to get the job done. Interesting, right before he was supposed to give a deposition.

2. Months ago, that same intel told us to watch for Scott Peterson to be in the news again. Scott Peterson was found guilty of brutally killing his pregnant wife, Laci, in 2002. It was a horrific case and done and over with quickly, and if I were to be honest, we all forgot about it. Imagine all our surprise when he mentioned to us that it will be back in the spotlight. Well, sure as shit its back in the news just like they told us it would be. The truthers exact words that were spoken, after announcing that it will be back in the news was, "Wait until you hear who really killed Laci." Sounds to me like the husband was the fall guy for the truth and his story will be coming out soon.

Chester Bennington, the singer for Linkin Park, committed suicide on July 20th, 2017. No, he didn't. He is alive and well. If you google him, any webpage that you see, you will notice that they list the parents as Susan Eubanks and Lee Russell Bennington. Nope. That's the wonderful world of misinformation at work. His real father is John Podesta. John Podesta served in the Clinton Administration and the Obama Administration. Not sure who is eviler, him or Hilliary Clinton. He is a big player in the Cabal, Illuminati, deep state or whatever you want to call these pagans these days. He is also a final marker, they said once you hear of his arrest, know that we are there. He has already had several assistants of his arrested for child pornography and pedophilia, but John is the one we need to be arrested. Chester knew who his real dad was, he always had, the false google information was for everyone else. Chester is a good guy– no, he is a great guy. He could not be corrupted into one of them and in addition, he was a threat to the deep state who feared he would blow the whistle. Chester knew his life was in danger, so he faked his own suicide. For all you Linkin Park fans, chill, sit down, relax and please know that Chester is living a great life in hiding.

I think it's pretty evident that there is nothing that the mainstream media or Potato Biden can say or do, that will shock me anymore, I am way past that. Or so I thought. I am aware that any negative feedback that Biden gets, will get blamed on Trump, or MAGA, I am aware of the constant hypocrisy, I am aware that he makes no sense whatsoever, in other words, I am aware he is a total fucking idiot. So, watching the fake SOTU should be easy for me, right? Yeah, I thought so too, but man was I wrong. That shriveled up, ice cream sucking moron hit a nerve. If I had a dollar for every time he said, "because of the previous administration," I could go retire on a yacht. He blew off the Laken Riley tragedy, made a comment that there have been lots of murders or crimes from the immigrants (that he allowed in) and then he proceeds to scream– yes scream– how we need to secure the border. I was so pissed at this clown show that they call the State of the Union Address, that it surprised me at how indignant I got. I know better. I felt a little better when I talked to Ella and she said the same thing, then further confirmation came in when I went to our channels and there were thousands of comments stating the same feelings. We all felt it. What I did notice though is the supposed Secret Service that was there as his protectors, all sported the United States Marshal pin tacked onto their lapel. Now, there is something you don't see every day. Biden also got there 17 minutes late, and he was announced at exactly 9:17 p.m., and his fake speech lasted 1 hour and 7 minutes >>17. Thats a lot of 17s. I wonder what the U.S. Marshals being there means, along with all those 17s? Oh wait, I do know, and you should immediately know by now too.

And oh yea, almost forgot, Nikki Haley has dropped out of the presidential race. Was she bullied, too? Inquiring for a side kick.

Enjoy the show.

March 19th, 2024

Something is brewing in the UK–King Charles has supposed prostate cancer; Kate Middleton went in for surgery and her and her children have not been seen since. They generated a photo that was circulating around that everyone said was so obviously photoshopped. They posted it after her surgery to show the world she was ok, and I saw the photo. One of her kids had only two fingers and another child's hand were slightly blurry and that one had only four fingers. As if that was not unnatural enough, she was sitting down in a pair of tight skinny jeans right after a planned abdominal surgery. Skinny jeans directly after an abdominal surgery? Man, that bitch is a trooper. I would have to agree that the picture was indeed photoshopped. Once everyone called them out on the photo, the British publications instantly took it down. December 25th, 2023, Christmas Day is the last time the public has seen her or her children. Three days later, there was an ambulance and police escort seen flying out of their home. No statement ever from the Royals. On January 17th, 2024, they reported that her situation is more serious, and she was admitted to the London hospital for a planned abdominal surgery. They also reported that the surgery was successful, and the Royals have not made any comment as to why she needed the surgery. Ok, I get it, everyone is entitled to their privacy, but wait, it gets better. They said she will have to stay in the hospital for two weeks. During those two weeks, no visitors. Not from the Queen, her husband, her kids, her siblings or even her parents. On January 26th, King Charles visited her, but no one else. On January 28th, it was reported by unnamed Palace Sources that Kate was in an induced coma. In February, they reported Kate's recovery time would be nine months. Prince William has been posting on his social media about the conflict in the Middle East, but no mention of Kate. He also is using the same singular emblem that he used to use before he was married. On March 4th, Kate is seen driving in a car with her mom, and she looks different. It started a social media frenzy, because the differences were so obvious. Then on March 10th was when the fake photo came out with the children that had missing fingers. And keep in mind, she still hasn't been seen. Then, Royal family member Thomas Kingston mysteriously died at the age of 45 and it is still under investigation on the cause of death, and Prince Williams ex-mistress is back in the picture. Let's not forget the obscure three horsemen in the street and that they have their flag hung at half mast, but no reason given. Truthers are saying, don't let what is about to come out about the Royal Family, distract you from the truth, which is the Federal Reserve collapse that is happening right now.

March 20th, 2024

The televised town meeting was two nights ago, very interesting.

Our very own military resident, the same one who vowed to take them down in the beginning, spoke with great austerity. He had stated that he is done playing nice. He is fed up, and so is the town. He reiterated to them that they work for us, and it's "We the People," not "We the Government." He mentioned he has top security clearance and that he made a few calls and hopes that the mayor has all of his financial records in order. He also revealed to the trustees that they are just as guilty and reminded them again that they signed a deal with the CCP, a communistic party. He also cited the 1st and 2nd amendments.

Now today rolls around. The mayor and his corrupt minions have decided to explore the possibility of gaining a restraining order on this individual. Their reasoning? Because by him citing his 2nd amendment right, he threatened the mayor. He quoted the 2nd Amendment, which is already public knowledge to the whole fucking country. This is good news, it shows that they know this patriot is on to them and the fact that they want to shut him up, speaks volumes.

March 21st=, 2024

I woke up this morning to some interesting news regarding the world. It looks like the Boeing whistleblower did not commit suicide. Like Chester Bennington, he faked his own suicide since there were attempts on his life before the deposition was to take place. He is giving the depositions in privacy while under Witness Protection.

For anyone entertaining the thought that there is no way, or things like that only happen in the movies, or whatever reality twisted fantasy land you might live in, let me share something with you:

1. John F. Kennedy, Jr. was the front runner for the NY Senate seat in 1999, days later his plane went down, and he was killed (no he wasn't–) and Hillary Clinton became Senator.

2. Mary Mahoney was a White House intern; she knew of all Bill Clinton's sexual escapades and was considered to be a star witness in the Clinton impeachment trials. She was then brutally executed at a Starbucks she was working at.

3. Then White House Counsel, Vince Foster, was found dead in a park after apparent suicide.

4. James McDougal, right before he was supposed to testify in a grand jury mysteriously suffered a heart attack while in solitary confinement.

5. Walter Scheib, a cook for the White House while the Clintons were residing in there–they feared that he might have heard too much. His body was found at the bottom of the river, and it was a supposedly an accidental drowning.

6. Seth Rich, Democratic Committee Staffer was shot and killed in D.C. He was linked to having information regarding emails.

7. Shawn Lucas, the lead attorney in a fraud case against the DNC, was found lying on the bathroom floor, dead.

That's only seven incidents. There are over 87 people that either are missing or found dead by Hillary Clinton.

The fact that Chester Bennington, the whistleblower for Boeing and so many others faking their own death, it is the only logical thing to do when your life is in danger with the deep state.

I discovered something that threw me for a loop, to say the least, but its ok. These Q boards, they started in 2017, they were intended for an eight-year plan. That would make it 2025. Let me rephrase that, I have seen that before, in fact right in the very beginning of this adventure, I noticed it, however, in this movement, there are so many codes, comms, hints, riddles and math that you so can easily lose track. If all those dates we were given in the past years, if it is an eight-year plan, that would mean those dates are intended for now until 2025.

So, let's back track, if since I first starting writing these notes, if it was intended for this year, does that mean everything that was supposed to take place immediately after the 2020 election, that's what will happen after the 2024 election, leading us into 2025? Will the elections happen, stolen again, then *EVERYTHING* I have been documenting will happen exactly that way after the 2024 election?

So many truthers have told us that the election will not happen. Let's face it, while there have been several things that have been told to us that actually did happen, there is more that did not happen, and I am not afraid to admit that.

When I came to the realization that this may, in fact, have always been intended for 2025, I in no way, in any capacity, got angry or discouraged. I would not trade this journey that Ella and I have been on for anything in the world. I would rather be awake, than sleeping and in total dismay when it comes out.

March 22, 2024

The awake have known for quite some time, that the Royals have already been removed and there was a lot of speculation how they would get rid of them in the public eye. Wouldn't you know, they have just announced that Kate Middleton has stomach cancer– great timing now that King Charles also has cancer. Pure genius. They released a video of Kate sitting alone on a park bench asking for prayers and discussing her supposed newly found diagnosis. Sitting alone–seems odd. They are a prominent Royal family and with the massive amounts of Royal etiquette rules, seems a little strange that she is sitting alone explaining something. Do you want to know why? It's AI. Already been confirmed that it is, in fact, AI by photo/video experts. They zoomed in and showed in detail as to why they knew that. They also explained, in detail, that AI is easier to master with only one person in the video. AI is not completely perfected yet and having two people in the same video is very difficult to project flawlessly. That is why she is the only one in the video, and in addition to that, she is wearing the same sweater that she wore during a 2016 video promoting a fund raiser. Pure royalty wearing the same sweater from 2016? Well, my exhausted chaps, it's because it is the exact same video from 2016, they just altered the words. Same sweater, same exact hair, same everything from the 2016 video. I saw the two videos played side by side– yep same video, different words. To top it off, look at the sweater, does it look familiar to you? Think of the building on Epstein's Island, blue and white stripes. On *X* (Twitter) The Yorkshire Lass posted a poll. The question was, "Who else thinks Kate Middleton is already dead?"

Astonishing enough, 82% voted yes and 18% said no. That is huge! See, told you, more are awake than not awake. There is zero excuse for the sleepers anymore. At the same time, they released that AI video, they staged a terrorist attack in Moscow. Don't know the relation, but undoubtedly there is one.

Weren't we told a few days ago, three days to be exact, not to let the news that will be coming out about the UK, to distract us? Yes, my dear Watson, we were.

Another conspiracy theory was proven correct this week. They are posting it on public websites. Hydroxychloroquine, Ivermectin and the generic Z-pack, all cure Covid–oh wait, we can call it the flu now–and very quickly, I might add. Funny, Democrats were able to block those three drugs from citizens but let Fentanyl come through with no problem.

Just another conspiracy though, right?

March 30, 2024

We are rapidly approaching April. Absolutely no relevance at all for me mentioning that other than the fact that time is flying, winter is over, and I am glad spring and summer are right around the corner.

Tomorrow is Easter. They have been saying for the longest time now that Easter is their timeline. Tomorrow is the 31st, Easter has never been and will never be March 31st. They have been messing with us every day for centuries, many holidays, holidays as we know it, are not what they seem. The real Easter date is April 28th. The dates line up nicely, if it is meant for this year. If Easter truly is their timeline, the eclipse and the eleventh are before the 28th, enough time to roll everything out. Also, that creepy Mickey Mouse clock, the hands are at 10 and 2, if you mirror it, the hands are at 4 and 8, April 8th. Not expecting anything tomorrow, but maybe, just maybe, on the 28th? Unless of course the ending to this brilliantly planned movie starts in November, rolling into 2025.

Speaking of the election, Nevada state senator says 130,000 people voted illegally in his state and is insisting that the people that were behind this must be prosecuted. The 2020 election fraud is dwindling down since six counts have been thrown out in Fani Willis' case against Trump. They are publishing now how Obama faked his name, religion, wife, kids, birthplace, nationality, education and career and then sealed the records to stop us from finding out. In addition to all of that, Kimberly Zapata was found guilty on all counts against her in voter fraud involving military ballots. Also, let's not forget we have been told several times that the election was, in fact, already overturned. General Millie stated to the world that the U.S. is a "corporation" and the Congress is the board of directors. Oops! Did he meant to say that? I think so, red pill… drip… drip.

Another huge coincidence is that:

The President of Vietnam resigned.

Prime Minister of Ireland resigned.

Israel's Army Chief of Staff resigned.

South Korean Official for the President resigned.

All on the same day. Did I say that was a huge coincidence? You should know by now, what I am going to say next, all tougher now– nothing is coincidence.

Who's next? President (fake) of the United States-Biden?

Video, upon video, upon video, upon newspaper articles, radio shows and even some news outlets about how whites are getting beat up, just because they are white. One young girl's head was slammed on the concrete several times by young black girls. Where are the riots? Oh, that's right, BLM was funded by the Democrats, and the Democrats won't round up people and organize anything unless it's something to make Trump look bad.

Jonathon Diller, A NYPD white officer that was killed by a career criminal black man. That's ok, though? The family allowed no democrats into the funeral. Trump went and was welcomed with open arms. Biden blew it off completely, didn't even acknowledge it.

Please tell me that whoever is reading this sees the screenplay by now? Or at least, if you don't believe it was a movie, tell me you see the differences in *EVERYTHING*?

If people don't see it by now, its ok, they were trained that way, they are conditioned. They learn that people like us are unhinged, dangerous, harmful conspiracy theorists, and they make sure not to listen to us. Whatever you do, don't listen to us, maybe it's for the better because once you go down that rabbit hole, there is no going back, you will never trust the system again.

I saw a quote recently and unfortunately it is going to be so true for many people, very soon:

"One day many will hang their heads in shame, when they realize the evil they defended and the heroes they ridiculed."

Great news for Trump! The appeals court ruled Trump can continue operating his businesses in New York, and the money he owed was reduced to $175,000,000.00 instead of $454,576,230.00. Of course, not shown on the news, so the normies still think he is banned from operating there, and surely, they are still gloating.

Trump's attorney exposed the judge that was hearing this case regarding him "lying" about his assets to get a lower rate, stating the judge took a 10-million-dollar bribe from Joe Biden to convict Trump. Are you connecting the dots yet? That is now public knowledge and is it too much to ask for if I want the liberals to see that? Will they figure it out then, or am I giving them too much credit? Oh, how could I forget, they also discovered another paper trail confirming that Biden is getting money from China. Wow, much like our little town officials. Maybe they can all get adjoining nooses, and can all drop together? Wouldn't that be sweet?

The bridge! It finally happened! All of these talks about bridges! We never knew which bridge it was, and it turns out it was Francis Scott Key Bridge. The name of the container ship was DALI. D=4 A=1. L=12 so (1+2=3) I=9. =17. There is that damn 17 again. And Q post 4139= bridge collapse. Damn, do you see it yet?

It collapsed at 1:28 a.m. This is 128 days after Francis Key's Birthday and it's on Nancy Pelosi's birthday. She is 84 years old and just happens to be from Maryland. The bridge is in Maryland. The ship apparently lost power and crashed into the bridge, causing it to collapse completely. Some of the containers on the ship carried hazardous materials, including corrosives, flammables and Class 9 materials such as Lithium-Ion Batteries.

That movie *Leave the World Behind* started with a ship losing its power due to an EMP, the same thing that they said happened to this ship. Also, very ironic that the ship in the movie looks eerily like the ship that crashed in the bridge.

Potato head is at again, this time is not saying that he is talking to dead people but when he gave a brief speech about the bridge, he reminisced about how he took a train over that bridge many times. There has never been train tracks on that bridge.

I am also thrilled to announce that there is another win for the conspiracy theorists! All of those "stories" about the Hollywood puppets being part of the Elite, in cahoots with the Democrats, the Royals and the Illuminati and child trafficking that the liberals laughed about for years, is coming out that they weren't "stories" at all. P Diddy was arrested! P Diddy is a rapper in the music industry, and while I certainly don't listen to rap, he is a household name. P Diddy was *the* Jeffrey Epstein in the rap industry. He was allegedly drugging and trafficking women and children across state lines. While searching his home, they found underground tunnels, and The Department of Homeland security is currently cleaning out bodies from the tunnels. It is a well-known fact that P Diddy is close friends with Obama, and it is circulating that when P Diddy got wind that his homes were being raided and they were detaining his sons, Obama helped him escape; he was originally headed to Cape Verde since they have do not have extradition treaty with the U.S. However, he was found and was arrested. He has also been linked to Rachel Chandler, the child handler for the Epstein's. For the people that have been following this, we were a little peeved that nothing was being done about the Epstein client list. We all knew there was a reason, waiting is the hardest part of all of this, and it does get trying sometimes. Ghislaine Maxwell was moved to a secure cell and treated very well because she is singing like a bird. The list is being used to go after these sick fucks, now all of the sudden high-profile names are getting busted for trafficking. Less than one week before this came out, Trump told Nigel Farage that he would consider deporting Prince Harry form America and now Prince Harry is being highlighted in the news for this.

The above coupled with the statement he made at one of his rallies is more than sufficient evidence that Trump knows everything and he is taking them down. He stated that, "Prince Harry is going to need a lot of luck, and I do wish him all of the luck, because he is going to need it." That was a while ago, then all of this came out.

It will be interesting to know if any liberal's notices yet that all of the people that condemn Trump publicly, are pedophiles.

Think past years–Mel Gibson came out in 2000 trying to expose the trafficking and corruption in Hollywood, he was blackballed from Hollywood and his life was threatened numerous times along with other intense repercussions including the threatening of his family. I remember when that came out, of course I remember because it was all over the news and that was before I was awake. Honestly, when I heard all of that, I thought to myself "Mel Gibson has lost his damn mind." Sorry, Mel.

Think of all the child actors that tried telling people; Corey Feldman tried several times, no one listened. Think of all your "one hit wonder" musicians that never went anywhere, or actors that you only saw in a couple of movies, then never again. Those are the ones that would not go along with their plan or sign the contract.

March 31st, 2024, Easter Sunday.

Happy Easter!

Question, am I the only that finds it odd that another bridge got hit in Oklahoma, a few days after Maryland, at the exact same time (1:30 p.m. not a.m. like the other, but still 1:30)? Yea didn't think so.

They have been telling us for years to "watch the waters." Is it the bridges? At first, we thought it was the Three Gorge Dam, then we thought the Navy Ships, then we thought possible tampering of water and now there are all these ships crashing into bridges. Another "water" is a news commentator of Fox, named Jesse Watters. Jesse has been blowing us away with comments on his show, once dropping the name of a town, allegedly on accident, that one of our big truthers lives in, so it is not a surprise that we are thinking "watch the waters" might be referring to Jesse Watters. One of our truthers showed us John F. Kennedy, Jr. on

March 24$^{th}$, and right afterwards Jesse Waters is talking about him, it was that same truther that Jesse mentioned his hometown. Watch the water– who is Jesse Watters? Also, Jesse has been known to make the same compulsory hand movement that John F. Kennedy, Jr. used to make.

Well, well, good ol' Biden made today, of all days, a huge holiday in addition to it being Easter. Easter Sunday is now national Transgender Day. Damn, this shit is so obvious! They want us to get exhausted, cave in and start complying. It is common knowledge now that transgenders are against Christians, and the President (fake) of the United States, just spat on all Christians by honoring a demographic that is against Christians, on Easter! Oh, to make matters worse, Biden banned children from submitting religious Easter eggs for the traditional Easter Egg roll out. Traditionally, New York City lights up the signs of the cross on their skyscrapers in the city, this year it was the gay pride colors. Will this wake up the rest? Damn, how many times am I going to have to ask that question throughout these notes?

I am thinking we are done at trying to wake people up. The sleepers now, are just done. Someone I know posted a quote from Biden stating how wonderful he is, the best economy– yada, yada, same old bullshit. But this person posted it in support of him. All the comments were positive Biden comments; they are all voting for him.

By Duncan O'Finioan: "This is the end game, we are not going to wake anybody up anymore. There are things about to happen everywhere that is going to freak them out drastically. By now, they are comfortable with being asleep, they want to be there otherwise they would have noticed something. Nevertheless, when shit does hit the fan, they are going to run around in distress and whine....'Why didn't someone say something?'"

At the risk of being cruel, I strongly feel that the people that are still sound asleep, are selfish. There are three groups of Biden supporters that still support him:

1. They are not affected at all. They still go on vacations and live in an area that has not been affected at all by immigrants. They may or may not see the fuckery in the world, but hey, it's not affecting them, their pedestal is still high up in the air and that is all that matters. That Trump

guy, he is nasty, and he offends them. They feel the world might be rougher for some, but don't care. They might even throw in a few "should have gone to college" comments or "get a better job." Selfish.

2. The people that do feel the higher prices, the division, the hypocrisy, but there is no way they will ever be for Trump. They would rather have the world go to shit than to have Trump and will never admit they were wrong. Selfish.

3. The ones that are somehow, someway benefitting from all the corruption, treason and pedophilia. Selfish.

Newsflash– a lot of Red "Trumpers" are not affected either. The higher prices suck but we are still ok, we still live comfortably, can pay our bills and go on vacations. Regardless of that, the big difference between us and the above-mentioned Liberals is we just don't think of ourselves. We see others hurting, we see the country going to shit. We love America, it's not about us, it's about We the People! We have not been affected directly by immigrants either, but we still feel utter remorse for Laken Riley, and she was one of us, that basically was killed by Biden. How can you post that you are for him? You might as well say you are defending the killer of Laken Riley. What if that was one of their relatives, would that wake them the fuck up?!

Please listen, this is very important, the division is unconstitutional.

I have explained several times how they feel about us MAGA, and now I just went on a rampage on how we feel. It was never like this. Never. Technically, I should not clump all Lefties into one category, and for that, I do apologize. But please don't mistake my apology for an apology about how I feel; that I will not apologize for. The world does basically "like" each other. They succeeded in the division of race and politics.

Whether you are black, white, brown or purple, whether you are straight, gay or a transgender, whether you are Catholic, Baptist, Protestant or any other religion, whether you are a Lib or a MAGA, whether you are red or blue…

215

We all have one thing in common. We all have been played by a master plan and lied to our whole lives. Let's hope for that sake of humanity, that once the truth comes out, that will be our common denominator that unifies us.

"Being awake isn't cool. It means having to dummy down 98% of your conversations every day so you don't sound like a lunatic" – Dave Chappelle

Maybe we are not conspiracy theorists
Maybe we just see something you don't.
Maybe we have learned something you haven't yet.
Maybe we understand a pattern that you don't see.
Maybe we aren't crazy–maybe we actually see through the propaganda and even in the face of ridicule are trying to translate it for you.
There ya go, in a nutshell. That's the world now.
Damn, what a great March!
P Diddy arrested for human trafficking
More of Hollywood being exposed
Bridge collapse
Julian Assange's trial
Prince Harry also involved in sex trafficking
Kate Middleton's fake stomach cancer
Easter is now transgender day
Nickelodeon kids speaking out
More pedophilias being exposed
Trumps bail bond reduced
Judges been exposed
Can hardly wait to see what April brings.
April 2, 2024
Some interesting new news about China. China is urging its citizens to prepare for unexpected situations in the U.S. since Chinese students and workers are being questioned and then deported from American airports, if necessary. This is extremely interesting, and it does insinuate that maybe the white hats are truly in control. What reason would they have to question the Chinese coming into airports when there are millions

of illegals coming over the border? China, of all countries, the one that we have been told are in bed with The Biden Crime Family and trying to take us over, and now they are questioning them when coming in– yeah, tell me that is not part of the plan, and we are cleaning up. Although, it could be because according to the Gate Stone Institute, China has unleashed an "unrestricted warfare" on the U.S.A. Damn, I hope it's for the first reason, otherwise I am telling ya, it's going to get spicy.

If "our way" is indeed incorrect, the social credit score will also be implemented. Social credit score is exactly what it sounds like. They grade you, or rather give you, a score on your social behavior. They know who everyone voted for, they know who got the vaccine and they will look at your social media. Needless to say, being a Trump voter and non-vaccinated, we will have a very low social credit score. Those with low scores will not be allowed to do certain things and they can even freeze your bank accounts. Does that sound way too severe and crazy? If so, please go back to page one and re-read this whole story.

Ok, enough of the sad parts, here is some good news! Dominion (the voting machine company) lost their lawsuit against Rudy Giuliani and Sidney Powell. Rudy and Sidney, two of Trump's attorneys, got sued by the company when they were claiming the election was stolen (it was). Well, the company lost, which means a lot! They were able to prove that Rudy and Sidney were, in fact, correct, the machines were tampered with. This is a win we haven't heard about yet!

New information about the bridge that went down in Maryland. Larry Silverstein, he is the same person that had a 1 trillion insurance policy on the World Trade Center. He obtained that policy six weeks before it went down; indeed, he did, because as you already know, 9/11 was planned. Larry Silverstein also had an insurance policy on the Baltimore bridge, for the same amount of 1 trillion. As far as the bridge goes, they found explosives on the bridge– ironic that the ship lost power just long enough to crash into it but then regained power and there is proof that they stopped cars from crossing the bridge prior to the explosion. Now there is proof that Silverstein had an insurance policy on it. In addition to that, the owner of the ship was Mitch McConnell's sister-in-law that died six days prior. Awful lot of odd elements surrounding this bridge collapsing.

An El Paso judge released illegal immigrants who stormed the border and rioted against our National Guard. The National Guard describes it as a "border riot," when Venezuelan immigrants overwhelmed all security measures and attacked the National Guard, pushing their way through and cutting the razor wire fence. Two hundred were locked up, 70 were arrested, the group consisted of approximately 600. The judge ruled that "all rioting participants will be released on their own recognizance." Hey, here is a thought, let's free the January 6 "rioters" on their own recognizance– you know the ones that are fucking American and did not "riot" nearly as bad as these Venezuelans, yea, you know those guys. Sleepers cannot ignore this anymore. Enough is enough, the release of these Venezuelans is also on the fake news, and I even heard it on the radio. No reason to be asleep, unless they feel the January 6rs are correctly imprisoned because they are Trumpers. If that is case, please allow me to revoke your American status.

April 8th, 2024

One of the things that I am most excited about is the verification of three different things that Trump has said since day one regarding the Covid.

First, they released the ingredients of Trump's "warp speed" vaccine. As suspected and we stumbled upon this before, his ingredients were Hydroxychloroquine, Ivermectin, azithromycin, doxycycline and zinc. There ya have it.

Second, he was urging people to ask for HCQ and almost begging people, to not let them put you, or someone you love, on a vent. That video of him saying that was made during the Covid era. It was shown on C-Span, and the filming of it was in hopes that every news outlet would show it as a way to help out "We the People" in dealing with Covid. It was not aired on mainstream media; it was removed immediately from C-Span and completely scrubbed from the internet. So, all of the people that thought it was ok to silence Trump and remove anything that he speaks of from social media and the internet, how did that work out for you? If they aired that, it would have saved a lot of lives, or at the very least, cut people's recuperation time in half.

Lastly, it has been confirmed that the biggest part of the vaccine was mind control. In addition to the turbo cancer and heart disease, it messed with everyone's way of thinking and that was their main goal. Dr. Nehls has stated that, "It wasn't so much about money or even death, it was all about conquering the human mind."

Us un-jabbed, truly do beat to a different drummer. They threw everything they could think of at us, and we didn't even flinch.

Would this be a good time to remind you of what being a true conspiracy theorist means? "Someone who can see a certain pattern and the truth before anyone else can."

More and more 2020 election fraud evidence being exposed. Garland Favorito of Voter GA testified on six affidavits alleging counterfeit ballots in Fulton County, Georgia's 2020 election. After three and a half years, it still has not been rectified and he further states that this is not the appropriate way to investigate. Mark Wingate, a Fulton County Elections Board member, also testified that he voted against certifying the 2020 election because they could not verify 147,000 mail-in ballots. How come we didn't hear about that? According to the mainstream media and the Liberals, everyone was on board with certifying since there was no proof of fraud. As with so many things in these past few years, we call bullshit, again. There is no denying the amount of so much truth coming out and the normies are going to have the shock of their lives, coming real soon to a theater near you. The ending of our movie will be the beginning of theirs.

Within the past four days there have been several earthquakes. The delta (past Q posts) for the day it happened was:

BOOM

BOOM

BOOM

BOOM

After the third earthquake, they told us there would be one more to equate to the four booms. Sure enough, a fourth earthquake was reported. According to the seismic scale, the way structures are built and the characteristics of the earthquakes, the truthers are telling us that they were not earthquakes, they were the destruction of the last remaining DUMBS.

John Wayne, a classic actor mostly known for his cowboy western movies–his daughter spent years looking into Obama. After a long and tedious investigation, she has discovered that Obama is using the social

219

security number of Jean Paul Ludwig, who was born in 1890. Ludwig spent the final months of his life in Hawaii, and that is where he died. How perfect for Obama that his grandmother worked in the probate office in Hawaii and had access to the SSNs of deceased people. The SS administration was never notified of Ludwig's death because he never received SS benefits– there were not benefits to stop, therefore, no questions were asked. That is how the birth of fictitious Obama got created. He was never a U.S. Citizen, and he has been using a fake SSN all these years. John Wayne's daughter has publicly announced and published it. Just when you think it couldn't get any worse for Obama, Tucker Carlson leaked a video where him and Michelle/Michael are "having fun" with a 10-year-old. The 10-year-old was screaming and begging them to stop, and both of them ignored her screams. On the same tape, there are officials raping children and committing other horrific crimes including the Obamas, who were having sex with child victims' multiple times.

More emails, texts, voicemails, photos and witness testimony proving Joe Biden was fully involved in his son Hunter's corrupt foreign business deals. It's all coming out at a ferocious speed and unfortunately for the fake deep state, it's really bad timing since a lot of the country is still pissed that he made Easter national Transgender Day.

Speaking of transgenders, an Illinois trans person has plead guilty to threatening to copy the Nashville school shooting, bomb churches and rape Christian children as revenge for transphobia. That is the group that is protected, and that is the same group that Biden wants to honor on Easter.

April 10, 2024

Trump is claiming that Beijing, China, is building an Army within the United States. He is concerned with the Chinese buying up our land in addition to the Chinese migrants coming across the border. At least 46,000 of the immigrants are Chinese. Very healthy, young men. He is concerned and with valid reason; he is pointing out that China is not like other countries, you do not leave without permission, therefore, indicating that they are being sent here. He is worried for our country, more so than the imbecile pretending to be our President. I am quite certain that will get turned into the mainstream media and normies calling him racist.

They also mentioned on Fox this morning that China's aggression is escalating. Quick reminder, CCP is coming to our town. Yea, there is nothing going on though. Oh, there is another border of concern; the fake Biden administration is worried about and wants to help secure the border in the Middle East Countries. They have agreed to grant $380 million in border security. Now, if that doesn't wake people up, it's getting a little old saying that, so many people still have uncommon sense instead of common sense. I am just trying to give them the benefit of the doubt.

This movement is starting to lose a lot of people, more so now, than previously mentioned. They are getting discouraged because he talks so much about the election, and what he will do when he takes office in January of 2025. I watched the most intriguing podcast last night. They said if you read the "Law of War Manual," you would understand everything. The manual was updated in July of 2023. It is sold in 2 volumes, each volume consisting of 700 pages. As much as I would love to read that, there is no way I could find the time to read 1,400 pages. Everything that we are living right now, everything that is happening, *everything*, is being done exactly the way it should be. Remember, centuries of corruption have to be removed and cleaned up, if everything was not done exactly the way it should have been, the plan would not have worked. I don't need to read the manual to know that. I don't need to know exactly how the military operates; I will leave that for the geniuses and the people in charge. I do, however, know for certain that everything had to be done a certain way.

` Well, well, well–guess what's on the FBI's website? After admitting that the Comet Pizza place was a main hub for pedophilia, they have also just posted the "codes" that the Elite used for their parties.

"hotdog" = boy
"pizza" = girl
"cheese" = little girl
"pasta" = little boy
"ice cream" = male prostitute
"walnut" = person of color
"map" = semen
"sauce" = orgy.

221

Think back to any social media posts that your favorite celebrity posted– if they stated they could not wait for their pizza party, or how they are craving ice cream, or at their party they will be serving hotdogs– you get the drift. They were advertising their evil because they are proud of it and no one ever knew. Now answer two questions for me.

1. Why would the FBI have that on their website if the truth was not about to explode?

2. Is it just me or do they show fake Biden eating a lot of ice cream?

Another win for us via the FBI is they are confirming that Ashley Biden's diary is authentic. The FBI and *New York Times* also verified that Ashley's father, Joe Biden, did sexually assault her. On May 17th, 2022, the FBI stated the diary was unethical and refused to acknowledge it.

Ashley wrote in her diary: "I am so afraid of him coming in the shower with me that I've waited until late at night to take a shower," and "My father molested me many times in the shower." Pages 67-68

FBI confiscated it to protect Joe. Joe was known as Pedo Peter, a nickname made up by his son, Hunter. But wait, there is more– Tucker Carlson, much like the video he leaked of the Obamas with a child, also leaked a video of Joe, with concrete evidence he likes to have "fun" with much younger girls. Poor Joe, his actor is not having a good week, the real Joe ought to be thankful he is already dead.

Now that the diary is considered authentic, the codes posted and the leaked video, in my opinion it's another indicator that the good guys are in control.

On *X*, formerly Twitter, the great Covid cover up is being exposed and trending. Liberals and pedophiles are, of course, blaming Trump. Wait until the day comes when they realize that "trust the science," which was embedded in their heads by Fauci and the Dems, has never meant anything other than "shut the fuck up and obey." The dots are practically touching each other, and people still cannot connect them, it's just "I blame Trump!"

Still more and more Boeing airplane issues and now they are saying that there will be many hi-jacked jets that will more than likely be flown into buildings worldwide. Another 9/11 event. That would line up with the predicted ISIS attack they had mentioned a couple of days ago. A podcast I watched the other day said there is still an imminent "scare event." I know I have tried explaining several times about a false flag and I think I described it efficiently.

Russia opened a probe on the West financing terrorism by sending funds to Ukraine. Russia claims that the funds that were received in Ukraine are from the United States firms that link to Hunter Biden. Billions of dollars were given to a long list of Democrats. Joe Biden alone received 92 million.

That is the people and the amounts that our wonderful government has been getting with every funding that was sent to Ukraine. So, you see folks, that is why they don't give a shit about securing our border; their pockets are getting lined, in addition to all the other corruption going on in Ukraine, that is far more important to them. And yes, this is public knowledge.

Also, Hunter Biden funded the terrorist attack in Russia.

The day they announced this, Trump posted "Biden Trials" on his Truth social media page. Approximately 15 others in his circle all posted at the same exact time "Get a warrant #FISA," FISA stands for Foreign Intelligence Surveillance Act.

While everyone was out, including myself, trying to catch a glimpse of the eclipse, the Biden impeachment inquiry hearing was occurring and broadcasted live at the same time. Damn! I didn't get that memo. I would have enjoyed that show much better. Yes, it's still going on, normies don't know this, but it is.

In Hollywood, Ben Affleck's daughter came out as transgender and Jennifer Lopez's daughter is non-binary. These are just two names out of thousands of celebrities. When you sell your soul to the devil, you're offspring are included as part of the deal. Jennifer Lopez was also in a serious relationship with P Diddy and Affleck's name is in the Podesta emails to Hillary Clinton about "pizza parties." Just a coincidence though, right? Let's all say it together again, nothing is a coincidence. Let's say it louder for the people in the back, NOTHING IS A COINCIDENCE.

Regarding history, more information about Mother Teresa coming out. Sweet little Mother Teresa, so everyone thought, was one of the largest human traffickers and sold babies and made between 50-100 million a year for the Vatican. Teresa's connections include Doc Duvalier, the Haitian dictator, Charles Keating (the criminal of Savings and Loan) and Robert Maxwell, Ghislaine's father. See how it is all connecting nicely? Mother Teresa opened a D.C. Toddler home with Hillary Clinton; the orphanage was silently closed in 2012. Again, it all comes together in a nice little perfect package. Oh, lets spruce up the package even more. The Walt Disney Company bought Epstein's Island. The company will open another theme park and make that a stop on their cruise ship lines. It has already been verified (even with the libs,) that they did horrific things to children there, but they have no problem opening it up as a children's theme park. All for show, it won't get that far, but if that doesn't open the eyes of the sleepers or the Disney lovers, I don't know–oh shit, there I go again saying that.

April 11th, 2024

Loving this movie more and more! Yesterday, UK Secretary of State David Cameron had a meeting with Trump. He quoted, "The meeting I had yesterday with Donald Trump was a good meeting. It was a private meeting."

A foreign leader meeting a "former" President of the United States to discuss ongoing wars, yeah, seems totally normal, right? Additionally, Charlie Ward who is the head of the QFS was at Mar-a-Lago–and this is the best part–Trump enrolled the United States in the BRICS this morning! BRICS is... or stands for Brazil, Russia, India and China. B - R - I- C.

Before you lose your shit, you must always keep in mind that you are watching a movie and this is all planned. The fact that Trump signed up the U.S. with countries like Russia and China, is a good thing. All bad players have been taken out. Even this bullshit going on in our own small town is part of the plan. And, important to remember, China itself is not bad, just the CCP. Several other countries have also joined, and now the U.S.A.!

Nations often use the U.S. dollar to trade between themselves. This was created to ditch the U.S, dollar, hence new gold backed Rainbow currency.

Leading politicians in Brazil and Russia have suggested creating a BRICS currency to reduce the dollar's dominance. However, this was not discussed at the group's 2023 summit. Why would it make sense for the

U.S.A. to join BRICS quietly behind the scenes? Because the U.S. Treasury will be putting U.S. gold backed notes in your QFS account at the RV. They cannot put money in something that is not legal tender. This had to be done for the new financial system and before Trump can come back in the public eye. And now it's done.

The price of silver and gold continues to go up. For every $1.00 that silver goes up, Bank of America loses $800 million. In the last seven days, silver has gone from $24/oz to $30/oz. Bank of America has lost $4.8 billion! They, along with Wells Fargo will be the one of the first two banks to collapse.

The Ponzi scheme against "We the People," is over.

We are to expect a raging inflation, a major crash, things to get worse for a short period of time, but then the opera.

Back to the fake disease–Senator Paul was noted to say that 15 Federal Agencies knew in 2018 that the Wuhan Lab was trying to create a virus like Covid-19, which turned out to be just that, Covid-19. That, my dear, was on the news. Also, someone please explain to me why Klaus Schwab wrote a book about "Response to Covid" long before there was even Covid? Sounds like I am talking in riddles, but sadly that is the reality.

Conflict in the Middle East is supposedly increasing. I say supposedly, well, because as you know by now, it's a fucking movie– and a most impressive one I might add– making sometimes even the ones that are awake question everything we have learned. Both Iran and Israel are literally calling out their attacks before they happen. If this was non-fictional, they would not telegraph their attacks. On the same note, if it was real, so many people in this country aren't even aware of the fact that we have been at war for a couple of years now. War is not like it was, there are not just guns and bombs. It comes in so many different forms nowadays– cyber war, the AI, CGI– it is more advanced and intelligent.

The pro-Palestine protestors in Chicago and New York were stopping traffic to the airport and making the travelers walk to the terminal to catch their flights. While protesting, they were chanting "Death to America" in the streets. Do they know they are in America? Of course they do, but our government is allowing this, supposedly for the normies to witness. Now, shit like that, it does not matter if it makes the news. Thousands of people saw it, heard it, witnessed it. Anyone who thinks that this would not be stopped by the military instantly had it not been planned, is in for a surprise. You cannot say "Death to America" in the country of America, then just go home. Think about it. They are openly threatening us, and nothing is being done. Please people, use your brain that God so graciously gave you.

New evidence that Fauci also manufactured the AIDS virus in the 1980's and conveniently, he is married to Christine Grady. Christine Grady is the head of the NIH Bio Ethics, which is the company that approves drugs for the FDA. Are you starting to get it yet? On top of that they also posted again the incentive pay that the doctors. and hospitals got for administering the Covid vaccine. Once they got up to a certain tier, they got as much as $250.00 per newly vaccinated patient. The whole schedule is posted for the world to see and as reported earlier, the $14,000.00 payment they received for listing Covid on death certificates, regardless of if they died of that. Just wait, at the risk of sounding repetitive, everything we have been taught has been a lie, I cannot stress that enough.

We need an opera.

April 23rd, 2024

Another bad day for the fake Dems. Hillary Clinton's and Barack Obama's former senior policy advisor Rahamim Shy has been charged with child sex offenses, and he is being transferred to Guantanamo Bay. Odd, so many being exposed as pedophiles. No, it's not odd if you have been paying attention.

However, with all these revelations and exposures of the deep state, it is still Trump that finds his way in the courtroom at every single turn. He is there again. Not for January 6th, the Russian collusion, documents in his home or a tax situation- those all failed. Now it's about hush money to Stormy Daniels. Stormy wrote a letter dated January 30th, 2018, admitting that she never had a sexual relationship with Donald Trump, nor did she get hush money to keep silent about the alleged relationship. She is silent about the allegations because it never happened. This supposed affair was in 2006. This is 2024. They brought it out the year of the election. Great script writing military, good job. This is by far the most interesting movie I ever witnessed.

The corrupt, fake judge put a gag order on Trump, which he, of course, violated. There have been many abstract messages today, mostly from Trump himself. He is insinuating that he will be thrown in jail. If that is not pulse-pounding enough, truthers are back to saying that there could be a fake assassination of Trump. If that happens, they are telling us not to go nuts and to remember everything that we have been taught. We have been preparing for this. The media will go wild, but we are not to believe a word of it and rest assured that the real Trump will be safe. This is not a definite narrative, it's a possible narrative.

April 24th, 2024

There is great news today! Venezuela has also joined BRICs and the RV is closer, could possibly even be this week. The RV is the re-evaluation of money, it is for anyone that holds bonds, not to be confused with NESARA. People that hold bonds will receive an email on where to trade it in; they will also have to sign an NDA. We do not possess bonds. That beautiful moment for those bond holders will not apply to us.

Alex Jones had a podcast and interviewed Pascal Najadi, the son of the World Economic Forum co-founder. Pascal verified that the real Hiliary Clinton, Barack Obama and Dr. Fauci were all executed at Gitmo and have been replaced with body doubles. We knew that already, but it was exhilarating hearing it from him. Is it wrong that I want to Scooby Doo their assess and have their masks be ripped off in public? They say it will go down that way, I hope that was not misinformation because that is a want and a need for us patriots.

Information that I also look forward to learning about is how everything was connected. Everything form the beginning of these notes, the social media being down, the cell towers being down, last week several states could not use 911, the odd storms, the overabundance of earthquakes, Trump's codes that he throws during his rallies that only MAGA understands, the stumbling and fumbling of Joe Biden, the Super Bowls, the Royal Family, Taylor Swift–*EVERYTHING* had meaning and everything is connected. How cool it's going to be to see all the dominoes collapse and the pieces of the puzzle will fall into place all on their own.

If you ever wonder, how did we deal with all these clues, riddles and disappointments almost every day, for almost four years, I assure you it was worth it. Knowing that our country would be patriotic again someday made it all worthwhile. The flip side of the coin would have been to not know any of this and truly believing that our country will be exploding with people chanting "Death to America." That, my fellow Americans, would have been harder.

May 2nd, 2024

We did something! Ella and I went to our first ever Trump Rally yesterday! Myself and my partner in crime, Ella, hit the road at 4 a.m. Sometimes the best things in life are done out of spontaneity. Adam worked last night, and he arrived back home just as I was done getting ready. Perfect timing for him to see me in my gear. I asked him if I looked MAGA enough. He smiled while trying to hold back his laughter and his exhaustion from a 12-hour shift, but I was able to get a "Yes, mom" out of him. Mission accomplished!

When we arrived and got in line, there were only about 100 people ahead of us. At that instant, our anticipation and excitement grew even more with the realization that we will get in and quite possibly snatch a very close seat. After securing our place in line, we now had four hours to wait outside until the doors opened, making us very thankful for the nice weather. I can tell you one thing that is a fact, and that is I don't think I have ever been in a place with thousands of people, where each person was nicer than the next. The camaraderie between all these patriots was extraordinary to witness. The four hours flew by as we enjoyed talking and listening to likeminded people and sharing our thoughts and input. Thousands of people defining the true definition of teamwork. It was unbelievable. We were all MAGA. Yes, the same MAGA that are considered domestic terrorists. Just a friendly reminder in case you were sleeping previously, MAGA means Make America Great Again. Yep, those people. The ones that love our country with every ounce of our soul. Let's put it this way, if every person in the world was like the crowd that day, the world would be a much better place. While everyone was obviously MAGA, there were some different beliefs. Some believe that everyone we are seeing are wearing masks (like we think) and some did not feel that way; they feel we are seeing the real Biden. Some are worried the election will be stolen again, some thought the election won't happen. However, even with the differences, *EVERYONE* got along, everyone there loved their country, everyone there was there to support our CIC. Nobody cared if we had different outlooks. I repeat, no one cared. We are all Americans; you can have your own beliefs. If it were a rally with all libs and they expressed a difference of opinion, there would be arguments. They would scream and yell at each other and maybe even throw a punch. What they accuse us of doing is in fact what they do.

Those who condemn us should learn from us.

We met two ladies that were fantastic, they just happened to have parked by us and walked up to the line with us. After standing and talking to them for four hours, we got to know them well and we all ended up exchanging phone numbers. While waiting, there was a man there dressed up as Uncle Sam and would occasionally entertain us with patriotic songs and "Amazing Grace" being played on his harmonica. In the near distance, we heard bellows of cheer and applause which promptly grabbed our attention. Turns out, Mike Lindell was there and walking up to people in the crowd. Before we knew it, he was walking in front of us, and we were able to grab him for a picture. A moment to remember indubitably. Then it was time for the doors to open. Once in, we captured our seats– our incredible seats that is– which were only about 50 feet away from Trump, the 6th row. I, Ella and our newfound friends were in for a treat.

For Trump's entrance, they always play "Proud to be an American" while our CIC walks in. If you don't get goosebumps during that, either check your pulse or check your American citizen status. It was a feeling that I will never be able to describe.

At his exit, they played the song "Don't Worry, I am Coming."

He shouted out how he vows to make America Great Again and the whole crowd cheered. Departing the auditorium, everyone was polite, pumped up and full of patriotism. They played "YMCA" by the Village People and only a few people walked out– the majority danced their way out to the blaring music. Of course I was in the group that danced their way out, causing Ella to remove the banners that were given to us out of my hands for fear of me wrinkling them. I was too naturally high to worry about the signs, but I am glad she recouped them since they are a nice keepsake.

I am still in awe at how incredible the day went. While I don't usually watch his rallies on TV, being there in person is a completely different ball game.

May 7th, 2024

Interesting thing I stumbled upon regarding the protests. Three years ago, I would state that it shocked me, but I am past that; nothing shocks me anymore. They posted more of the deep state's agenda. In November of 2023, they have a list of all the colleges to protest and camp out at. A list of colleges to be "activated" is what it is labeled as. They planned this in 2023. Are you getting it yet?

The riots, the diseases, the fake indictments against Trump– it is identical to 2020. Identical!

Because the riots are for different causes, that helps camouflage the agenda as well. The first riots were because of George Floyd and all the BLM; these riots are because of the war in Israel. But it is the exact same thing. Just like I told you that most kids that marched in BLM did not have a fucking clue why they were marching, it is the same with these college kids. An interviewer went to the colleges and interviewed them. The reporter asked why they were protesting, and they literally said, "I am not sure. I am thinking we are opposed to the war in Palestine?" Fucking idiots.

They have been saying that when this over with, a college degree will be as worthless as a piece of paper. When Andy lost his job in 2008, we swore we were going to make our kids go to college to get some sort of degree. Then as time went on, we had a change of heart, and we felt blessed that our boys decided to go into the trades. That was before we were awake; our reasoning for having a change of heart was because little by little, we saw so many people with hefty student loans and start off with a shit paying job. Then when we woke up and learned more about the deep state, the indoctrinated educational system and the liberal woke ways, it was an ah-ha moment for us.

May 9th, 2024

Two states have admitted, for sure, that the 2020 election was stolen. Claire Woodall-Vogg was fired. Claire was the most corrupt election clerk from the biggest city in Wisconsin and, the key player in stealing the election of 2020. She printed 64,000 ballots in the back conference room of City Hall in room 501.

The second state was Georgia. The Georgia State Election Board admitted they found the hand and certified machine recounts in the 2020 election, to be in violation of the law. It has also been proven without a shadow of doubt that Dominion voting machines switched 221,000 Pennsylvania votes from Trump to Biden, 941,000 votes were deleted, and other states switched 435,000 votes from Trump to Biden. Yes! I will take my popcorn back now.

Trump's classified documents case has been delayed indefinitely. In other words, thrown out. This came after Jack Smith pretty much admitted the documents were falsified and planted in Trump's home.

We were told there will be an assassination attempt on someone of importance but were not told who.

Lastly, (for now), AstraZeneca is withdrawing their Covid vaccine because they are now admitting that it can cause a rare and dangerous side effect.

Everything is getting exposed. VINDICATIION!

There was a meme that said that Trump needs more haters because all the ones that hated him before now love him. Not the people I see, but I am sure there are several people that flipped to Trump now. I truly admire Patrick Byrne. He is an admitted ex- lib–was always Democrat. He despised Trump. On the night of the election in 2020, he saw the number flip right before his eyes (like most of us did); he knew right away that they stole it from Trump and didn't like it or approve of it. He knew right from wrong, regardless of his personal feelings. He has been dedicated to uncovering the truth ever since. Michael Rapaport also admits he was wrong about Trump. Yeah, I guess that meme was true, while there are still haters out there, he does not have nearly as many as he used to. The active haters that are still present are so corrupt that they fear him, or some are too easily offended, while others have issues with admitting they were wrong.

May 10th, 2024

Wait? I thought it was white lung disease? No, wait, Disease X, right? Well, now they are saying bird flu is coming back–wait for it, wait for it– and they miraculously will have a vaccine for bird flu within two weeks if needed! Oh, wait, what? It's now H5N1 disease? Please fake Cabal, please make up your mind; I am losing track of which disease to make fun of you for. But man, thank you, thank you for having a game plan for a vaccine already. But wait again, wasn't bird flu around years ago and we all survived with no vaccine? Shut the fuck up Sidney, they don't want you to use your brain, just pretend you forgot about the last round of bird flu and go with the revised bird flu theme. Sadly, if the white hats don't do something publicly, people will do just that. They will again turn a blind eye to the pattern and not even see that everything is being done exactly as 2020.

We no longer consider ourselves conspiracy theorists. We consider ourselves to be the fuckers that were right all along. Nothing can stop what is coming!

Tonight is a solar flash. What does that mean? Probably nothing, however, truthers are saying that several emails were sent out by the DOD via the Pentagon Force Protection, notifying people that the solar flash might take out the grids. I know nothing about solar flares.

According to Wikipedia: "A solar flare is a relatively intense, localized emission of electromagnetic radiation in the Sun's atmosphere."

Yeah, ok even with seeing the definition, still Greek to me. Although even if I understood it, it doesn't matter anymore since literally nothing is as it seems. Are they going to use the solar flash to knock the grid out, then it will escalate from there? Thinking not since it does not line up with everything we heard. If the world thinks the solar flash took out our grid, it will just look like an act of God, the sleepers won't be able to connect the dots. But, hey, they know the plan, not me.

May 17th, 2024

Earlier this week, the Board of Elections concluded that Biden did in fact steal the 2020 election. No shit. The whole Pandora's box was opened that Biden is an illegitimate President. Ah, we can breathe now. Now show the damn results and end this four-year-long movie. Roll the credits already!

Additionally:

Biden is going to be removed.

RV has rolled out. Bond holders can cash in, and foreign currency holders can exchange it for the new rate.

The citizens of the U.S, Republic and Israel call for the removal and arrest of Netanyahu and Biden.

It's getting frosty out there, peeps! Each day gets better and better.

Amazingly, there was the predicted assassination attempt. It was on the Slovakian Prime Minister, who apparently was shot twice in the abdomen. If that shit is part of the "plan" and in fact real, that is pretty fucked up. From this point of view, of course, I am sure Military Intelligence has a whole different outlook and reasonings. And as always, everything is connected.

Just today, breaking news is that Congress wants to abolish the federal reserve. Woot woot! It's happening, friends.

.

June 3rd, 2024

I sit here typing while still in an extremely high-spirited mood. Yes, it is still present, although I must confess, it was diminished slightly this past week but first allow me to catch you up on what has transpired since my last entry, many events have happened.

Iranian President Ebrahim Raisi was killed in a helicopter crash. World leader deaths are more common than people realize, unfortunately. Although the Slovakian Prime Minister did not die, we have had two world leader tragedies within a short period of time. Trump was the one briefed about Iran shortly afterwards.

Shortly after those incidents with the two world leaders, 45 U.S. states have dropped the taxes on gold and silver because you can't tax currency, and these commodities can be used as currency! Soon, people, soon. Soon it will be announced that our new currency is backed by gold and silver. As mentioned in a podcast, when you hear that Deutsche Bank or Bank of America is in the news, you know we are getting closer. Well, we hit the trifecta, Deutsche Bank was mentioned twice and Bank of America once. Former Deutsche Bank board member Frank Strauss died suddenly and unexpectedly; he was only 54 years old. By the same token, former Deutsche Bank CEO, Rolf Breuer passed away after a long illness at the age of 86. Two deaths of high-profile figures of Deutsche Bank within 2 days of each other. What are the odds? After that, you guessed it, Bank of America was mentioned in the fake news regarding financial problems; SCOTUS decision confirmed the U.S. has a dual banking system with Federal and State chartering. If silver runs up one more time, that will be the nail in the coffin for BOA! As predicted, they were in the news.

Saudi Arabia will no longer take the U.S. dollar for payment for their oil, after June 9th, of this year (six more days). A 70-year contract will end. The Saudi Prince has already notified the U.S. that this agreement will *NOT* be renewed. Is that what will move things along? Furthermore, just this morning, it was reported that 517,000,000,000 in unrealized losses hit the U.S. Banking System as FDIC Warns 63 lenders on the brink of insolvency. Possible collapse very soon then all the war events will begin. Rapid fire.

Japan's former Interior Minister became the first major politician to apologize to anti-vaxxers. He stated," You were right, vaccines are killing millions." Japan is also demanding an investigation into the origin of Covid and questioning the jab. Around the same time, a physician who used to be pro-vaccine, has admitted that the Covid vaccine is poison and is also apologizing for being fooled. She goes on to say how they were lied to, and she wishes she could go back in time.

Now for the reason as to why my joyful mood lately was temporarily diminished. The infamous Trump verdict came in. Guilty on all 34 counts. All felonies. This is what we wanted! I, Ella, and all other that are awake were jumping for joy! We have been waiting for this! We knew he was going to either be found guilty, or an assassination attempt. Honestly, an assassination attempt is not off the table either. He had to be found guilty for three reasons.

1. It sets a precedent. If Trump does not get immunity, that means all others don't either. Now he can go after Biden, Obama, Clintons, Bushes, etc.

2. He must be completely removed before the truth can come out; this way the Libs cannot blame him when the truth is exposed. In their eyes, now that he is a felon, he is gone.

3. The injustice was extremely evident to most, even Libs. The charges were absurd, a Kangaroo court to say the least. The judge told the jury that the vote did not have to be unanimous. He also told the jurors that if they wanted to move the misdemeanors to felons, they can.

Another *Saturday Night Live* skit at its finest. Many that were anti-Trumpers, now realize that this was all so unfair. Many have flipped to him now and they are referring to May 30th as the day Trump won the election. Trump has already received 200 million dollars in donations. So, if I was happy with the verdict why the drop in excitement? It is what came afterwards–the podcast. The same person who is always right, except when he purposely gives misinformation, the same guy who told us to buy silver and now it is skyrocketing and the same guy who told us to look for the two banks in the news, gave us a harsh reality. Trump's sentencing is for July 11th. He blatantly told us that he will be sentenced to jail time. Again, he must be completely removed. I quickly snapped myself out of it when I followed my own advice–trust the plan, and this is just a movie. Most importantly, it could be misinformation again. But, hey, I am human, we all have our periods of doubt in life. As always, a good dig and conversation with Ella, always helps.

If Trump did this to Biden before the 2020 election, the Libs would have burned this country to the ground. It should be evident by all that MAGA is not violent. Any riot or extremism was generated and funded by the Dems. We were set up and the sleepers will never accept that.

Conversations are still rough. A liberal that I know just found out she is going to be a grandparent for the first time. She is excited, except for one aspect of the pregnancy– the due date. The baby is due Jan 6th, 2025. She is traumatized by that. The thought of her grandchild being born on insurrection day, a day that "he" ruined, is too much for her to accept. She expressed so much concern, that if it looks like the baby will be born on that day, she is going to have a talk with the doctor because "that simply cannot happen." I sat there with my head down and I seriously pondered whether these people hear themselves. In addition, to sounding like an idiot, it answered the question of whether people know now that January 6th was not MAGA. I don't think she would even be that upset if the due date was 9/11. Imagine if you will, two conservatives talking about having babies due date on November 5th, and that cannot happen since that is the day the election was stolen. First, that conversation would never happen because we are not that trivial or superficial, the excitement of our grandchild would supersede all the above. Hypothetically, if that conversation did happen and a Lib overheard us, they would ream us a new one and tell us how crazy we are. In this situation, it was reversed; I sat there calmly and listened to her never telling her how insane she sounded. Thats us domestic terrorists–MAGA.

Trump called upon the Supreme Court to step in before the July 11th sentencing. Also, he is still under a Gag order, all he has to do is say something he is not supposed to and BAM! This is a movie that we have been preparing for now for almost five years. Envision if you will, in everyday life, when a perpetrator is sitting in a courtroom waiting for a verdict, if they are found guilty of a felony, do they let the accused leave the courtroom? Well, now, envision 34 felonies, but he was not cuffed and sent to jail at that moment. Something to think about. The same evening on the *Gutfeld!* show, he made a joke about Biden being dead and replaced by an actor. Another commentator of Fox news made a comment about it's as if we are watching a movie. Trump himself uses the term "Central Casting," all the time. Damn, this gets better every day!

Amazing day also with fake Dr. Fauci. They televised his live trial all day. Well, not on regular mainstream media of course. It was incredible the way they tore into him. They mentioned everything that awake people have known for five years now. He basically made all the restrictions up as he went along. He made up the six feet rule, the imbecilic arrows on store floors, the masks and he knew the masks could in turn harm you more. Sleepers are not even aware in any shape or form that the trial even happened. The best part is that he confessed this! This is the biggest crime against humanity ever to happen in the whole world! The plandemic killed more people than the Holocaust. Biggest sign that this is a movie is the spectators in the room. There was a young man sitting directly behind him making sad faces and googly eyes. There was another man sitting behind him, his name is Ivan Raiklin. Ivan is a diehard patriot and has a part in taking down the Cabal. It has been discovered that the man sitting right behind Fauci making those faces had been identified as one of the J6ers, Brandon Felllows. He was sentenced to three years in jail, and he was recently released. How on earth could those two be in a courtroom in a world that is supposedly still ran by the Cabal and Democrats? Nah, not buying it, there is no way they would let a man who has vowed to take them down sit that close to Fauci, and definitely not a man they put in prison for January 6th. Impossible. Those seats are VIP seats; they would not be able to secure them if white hats were not in control. The arrogance on the face of Fauci was eerily similar to our town mob—absolutely no remorse. While Fauci is an act, sadly the Cabal in our hometown are not. It is highly doubtful they will still be flaunting that same smirk when the hammer comes down.

June 5th, 2024

Just when you think the situation in our ideal town could not get any worse—they barked up the wrong tree this time. They awoke a sleeping bear because it personally hit a townsperson, a townsperson that is greatly respected. The local baseball coach was fired. He has been a coach for 13 years and just so happens to be a patriot. He has no problem pledging his loyalty to America and has been noted several times to speak up against the CCP coming in. At the same time, the cabal in our town miraculously discovered mishaps with him in the coaching area. He was terminated. The townspeople are livid and of course they all realize that it was a political retaliation.

There are also reports of several Chinese walking our streets wearing black hoodies with the hood pulled securely over their heads and not moving for traffic.

The people fighting this were interviewed on Fox News recently. The real icing on the cake is that we also just found out that the CCP bought another 223 acres here in our town. Safe assumption is that if our way is incorrect, we will be the new Little China. I might start looking now at homes in Texas— it's always smart to have a backup plan. Additionally, Andy has mentioned to me how hard it is having to go to work and seeing all of the Communistic loving and corrupt people on a daily basis. It makes him sick sometimes and he comes home disheveled. He feels trapped. He said to me recently, "Can we look into leaving soon?" We sure can, Andy. We sure can.

In this line of work, your day is always different and that's what I love about it. While meeting with a mother and daughter to review price of packages regarding mechanical issues on their Industrial building, they looked at each other and were giving signals to one another with their eyes, yes, that's possible. Finally, daughter looked at me and said, "Well, here is the thing, we would like to pay cash for a 5-year contract, however, our money is not liquid."

237

I was cautious with responding as I did not want to get too personal, so I left it generic. "Ok, I understand. Do you need time to call your accountant or employer if it is tied up somewhere else?"

They again looked at each other, thought about it, then daughter just blurted it out, "It's stored in our house, but it is in precious metals. We pulled out our retirement and transferred it all to gold and silver. I know you probably don't understand that, but just trust us, we have a reason, and we will have to sell it to get the cash."

My heart fluttered. Only the awake will understand this next part. It is so hard to find someone fully awake. Ella and I have been struggling with it for so long now. A Trump supporter, no problem. Someone who knows the election was stolen, they are a dime a dozen– but to find someone that is fully awake, even though there is 9 million plus people out there, they are hard to find. Only a fully awake person knows that the financial institutions, as we know them, will be null and void soon and the new currency will be backed by gold and silver.

I responded, "I do understand, my fellow patriot." After they picked up their jaw from the ground, mom asked, "How much of a Patriot are you? Are you fully awake?" My response was easy.

I said, "I was thinking the same thing. I'll tell you what, I will say 5 words. If you recognize them, I will know how awake you are and in return, you will know how awake I am."

They nodded in agreement, and I then said these five simple words, "Adrenochrome, actors, masks, movie, Nesara."

After saying those words, I had an oh shit moment. What if they only knew about the financial end? What if now they will want me to explain those five words? Nope, was not the case at all. They both jumped up and down– I mean literally, jumped up and down! They knew exactly what I was talking about. They felt so relieved to finally meet someone that was on the same page as them; I must admit, I was pretty thrilled myself. We then carried on with a very long conversation on how to proceed with their situation.

June 20th, 2024

While us conservatives know that other countries are sharing our truths, it still pings in the stomach a little when you see a new one. On the front page of an Australian newspaper today was " Biden Porn Shock."

Americans are the last ones to know what is going on in their own country. Other countries can hear about the corruption in our homeland, but we can't. I guess we need to just sit back, wait and enjoy the show. Easier said than done at times, but that is really all we can do.

It appears that good ol' Joe Biden will be stepping down from the presidential race at some point. No word on who or what will replace him; more than likely it will be Kackling Kamala, due to timing. Joe was horrible, but Kamala is an even bigger joke– at least we won't have to worry about it getting stolen again, no one in their right mind would believe that.

In our little town, the meetings are getting more intense. The usual patriots stand up to the podium with all their heart and soul trying desperately to relay how serious this CCP deal is. They get sniggers and no eye contact in return. The board is still arrogant as usual, and they truly do appear to feel untouchable. After the interview I watched with Trump, our local mob is going to have a real eye-opener. During this interview, they showed a map of the United States. On this map, there were several red dots. The red dots signified all the locations of the CCP owned land. Our state was on there. The interviewer asked Trump if he was aware of this. He replied," Oh, I know exactly where they are. I know."

He then went on to say that he will not allow the CCP to own our land. They will be taken down.

July 13, 2024

Assassination attempt on Trump! Just like we were told. It happened live at one of his rallies. While you might think that Ella and I either lost composure or cheered for joy since it proves that what we were told was correct, that was not the case. You see, when you are awake, you are prepared for news like this. We heard the announcement, then continued with our normal weekend barbecue. Where this facade takes us is when the real thrills will begin. Will it prove that the Dems were behind it and that it will be their demise? If it was a perfect world that would be the master plan, but we all know this world is far from perfect, but positive thoughts for that to be the consensus in the near future. Please absorb this fun fact- with all of Trump's rallies, this is the only one that CNN aired. Coincidence? I think not.

July 18th, 2024

The RNC. What can I say other than it was off the charts incredible. There were many great speakers, and the mood was so astronomical that it pulsated through the airwaves making us at home viewers feel their energy. Additionally, comms galore. He mentioned free energy, that we have gold under our feet, paying off debt and then emphasized how we have "loads and loads of money." That is the same way they described the 650 plane loads of gold and artifacts retrieved from the Vatican. My favorite part was when he sternly stated that, "No Chinese plants will be allowed here and no electric car mandate!" I am sure you can guess why that was my favorite part. He ended the night with gold balloons being dropped from the ceiling.

July 21st, 2024

It's official! As predicted, Biden dropped out of the race. Kamala will take his place in this crazy script. I would rather see him getting publicly arrested instead of just removing himself, but that day will come.

Right after he removed himself, past quotes from Democrats are being posted everywhere.

"If American people ever find out what we have done, they will chase us down the streets and lynch us." said George W.H. Bush in1992.

"Those Trumpers think we care about the Constitution. We have the power now; it's time to end this. They really don't get it. We will block them in courts; we will use Federal Law Enforcement and the Military. After Joe inflicts the death blow, I will take over the reins. They will beg me for a loaf of bread." said Kamala Harris in 2021.

Those past comments were released while Joe Biden stepped down. They are everywhere. For those still not seeing through the charade, their ignorance is on them. It is in our face every day.

September 1, 2024

The ugliness in people is getting worse. On both sides, to be honest. The Liberals are still in havoc worried about Kackling Kamala not getting in and the patriots are exhausted. Liberals bring up politics even more so and people that I know that are patriots are fatigued more and getting cranky. I see it, I feel it. People on both sides are fearing for the future of our country, and it is reflecting in their actions. The division is strong and when people are out with others in a mixed crowd, you can tell the phoniness. It's very eerie.

Robert Kennedy joined forces with Trump. We knew there was a big announcement that was to be had, but we did not know what. Prior to the announcement, there were a lot of purple comms. No one knew what it meant. Then the announcement came. What do you get when you mix red + blue? Purple. Kennedy vowed to clean up our poisonous food and to take down Fauci. The same day he announced that, Fauci was hospitalized. Pay attention.

I had a very interesting conversation with my cousin, who just happens to be a Trump delegate and had VIP tickets for the RNC. Turns out she was well aware of what's going on in our town and informed me that she sits at the roundtable discussions regarding it. She agrees with me that they will all be taken down. We then had a long discussion about how I am the silent cheerleader and detective for those patriots that are fighting this cause. I never looked at it that way, but I like it.

September 13th, 2024

Three days ago, was the scripted presidential debate. It was a combination of a comical, aggravating, disappointing and a nauseating cocktail all combined into one putrid beverage. Kamala's mouth shot out lies faster than a tennis ball launcher but then called Trump a liar. Trump mentioned how the Haitians in Springfield, Ohio, are eating neighborhood pets. That sure sent a whirlwind of memes and jokes for the libs. I cannot wait for the day to come when the world realizes that everything he says and does is for a reason and has a meaning. First, it's true, but of course since their precious mainstream media didn't show it, it did not happen. The mainstream media did show, however, how the Haitians and Venezuelans have infiltrated that town and seeing how that is their custom to eat animals– why would that be so hard to believe? While those gangs are hurting people in Ohio, all the Liberals concentrated on was Trump's eating animal's story. Someone please explain it to me as if I was a 5th grader, please help this make sense to me. Impossible to do since it makes absolutely no sense.

Kamala had a rally. Not going to elaborate on this because it doesn't deserve it. She told a patron that she was at the wrong rally when the guest mentioned God.

'Nuff said.

November 4th, 2024.

The night before the election. Honestly, I will be the first to admit that I did not think it would get to this point. But it did. That prompts the same question that has been asked so many times before– do I still trust the plan? And I can answer that without even thinking twice. The answer is the same as it has always been. Yes. Yes, I do. Not only do I still trust the plan, but I have also completely thrown Kenny and Mac's theory to the wayside.

If anything, keeping up with this crime show kept us busy and gave us hope. The positive that will come out of the full disclosures, lifted our spirits and made us temporarily forget about all the evil in the world. Maybe that was the intention all along, a form of a PSYOP. But it worked. If I could go back in time for the past five years, I would do everything the exact same way. I choose to be awake. Additionally, since finding out the Q drops were an 8-year plan, it made the anticipation of the election much easier to handle.

If you think that everything that you have read so far is too fantasy-like, and not even close to being a reality, then let me ask you something:

If I were to say to you 30 years ago that we would be living in a world where pedophilia is so large and it is actually covered up, a world were selling humans is an everyday occurrence, a world where God is taken out of the equation, a world where a human is confused on whether or not they are a man or a women, a world where that same human might decide they want to be a cat, a world where schools have to put in litter boxes for the said feline/human so they don't get offended, a world where the men are so flamboyantly dressed in cartoon colors and they are protected, a world where there is so much crime and the perpetrator is set free. Wouldn't you call me crazy and a conspiracy theorist?

The way we feel things will be is no more far-fetched than the above, which is occurring right now. The only difference is the current matters are an overt operation. You see them, they are tangible. Our hopes, dreams and plans for the future are still a covert operation. They are still hidden, concealed.

November 6th, 2024.

Trump Won.

A quote from one of my favorite songs, "May we all do a little bit better than the first time. Learn a little something from the worst times."

Biggest question is what now?

No one knows when it will happen, but it will happen. The day of reckoning is upon us.

With liberty and peace, keep your head on a swivel and when the pendulum does swing, I suggest you find yourself a conspiracy theorist.

You are going to need one.

www.ingramcontent.com/pod-product-compliance
Lightning Source LLC
Chambersburg PA
CBHW052125270326
41930CB00012B/2760